D1237021

Stephanie on Trial

by the same author

THE JAIL DIARY OF ALBIE SACHS

Stephanie on Trial

ALBIE SACHS

Harvill Press, London

© A. L. Sachs 1968
Printed in Great Britain
Collins Clear-Type Press, London and Glasgow
for the Publishers
Harvill Press Limited, 30a Pavilion Road, London SW1

TO DENNIS

Contents

Part One

ROMANCE
Cape Town 1964

Chapter 1

During the early part of 1964 my life was strange; I practised in courts in which I had nearly appeared as an accused, interviewed clients in cells where I had been held prisoner, and casually bumped into security policemen who had battled for months to break down my mind. While friends of mine were on trial for their lives, I was able to stay on at my work and to walk freely in the streets of Cape Town.

One day on my way to court I saw striding in my direction the man who had been my chief interrogator, Captain Rossouw. His body was massive, his face large and unhandsome, and yet he moved lightly and wore an elegant shirt and finely tailored suit. During the five and a half months of my detention he had frequently interrupted my solitary confinement to shout at me, threaten me with execution, make jokes, watch me and laugh at my occasional ripostes. Now as he bore down on me he kept his eyes firmly ahead, apparently determined to ignore my presence in his path. As we reached each other I nodded abruptly towards him, and he halted, swung round to face me, and thrust his hand forward in greeting.

'Hullo, Mr Sachs,' he said in a harsh, effusive voice. We shook hands. 'I'm pleased you're prepared to greet me,' he continued warmly and loudly. He held on to my hand for a long time before releasing it and allowing me to go on my way.

11

It was gratifying to feel that his need to be loved was greater than mine.

This was a time of great personal elation for me. People would come up to my chambers to have a look at me, and I enjoyed the attention. I was the man who had sat it out for 168 days in solitary confinement, insisting that I be charged or released. I had refused to answer any questions except in a court of law, and on being released had run six miles to the sea and jumped into the waves fully clothed. Euphoric at my triumph over the political police, I would tell visitors stories of my detention; so great was my enthusiasm that invariably they would comment afterwards on how strong and un-affected I was.

In fact, however, I had been deeply affected by my deten-tion and beneath my buoyancy there lay terror and confusion. I had decided to flee the country—that had been the reward which I had promised myself for holding out during solitary confinement. Yet I was ashamed of planning desertion and seemed to lack the will to carry it through. Over the years I had seen others preparing to quit, and had argued with them against it. Some had panicked wildly, throwing over the rules of conduct of a lifetime, while many had advanced sophisti-cated rationalisations for their actions. I must join them, they had urged; I could achieve nothing further by staying and would merely become a useless martyr. I had replied indig-nantly that South Africa was my Spain, and that people should right the wrongs around them and not run away as soon as the pressure became great. But the Africans won't appreci-ate what you're doing, they had answered. One does something because it is right, I had responded with great certainty, not because it is appreciated.

Now I was mentally committed to doing something which I knew to be wrong. I had lost my nerve for political action and dreaded the prospect of being subjected to isolation and stress

12

once more. I could no longer tolerate the idea of secret meetings and conspiratorial procedures, and yet at the same time hated myself for not doing anything about the indignities being perpetrated all around me. Too weak to stay, too strong to go, I felt that I was waiting for the intervention of an accident or some superior force to determine my future. It humiliated me to feel that I was losing control of my life and my destiny.

I carried on my practice as an advocate (barrister) from an office in a tall new building opposite the Supreme Court. Though I had been at the Bar for seven years since qualifying at the University of Cape Town, my chambers were as shabby as they had been at the start of my career. In the perpetual expectation of being disbarred on political grounds I had held back from buying decent furniture; the curtains were inappropriately bright, the carpet was worn in many places, and the chairs creaked and tore clients' clothing. A long, low, faded couch which stood against the wall near my desk had been useful during the years when crowds of African men and women from the locations had come to my office to seek advice or defence, but now that my practice was quiet, it seemed ugly and out of place.

The discomfort was not only physical—all the time that I worked there I had the feeling that there was a police microphone hidden somewhere. Similarly, when I stood by the window, looking over pretty rooftops and gazing at the huge, serene bulk of Table Mountain, I always wondered whether a police telescope was not scanning my office from one of the buildings below.

The Supreme Court was so close that I was able to look almost straight down upon its roof, and the conglomeration of glass, tile and metal which I saw made that otherwise austere building look absurdly piebald. For seven years, fat in clientèle, lean in remuneration, I had practised in that building, descending into its tunnels to interview imprisoned clients, rushing with gown flying behind me along stone-mosaic corridors, and cross-examining, arguing and pleading before grandly-robed judges in high-ceilinged court-rooms. During lunch-hours judges and advocates would stroll out of the solemn grey-stone buildings into a large nearby park known as The Gardens, where, parading up and down beneath oak trees planted three centuries earlier by the first Dutch colonists, we would digest the morning's evidence and argument.

From my office the tops of the trees appeared to stretch in a thick pile from the roof of the Supreme Court to the pink-brick late Victorian Parliament buildings a little further away. The scene was so peaceful and attractive that I would be overcome by rage that so much loveliness and calm could shroud the source of so much injustice. Sometimes when feeling particularly trapped and frustrated I would in fantasy even plant a mortar on my sill and lob round after round of explosives on to the heads of the oppressors in the distance. A Whites-only institution in a multi-racial land, Parliament had for fifty years passed law upon law to ensure that it retained this racially-pure character. In recent years African pressure for the vote had increased, but the Government's response had been to declare that it would act as resolutely to keep a single African from getting into Parliament as it would to prevent someone like Chief Luthuli from becoming Prime Minister. No area of personal or social life had been left exempt from apartheid laws, neither residence, movement, land ownership, education, job opportunities, access to public amenities, nor sex.

Half of my practice had been devoted to the ordinary run of civil and criminal matters, but the other half had been taken up entirely with defending people charged under various apartheid and political laws. Finally I myself had been caught up under the provisions of one of these statutes. This particular law, known as the 90-day law, was passed in 1963 to empower political police to detain suspicious persons whom they wished to interrogate, and any person so detained could be kept in solitary confinement for successive periods of 90 days. It had quickly integrated itself into the consciousness of all South Africans, and its author, Minister of Justice John Balthazar Vorster, was reported as having raised loud laughter at a dinner when he had jocularly warned golfing opponents that if they continued to beat him he would have them locked up for 90 days. Every few days we read in the newspapers of persons who had been detained, though often the names were not given, so that rumours were rife.

Most of the several hundred people detained in the first few months of the law's operation were Africans, including a number who had gone underground after their organisations had been outlawed at the time of Sharpeville in 1960, but there had been scores of Indians, Coloureds and Whites as well. Each month the news had grown worse. An African detainee had died, and the police said he had been found hanged in his cell; later a young Indian was to jump to his death from a seventh-floor room in which he was being interrogated. Stories of beatings and electric torture began to circulate, and it soon became clear that some of the detainees had broken down at the hands of the police. Many of the leaders of resistance had slipped out over the borders, but a core remained, and to the jubilation of the police and the dismay of their supporters this nucleus had been captured in a swoop on a house at Rivonia, near Johannesburg.

It was three months after this that I was detained. Seven security policemen had searched my office, and after examining my briefs and personal documents, had taken me into custody. From October 1963 to March 1964 I was kept in solitary confinement in various police cells. No charges were laid against me and the police at no stage told me precisely why they had arrested me. For my part I consistently refused to answer their questions, insisting that I be brought before a court of law or released; eventually I was released unconditionally.

Many of the other detainees had been charged with political offences; some became demoralised and agreed to be State witnesses, and a few had serious mental collapses. Of nearly a thousand persons held under this law within the year, I was almost alone in having survived without either having made a statement to the police or having been charged. I had returned to my practice as an advocate, and as I waited for work to come back to me, I had much time to speculate on my future.

In moments of fantasy I would visualise myself going underground and with a new identity continuing the fight against apartheid. A man could bear any hardship, deprivation or pain, I would tell myself, provided he tried hard enough. Courage was a question of will and belief and there was no reason why I should not endure the rigours which would result from further activity. Then I would recall how weak I had become during my detention and would reply to myself that courage was not only a question of subjective strength, but also a matter of what a body could bear. Although I was subjected to restriction and harassment, the luxury of being able to walk in the streets and speak to people was something which even during my most intense upsurges of spirit I could not easily consider forgoing.

As it was, I was debarred by Ministerial decree from leaving Cape Town, from attending social gatherings, communicating with a number of specified people, preparing anything for publication, being on various premises—altogether there were six pages of prohibitions above the signature of J. B. Vorster. To add to my sense of restriction I was fairly sure that my office was bugged, my telephone tapped, my mail censored and my motor car followed—all by the Security Police. Finally, people whom I discovered to be police traps came up to my office and tried to involve me in discussions about explosives and escape routes. One of these men, who claimed to be an Englishman, fascinated me with his mode of operation. First he steered the conversation towards the police and opposition to apartheid and then when I began to give him my views, took out a cigarette lighter and clumsily flicked it to light a cigarette. As soon as that part of the conversation was over he flicked the lighter again, and then I had no doubt that it contained a tape recorder. I was so infuriated by the next provocateur who came to me that I wanted to scream at him and hit him. He was a young, smiling Coloured man whom I had met at parties in the days when I had been permitted to attend social gatherings, and as he feebly told me of how he wished to cross the borders to be trained 'to do something useful,' I felt like shouting; 'Traitor! Liar! You lousy, bloody traitor!' but all I said was that he should study for his matriculation examination and then try to get into a university overseas.

Yet for all these prohibitions, hidden ears, and police spies, I was still relatively free. I could carry on my practice in a limited way, move in an area of several square miles, lie on the beach in the sun, and climb Table Mountain.

One of the more lasting effects of my detention was a weakening of my ability to tolerate stress, not only as it affected me but as it affected others. Every day the newspapers carried reports of political trials held throughout the country. In the past the police had had a struggle to get convictions in political cases, and the largest of these trials, the Treason Trial, had collapsed in fiasco after four years of evidence and argument. Now, however, the powers of the police had been increased, the laws of evidence and procedure had been changed to help them, and a climate had been built up in which people

17

were either afraid to criticise them or else eagerly supported everything they did.

The case on which most attention was focused at that time was the 'Rivonia trial', at which Nelson Mandela, the most famous of the younger African leaders, was the principal accused. With him in the dock were a dozen men, all charged with having planned sabotage and having prepared for guerilla warfare. Against two of them the evidence was very slight, but for the others there was only one issue: would they be sentenced to death or not?

One of those in most danger of being hanged was a close personal friend of mine. At 30, Denis was a year older than I; we had known each other as children and had later become good friends at the University of Cape Town. There were many parallels in our lives. We had both come from left-wing homes, reacted away from politics, and finally ended up deeply involved in anti-apartheid activities. In the days when open protest had been permitted we had worked together as supporters of the African National Congress, led by Chief Albert Luthuli, and had participated in campaigns against the Pass Laws, for the Vote, against divided education, for a National Convention, and so on. I had done much public speaking, while Denis had become a reliable and imaginative organiser. When the Government outlawed radical opposition by banning organisations, proscribing newspapers, prohibiting meetings, and placing individual activists under restriction, the political atmosphere changed drastically. Public meetings at which thousands of Africans had voiced their protest in lively speeches and sad songs, gave way to small, clandestine gatherings at which people gravely discussed new methods of action. In this situation Denis, the engineer, had become a more valuable person than I, the lawyer. It was a time of secrecy and caution; contact with Africans had become dangerous, and people learnt not to ask what others were doing. Thousands

18

of individuals had to take decisions which were seriously to affect their whole lives. For each of us the question had been posed: how sincere were we in our beliefs, how much of our energies and remaining freedom were we prepared to invest in the battles necessary to free South Africa from minority rule? Until then the risks for us had been largely ones of inconvenience, embarrassment or losing a job, and we had been able to accept these hazards quite easily; now the possible penalties were detention, torture, imprisonment and, even, death.

After years of campaigning for a non-violent struggle, we had to see if our faith in what we were doing was strong enough to include new methods of action. It was not easy to re-orientate to a situation of increasing violence. The police had armed themselves with rifles, sten-guns, saracens (armoured cars) and helicopters, and at Sharpeville in 1960 they used them all against a crowd, as one reporter observed, armed only with newspapers and umbrellas. Sixty-seven African men, women and children had been shot dead on that occasion. Later in the same year, a meeting of Africans at a place called Ngqusa Hill was surrounded by police who opened fire with sten-guns and killed twelve men. The lawyer who appeared for dependents of the deceased at the subsequent inquest was prevented by a banning notice from continuing with the matter, so I had been briefed to take over. The magistrate eventually found that one of the policemen had fired recklessly and unnecessarily, but despite this, the policeman concerned was not punished in any way, nor were the relatives compensated.

The confrontation of angry population and armed police made violence inevitable. More and more Africans complained that their hands were tied by the policy of never hitting back at the police, and gradually we saw the emergence of a new approach: selective violence aimed at Government property.

19

Electric sub-stations were blasted, telephone poles sawn through, and segregated post offices bombed at night. Violence and counter-violence followed. The Sabotage Act of 1962 defined sabotage in a wide way and provided for summary trials, death sentences, and minimum sentences of five years imprisonment. Students and others protested; the underground organisations declared that the Act would lead to more sabotage, not less. In the next year the Government followed up with the 90-day law; Africans responded by going abroad to receive training in guerilla warfare.

As the situation grew more serious I had begun to see less of Denis. On one occasion he had come to my chambers to find out about the full legal implications of the Sabotage Act. Though normally athletic and jaunty in appearance, he had been grave and tense. Some months later I was told that he had disappeared and then on the dread day of the police raid at Rivonia I read that Denis had been one of the captured men. According to a later press report, he had subsequently managed to escape from his police cell and climb over the high perimeter wall, but after being at liberty for half an hour had been recaptured. Some time later his wife Esmé had been allowed to see him and I had nearly cried when I heard how they had tried to cheer each other up, he hiding his chains under his trousers, she battling not to look at them. Shortly thereafter Esmé had been detained, and on the same day the police had arrested me.

Most of the Rivonia trial had taken place during my detention, with the result that although its outcome and in particular the fate of Denis were now of overwhelming concern to me, the details of the evidence affected me very little. Even the challenging declarations of the accused in their defence, when they proudly fought for their lives whilst proclaiming their willingness to die if necessary, seemed remote. Their dignity and the honour of the movement they represented

20

were preserved—all that mattered was whether they would be executed or not. Reports of demonstrations throughout the world raised hopes in their favour, and it seemed inconceivable that they should be hanged. Yet we had to face up to the fact that we were living in a period in which people would kill and be killed, not in isolated outbursts of anger, but as a matter of policy and over questions of principle. Violence had become a part both of the defence of privilege and the attack upon it, and many of my generation would die in the conflict.

The tension of the last days of the trial drove supporters of the accused into a state of anxiety made almost intolerable by our inability to make even gestures of solidarity. Two of the accused were eventually found not guilty on any charge, but as expected, the others were convicted of most of the charges against them. Each newspaper report was carefully scanned for some pointer as to the sentences likely to be imposed. We searched for a concession by the prosecutor, or a meaningful intervention by the judge, but no substantial clues were to be found. The prosecutor consistently stated that the accused had planned revolution and had unscrupulously sought to disturb a contented Black population. The leader of the defence team, a prominent Afrikaner Q.C., who was himself later to go underground, and then be imprisoned for life, did not himself make the final plea in mitigation, but an equally prominent Q.C., after calling the liberal author Alan Paton to give evidence, declared that South Africa had a tradition of not executing rebels, many of whom had come to be viewed more sympathetically by later generations. The judge listened in silence and promptly gave his reasons for sentence.

Newsmen from all over the world crammed the press benches to hear the final pronouncement. The spectators' galleries were packed, with Africans sitting in the area demarcated for them, and Whites in their special section; outside the court policemen armed with sten-guns stood on guard. In a slow, quiet voice the judge addressed the accused. He had considered the matter very seriously, he said, and had decided not to impose the supreme penalty. All the accused would go to prison for life.

Later we read the reports and celebrated. Denis was taken to a White prison in Pretoria to sew mailbags, while Nelson Mandela and the others were escorted to the non-White penal settlement on Robben Island, just off Cape Town, to break stones for the rest of their lives. The Government, we calculated, preferred live hostages to dead martyrs. All was quiet in the country and the police happily proclaimed that the forces of sabotage and subversion had been dealt a fatal blow from which they would never recover.

Then one day in the press there appeared reports that electricity pylons had been toppled in various parts of the country. Six had fallen in one night; another one was to hit the ground two nights later. The police announced that explosives had been used. Many people were angry at what they regarded as new outrages, others were delighted by the evidence of continuing resistance, but everyone, including myself, wondered what organisation had been responsible and what sort of people had had the daring to organise such activity at a time of such danger.

Chapter 2

Tap, tap. Someone was knocking softly on the door of my office. 'Come in,' I shouted, straightening up in the chair in which I had been huddling. The office was cold, for though it had a fine view of the city and of Table Mountain, it faced away from the winter sun.

Tap, tap—the knocking was repeated. 'Come in,' I yelled more loudly, rubbing my calves for warmth, and cursing my failure ever to have bought a heater.

The door opened and an African man walked in, smiling and holding out his hand in a tentative greeting. His appearance puzzled me, for I knew him well yet could not identify him. A lean face with skin pressed tightly on his cheekbones, hair grizzled and short . . . Then I realised who it was—I had known him over many years as a jovial, heavily-built man, but now his frame was taut and hard, as though the months which he had spent in prison had flushed all flesh and laughter from his body.

'Hullo, Mr Sachs . . . I hope I'm not disturbing you . . .?' During the many years of our acquaintanceship he had always called me Albie, yet here he was addressing me with the caution Africans habitually felt when speaking to a White lawyer.

I took his hand and shook it warmly, feeling his rough, calloused palm rub against my pale lawyer's fingers. I told him it was wonderful to see him again, and then, before saying anything more, shepherded him from my office into the passage, so that we could talk without fear of being tape-recorded. We shook hands again and again, eager to demonstrate our affection for each other. In earlier days he and I had frequently spoken from the same platform; afterwards we had occasionally met in the bush or on a dark street corner to pass on messages, or leaflets, or a duplicator. Then as contact between Africans and Whites had become more hazardous, we had lost touch, seeing one another only on such occasions as a political trial.

'You're a bit thinner,' I remarked to him, accustoming myself to his new appearance. 'I believe you had a very hard time.'

He had been one of the first of the 90-day detainees and on his release from solitary confinement had been held for several more months as a prisoner awaiting trial. In the end the case against him had collapsed, and after having spent more than a year in prison he had been allowed to go home.

It had been very hard, he answered gravely, but it had been worse for the others. He shook his head and told me how friends of ours had been sent up to Pretoria where the police had put bags over their heads and had subjected them to repeated doses of electric torture.

I remained quiet for a while. It still astonished and angered me that people could be deliberately cruel to other people.

Suddenly shaking my hand again, he broke the mood of sadness and beaming with friendliness told me how his wife had cried when she had read of my arrest and how happy she had been when she had heard of my release. The African people had all been very excited when they saw in the newspaper that I had been set free, he added, and even the reactionaries had said that the people now had their lawyer back.

His words moved me deeply, though I realised that at the centre of his praise was the hint that I should continue to fight

24

in the courts on behalf of his people. I asked him how he was getting on, and it was his turn now to become angry. The police were stopping him from working, he told me. The Government claimed the Africans were lazy, but every time he tried to get a job the police interfered. Twice he'd been taken on by employers, and both times he'd been informed afterwards that they'd changed their minds. Workers at both places had told him that they'd seen the police going to speak to the bosses, and one of the bosses had even admitted it, saying he was sorry and he didn't have anything against him personally, but that he wasn't going to employ someone who might cause trouble in the factory.

The police wanted to chase him out of Cape Town, but nothing would make him go. What was there for him in the Transkei? He would have no land, no cattle, no work, not even a hut of his own. Where would his children continue their schooling, and if they got sick, where would he find a doctor or a hospital for them? No, he said with feeling, he would never go there. Rather he would hide in the bush and live like a beggar than go and starve in the Transkei.

I grew silent again, and felt my indignation rising. Some of the passion which had accumulated in me over the years revived, and I felt that the prime source of my commitment was not the pursuit in itself of an abstractly beautiful society, but involvement in the lives and feelings of persons like him.

Noticing my seriousness, he laughed and apologised for troubling me with his worries when he was sure I had enough of my own. His wife and the people in the locations wanted Albie to know, he informed me heartily, that they thought of Albie all the time. That was why he had come to my office, and that was why he was so pleased he could now tell the people he had seen me.

I was amused by his reference to me in the third person. Most of my troubles, I said, seemed to be those that I made for myself, but I wanted him to know that whatever happened I would never, never, forget the people in the locations.

Once more we shook hands warmly, and once more we enthusiastically told each other how pleased we were to have met again. Finally we let go of each other and he hurried away down the corridor while I returned to my office.

For several minutes I paced up and down, waiting for the excitement of the encounter to wear off. We had done little more than exchange greetings, yet so starved had I been for contact that even those few words were to glow in my thoughts for a long time.

Chapter 3

My nights and week-ends were devoted solely to one task, trying to set down in an alive form exactly what it had been like living in solitary confinement. Writing with fanatical effort, I found myself pouring much of my anger, fear, hope and doubt into the labour. Always I had to be careful, for at any minute the very police about whom I was writing could have walked into my room and seized the manuscript. I bought paper in small amounts, so as not to arouse suspicion, and worked at home. As soon as I finished a chapter I would give it to a friend to type; then the two typescripts would be hidden separately in case one copy was discovered. In fact moving the different sections of manuscript and typescript safely from one place to another caused me more nervous strain and required greater inventiveness than the writing of the book itself.

When I was well over half-way through the project and had started to plan how I would smuggle the manuscript out of the country, all the batches of carefully hidden writing suddenly flooded back to me. It took me some hours to find out what had happened. The police had conducted raids throughout the country, searching more than a thousand homes and concentrating their interest mainly on respectable white citizens who had voiced disapproval of apartheid. Although none of the persons assisting me had themselves been raided, the

27

atmosphere of fear generated by the police action had led them all without exception to drop their contact with me. Fortunately for me a friend who was soon to leave the country was willing to help, and by taking over all I had written he gave me the chance to make new arrangements.

The police refused to comment on the purpose of the raids, but they did disclose that Adrian Leftwich, a former head of the National Union of South African Students (N.U.S.A.S.) had been detained and was being held for questioning under the 90-day law.

Adrian was a young liberal whose unusual drive and personality had quickly made him a leader of thousands of White English-speaking students angered by Government interference with their universities. He had fair, wavy hair, protruding lips, a pale face and a short, springy body, which gave him a distinctive and engaging appearance. At the many public meetings which he had addressed, his fervent, and witty speeches had invariably aroused his audience to passionate opposition of apartheid. Both young and old were attracted to him, and so patent were his resilience and integrity that he seemed to typify a spirit of urgent and indestructible idealism. It was distressing to think of him all alone in a bare concrete cell, but if anyone was capable of standing up to police pressure he seemed to be the one.

In the days that followed more students and ex-students were detained. I had difficulty in concentrating on my writing, for I kept visualising these young men and women battling against their isolation. Each day I opened my morning newspaper with a sense of dread, wondering who had been taken in on the previous night. The reports of the arrests were more detailed than usual, no doubt because the detainees came from what the press regarded as backgrounds more respectable than usual. On one occasion the headline read, SABO-TEUR CONFESSES, and a police officer was quoted as claiming that explosives had been found in Cape Town and that one of the detainees had made a full confession about his participation in sabotage activities. It was impossible from the report to guess which one of the half a dozen young men who had been taken into custody by then was the one concerned; possibly, however, the whole story had been made up to frighten people and justify the widespread arrests.

The detentions produced great excitement and anxiety in Cape Town, especially amongst students and staff at the University. Several campus protests were organised, and student representatives demanded that the detainees be either charged or released. There was no immediately discernible pattern to the arrests, and even people whose political activities had long since ceased began to panic and wonder where the detentions would end.

It was during this period that I was asked to be available one Sunday to meet a young physiotherapist who wanted to receive informal legal advice from me. I waited all day in my flat, but she did not arrive. Two days later, when I saw newspaper posters proclaiming that two more ex-students had been detained in Cape Town, I immediately guessed that she had been one of them.

I approached the newsagent apprehensively, straining to glimpse the headlines. The morning papers stood in a crisp pile on the counter and the moment I looked at them I saw her photograph—hair pouring gently round a soft, happy face, eyes innocent and touched with sparkle, cheekbones and brow luminous with the joy of early adulthood. TWO FORMER STUDENTS HELD IN CITY, the headlines declared. 'Two former university students, both of them aged 23, were detained by Security Branch police over the weekend,' the story read. 'They are Miss Stephanie Kemp, a physiotherapist and former U.C.T. student, and Anthony Trew, a Witwatersrand University B.A. who settled in Cape Town recently. Mr Trew's detention, under the 90-day regulations, was confirmed last night by his father, Mr A. F. Trew, general secretary of the Automobile Association. A senior Security Branch officer declined to comment on Miss Kemp's detention yesterday, but it is believed she is being held under the 90-day clause.' The story added that Anthony was the grandson of a former Deputy-Commissioner of police in the Cape.

Stephanie's picture entranced me, and I felt a simmering protectiveness towards her. It seemed monstrous that such loveliness could be thrust into a cell and subjected to the terrors of loneliness and police bullying. I wanted to shield her from the wrath of her interrogators and to urge upon her courage and the will to resist, yet there was so little that could be done that the only practical gesture which I could think of was to send in to her with her weekly laundry a cheerful red jersey which had in fact been knitted and sent to me during my detention.

The arrests, now mainly of junior lecturers at universities in various parts of the country, continued for weeks afterwards. It seemed that the police could do what they liked—their only failure was their inability to stop people from fleeing the country.

Then came news which shattered the complacency of the police. A bomb exploded on the main concourse of the White section of Johannesburg's railway station. Many people were injured, including an elderly woman who was not expected to survive. Gruesome pictures appeared in the press, and the Government assured the public that the persons responsible would be ruthlessly dealt with. Several people were in fact immediately taken into 90-day detention and not long afterwards one of the best-known of them, a young White teacher and sports administrator named John Harris, was seen by another detainee: his face was bloody, his jaw broken, he was dazed and complained of pain in his testicles. The police let it be known that as far as they were concerned the crime had been solved and that someone would soon be charged.

As the days passed, tension over the incident gradually subsided. For my part I was pleased that my work distracted me from painful but useless preoccupation with the fate of the detainees. My practice was building up strongly and all my spare time was devoted to writing. Occasionally, however, I lapsed into reverie. The closer I got to the end of the book the more my mind drifted away into fantasies of escape from South Africa and entry into a world where I would be released from perpetual strain and conflict. I imagined myself crossing the border in a variety of disguises. At times I would be hidden in the boot of a car, at others I would creep through the bush, on yet other occasions I would crash my way through a frontier barrier. I thought of airports and harbours and trains, of people helping me and of people pursuing me. Yet I could never really visualise myself outside South Africa; my fantasies would carry me up to the border but not over it. I decided that when the book was finished I would set about seriously planning my escape. It meant leaving the African who had visited me, and Denis and Stephanie and the other prisoners, but it would also mean getting away from the police and the threat of further detention and crack-up.

Chapter 4

Himie Bernadt, senior partner in a firm of attorneys with a large commercial practice, telephoned me one day to ask if I could meet him for lunch. I agreed, and after replacing the receiver, wondered what it was he wished to see me about. His firm handled a large amount of commercial, matrimonial and criminal work, but in recent years had also undertaken many defences in political matters. In a period when things were going badly, news was generally disheartening, and it was with some anxiety that I went to keep the appointment.

The restaurant where we met was large and crammed with old-fashioned dark-brown tables partly hidden by stiffly starched white cloths; in the corner a band played loudly, and everywhere white-aproned waitresses rushed busily to and fro. We settled down at a table as far from the band as we could get, and I waited expectantly to hear why Himie had asked to see me.

He began by apologising for giving me such short notice, explaining that he was 'completely snowed under', a favourite expression, at the time, of Cape Town lawyers.

Next he enquired about my work, and although I was eager for him to get to the business of our meeting, continued to chat amiably until we had placed our orders. When at one stage I observed to him that there were so many lawyers either in prison, underground or over the border, that the Government hardly needed to proceed with its plans to disbar 'undesirable' people from the profession, he smiled and asked if I had heard the latest Jewish New Year greeting: 'Happy New Year and well over the border.' He laughed with the wheezing chuckle of a heavy smoker, and I began to relax slightly.

The food arrived, and still he did not mention anything of special importance. We spoke of an appeal which I was due to argue against a prison sentence which had been imposed on a journalist friend of ours for being in possession of banned literature, and also discussed an application we were making on behalf of a client who wished to vary an order relating to the custody of her two young children. Nothing in our conversation seemed to justify the special meeting.

Himie was a cautious man, with a modest demeanour and a soft voice, so soft in fact that it was joked that he never had to worry about hidden microphones. Yet his determination, shrewdness and equability, together with his many years of experience, enabled him to handle difficult situations in a remarkably calm and effective manner. Though he had never, to my knowledge, been a member of any political organisation, and though even the police appeared to admire his integrity and professionalism, he always faced the danger of being penalised simply because of the cases he was willing to take on. He had once told me that in his youth he had been a long-distance runner, and the vision of a short, dogged athlete lurked inside the grey-suited, cigarette-smoking, middle-aged man who sat opposite me.

The band gaily pounded out pop tunes and the restaurant buzzed with chatter, so that I had to strain to hear what Himie was saying, especially since his voice seemed to have become particularly soft. His firm had been instructed to look after the interests of three of the young 90-day detainees, he was telling me. Adrian Leftwich I would, of course, know, but

33

did I know the other two, Alan Brooks and Stephanie Kemp? I nodded, and the vision of Stephanie's tender and beautiful features came back to me.

There wasn't much he could do for them until their 90-day detention was over, he continued in his quiet methodical way, but something had happened which required urgent attention and he thought he should get a second opinion. The gravity of his voice as he said this made me tense.

Messages had been smuggled out of the police cells, he continued. My anxiety increased. Both Brooks and Miss Kemp alleged, he informed me quietly, that they had been assaulted by members of the Security Police. I said nothing, but felt my lips tighten.

Did I know a Sergeant van Wyk—they called him 'Spyker'? I nodded again—van Wyk's name invariably cropped up when there was mention of violence.

Well, it seemed that van Wyk had beaten up both of them to force them to make confessions. The assaults had been quite severe and they had each been seen by the prison doctors. It was better not to mention who had brought the messages, for there was no reason why that third party should be involved more than was necessary. The question was, what could be done to expose what had happened so that Brooks and Miss Kemp could be protected from further violence?

The news of the assaults startled me, and I was unable immediately to respond sensibly to his question. Physical violence had been used extensively in the past against African and other non-White prisoners, but its infliction on White political prisoners was something new and represented a further deterioration in police standards.

The lunch-hour was nearing its end, and with elbows resting on the table, we anxiously began to consider what steps Himie could take. There would be no point in approaching the courts because they had already refused to intervene in similar cases, laying down that allegations of torture could be investigated only after the person concerned had been released from detention. Until then, the judges had emphasised, the police were in sole charge and no court would interfere. Not much help could be expected from the press either, since the papers would be too cautious to publish such a story. Finally there was no public body or authority to whom the matter could safely be referred, and to add to Himie's difficulties, the third party who had transmitted the messages had to be protected until he or she left for England, which he or she was due to do in a few days. We were beginning to feel increasingly frustrated and gloomy, when Himie eventually came up with an idea. Brooks had been born in Bristol, he pointed out, and being a British subject was entitled to the protection of Her Majesty's consul . . . I grew excited as I considered the implications: the consul could be expected to act on the basis of *prima facie* evidence, and although the press would not publicise the actual allegations, they might well mention the fact that the British consul was investigating certain complaints. If the consul were to intervene it was unlikely that the police would do further injury to Alan, and the publicity in his case would probably help to protect Stephanie as well. In the meantime her mother could be encouraged to keep requesting the police to be allowed to visit to her.

Himie puffed away at expensive cigarettes. His tact and skill would give the project a good chance of success, and he seemed encouraged by the enthusiasm which I showed for it. I was pleased that I had been of some assistance, even though I had merely acted as a sounding-board, and yet at the same time I felt anxious at having become involved in the matter.

The band had stopped playing, and the tables began to empty as diners hurried back to work. I looked around to see if I could discover whether we were being kept under observation, but could not see anyone taking special notice of us.

Himie was thanking me for having given up my lunch-hour, but I was only half-listening to him. In ordinary cases, he continued, he knew what the rules were and where his client's 'remedies' lay, but under the 90-day law there were no rules and he had to rely on people who, and he smiled as he said it, had inside experience. I smiled back at him. There did not seem to be much point in trying to describe to him how horrifying I found news of the assaults or how frightening the prospect was of being put 'inside' again.

Chapter 5

Carrying people for hire without a licence. Receiving a stolen drum of cooking oil. Damage to a motor car. Murder. Divorce. A psychologist's report on the best interests of children. Insurance. Fire. Debts. Company law. Salary owing. Drunken driving. Signature. Fraud . . .

My practice was growing more respectable each month. Instead of spending half my time fighting for persons charged with political offences, I was devoting all my days to the affairs, squabbles and ambitions of ordinary, middle-class citizens. My diary was filled with reminders of consultations and trials, and gradually my fees began to increase. For the first time in years I felt I could spend money on clothing, and bought a new suit and some shoes and ties. I also dropped my sixpence-saving rule of never buying tea or coffee after meals, and even spent a few pounds on acquiring a small abstract water-colour for my flat.

The work itself no longer gave me much satisfaction. It now seemed a mere game played by lawyers amongst themselves, which entirely ignored the pain of the victims. But at least my new kind of practice did not involve me in cases in which I was subjected to heavy stress. The period before my detention had been a particularly strenuous one. Two mass trials of a political character had kept me in court for weeks on end. I had had what in the gruesome language of my profession was known as my first 'swinger'—a client sentenced to death—followed shortly afterwards by a second one. These death sentences had upset me profoundly; I had previously appeared in more than thirty murder or rape trials in which capital punishment could have been imposed, but had not. Now within months two clients had been condemned to death, and although one was eventually reprieved, the other had been one of nearly a hundred men and women hanged in Pretoria Central prison that year. My last court appearance before my detention had been in connection with the defence of an African man charged with sabotage. According to the police he had been shot in the head by them while running away late one night from a post-office at which he had thrown a petrol bomb. With a large crater in his skull and with his vision, memory and coherence seriously impaired, he had shuffled slowly into court, where the judge had accepted complicated medico-legal evidence to the effect that he was unfit to stand trial.

Against such a background it was like being on holiday to fill my days purely with problems of matrimony, property and insurance. My most exacting work was in fact now being done at night, when I worked furiously to finish my manuscript. The end of the book seemed to come very suddenly and I felt proud and elated as I described my triumphant run from my cell to the sea. I was unable to share my elation with anyone, but privately I rejoiced as I recalled my release from prison—and celebrated the end of my enslavement to the book. A few weeks for typing and a couple of nights on revision, and I would be able to smuggle the manuscript out to a publisher in London, and then set about getting myself out of the country.

The 90-day arrests seemed to have come to an end, and I found that I was sleeping and eatine better than I had done for some time. A heartening headling appeared in the newspaper one day. SMUGGLED MESSAGES TOLD OF ASSAULT it read, and above it in smaller type were the words: 'Brooks: report to Embassy.' Himie's approach had obviously been successful. The paper stated that the British consul had visited a 90-day detainee, Mr Alan Brooks, and was sending a report to the Embassy in Pretoria. 'Mr Brooks' attorney,' the story continued, 'said today that Miss Tina Fiedler, a student who sailed from Cape Town last Friday, told him she received smuggled messages from Mr Brooks in which he alleged that Security Police had assaulted him. The attorney said he planned to take steps to have the allegations of ill-treatment investigated . . . Security Police in Cape Town declined today to comment.'

A few days later I saw Himie and found out more. Apparently Alan had confirmed that he had been subjected to physical torture. A week after the assault his ankles had still been swollen and sore, and the consul had asked that he be examined by a specialist. An X-ray had revealed a fracture and he was now hobbling around in plaster.

A short while later further relevant news appeared in the press. A meeting of more than two thousand students and staff of the University of Cape Town urged the authorities either to bring the detainees to trial or to release them at the earliest possible moment. While violence, subversion and sabotage could not be tolerated, the principal had said, it could not be countenanced that a single soul should be made to suffer hardship and indignity without being brought speedily to trial. The president of the Student's Representative Council had been more direct. He had declared that the students joined with religious leaders who stated that the 90-day law was morally indefensible; lawyers who regarded it as a negation of the rule of law; and medical specialists who labelled solitary confinement as torture. For those who asked what good it was to protest, he had gone on to applause, the audience should remember the words of Edmund Burke: 'For evil to succeed it was enough that good men did nothing.'

Yet despite these pleas and protests further weeks went by without any of the detainees being brought to trial. In Pretoria, however, the Station Bomb case commenced amidst much publicity. John Harris, charged with murder and sabotage, was the sole accused, and former friends and political associates of his were called to give evidence for the prosecution.

Rumours spread that all the other detainees would soon be moved to Pretoria, where they would be charged in one major conspiracy trial, and people began to speculate about who the witnesses would be in what was by then becoming known as the 'Leftwich case'. Himie and I discussed the matter from time to time, and thought that it was unlikely that either Alan or Stephanie would agree to be witnesses for the State against Adrian. And unless someone like them gave evidence it seemed that the prosecution would be unable to get a conviction against him.

We learnt one day that Stephanie had been moved to a prison seventy miles from Cape Town, which confirmed our feeling that special pressure was being applied to compel her to become a witness. It seemed inconceivable that she should succumb to the police and dishonour her ideals, and yet I had to allow for the fact that she was alone, isolated and inexperienced. 'You can't tell where it will all end,' I used to urge her in imagination, 'but you must keep on doing what is right at each stage and hope that ultimately everything will work out properly.'

For a time I was distracted from thoughts of Stephanie by an extraordinary murder case in which I was involved. Ten years earlier a White storekeeper had been stabbed to death in a village several hundred miles from Cape Town. Now, suddenly, four Coloured prisoners serving long sentences in a

40

Cape Town jail had one after the other confessed to having committed the crime: each had claimed that pressure of conscience had forced him to tell the authorities what he had done. My particular accused, a battered man with a long history of crime, soon unravelled the mystery of their sudden confessions. He explained to me that he had had nothing to do with the crime, but that conditions in the jail where he was serving his sentence were so bad that he and his mates were prepared to do absolutely anything to get transferred to another prison. Didn't he realise he would probably be hanged if found guilty of the murder? I asked. Yes, he replied, but anything was better than staying on in that hell. Apparently his main criticism was not so much the actual ill-treatment, since he had been in many jails and had got used to that, but the absence of a single person who would listen to their complaints.

The matter duly came to trial and an astonished judge and incredulous Attorney-General asked the same question that I had asked and got the same answer. The prosecution witnesses testified to there having been only one killer, so that when the time came for my final address I found myself in the unusual position of urging the court to believe all the prosecution evidence, and to hold that my client was a liar without a grain of genuine conscience. The judge took the point and the Attorney-General left the court shaking his head and declaring that he had never come across anything like it in his life.

Immediately after the conclusion of this trial—I heard later that the accused were going to be transferred to another prison—I found myself fully absorbed in an arbitration, for which Himie Bernadt's firm had briefed me, to settle a dispute between our client and the company which had built his at first sight magnificent house, splendidly situated on a mountain slope over-looking the sea. Eventually, after hours of snooping around searching for cracks, bad painting, or wrong levels, and wondering if I was to spend the rest of my life hiring out my energies to people engaged in squalid proprietary disputes, the arbitration was settled, and a short while afterwards I received a phone call from Himie's office. I assumed that Himie wished to discuss the details of the settlement, but as soon as he began to speak, realised that there was something more important in the air.

'They're being charged tomorrow,' he declared happily and cryptically, on a note of what was for him quite unusual excitement. Though the news was unexpected I guessed immediately that he was referring to his three detained clients. I too began to feel excited, for after three months of helpless waiting we would now at last be able to see them and give them legal aid.

Restoring his voice to its normal professional tone, Himie went on to tell me that the respective parents had given him written instructions to handle the defences of Leftwich, Brooks and Miss Kemp. He expected that they would be remanded for summary trial in the Supreme Court in about a month's time, and wanted to know if I had any suggestions about what could be done when they first appeared before the magistrate the next day.

I suggested that he might ask for bail; even though there wasn't much chance of it being granted, the application would give him an opportunity to mention how long the accused had been in solitary confinement and how necessary it was for them to enjoy ordinary society before being called upon to face the rigours of a serious trial.

We had to be cautious when speaking on the telephone, and we chose our words carefully. I felt confident that Himie would find the right note on which to make the application. Some years earlier, in what had been regarded as Cape Town's most sensational murder trial, he had prepared a bail appeal on behalf of the accused, a young girl who had shot her lover. The application had presented her in such a sympathetic way that from the moment of her arrest a climate had been created which eventually had contributed towards her acquittal. But she, I told myself wryly, had only shot a man, not engaged in politics.

Could I do him a favour? I heard Himie ask politely. He would go to the court in the morning so that he could see the accused as soon as possible, but unfortunately he was so snowed under, he wouldn't be able to spend much time with them: would I possibly be able to visit them at Roeland Street prison in the afternoon? I said I would gladly do so, and decided to tell him later of my reluctance to be drawn further into the case. I needn't worry about taking statements, Himie continued, he would do that as soon as he was free. All he wanted me to do was to chat to the accused, find out what they needed, and possibly answer any queries they might have about the trial procedure.

The next day I dressed with special care, pleased that I had decent new clothing to wear. I felt that because I identified so subjectively with the accused I would not be a good person to appear on their behalf at the trial, but there seemed to be no reason why in the meantime I should not do what I could to strengthen their morale.

As the morning progressed I sat impatiently in my office and imagined how I would greet the accused when I saw them later in the afternoon. It was a bright spring day and I looked forward to the trip. Briefs lay unattended on my desk and I visualised myself exuding warmth and strength in the consulting rooms of the prison.

The telephone rang. 'Hold the line for Mr Bernadt,' a lady's voice told me.

'Hullo, Albie, Himie Bernadt here.' His voice was hard and brisk. 'Can you still go up to Roeland Street this afternoon?'

'Yes, of course,' I replied.

'Well, you needn't bother to ask for Adrian Leftwich. He didn't appear in court this morning and the police say we can't see him under any circumstances. It doesn't look as though they're going to charge him at all, and if they don't, my mandate to look after his interests falls away.'

Hidden in this careful language was the shock he felt at the implications of his statement. The only reasonable explanation for Adrian's absence from the court seemed to be that he was going to be a witness against the others. This was incredible. He should have been the chief accused, not the principal witness for the prosecution. The earnest speaker, the buoyant, youthful, sincere organiser . . . no, it seemed impossible.

I told Himie that I would definitely see the others. My voice too was hard, and we ended the conversation abruptly. There was no reason why the police who listened in to my calls should know of my disappointment and consternation.

Some of my anger still remained when I later drove to the remand prison, but as I parked my car near the main entrance, I felt a renewal of my earlier excitement. The most important thing at that stage was not to think of Adrian, but to talk to Stephanie and Alan and to act as a lifeline between them and the world outside.

At the main door of the prison I tapped a brass hammer. A flap opened, a face peered at me, and then I heard the rasping movement inside of the iron bar which bolted the door to the wall. A lock turned, and the massive steel door swung open.

I stepped into a passage, signed the visitors' book, and proceeded to the next door. After ringing an electric bell I waited patiently for the guard at the other side to let me through; for years I had come to that prison to interview clients and I had learnt that jails had a pace of their own which nothing

44

would speed up. After a while a flap was opened, an eye appeared at a spy-hole, and the door was unlocked.

I told the guard that I wished to see Alan Brooks, and was conducted through two more doorways to a consulting room. The walls were bare and glistened with cream paint; I sat down at an old table and waited patiently in the austere room. The prison had been constructed in Victorian times and was cold, ugly and sunless. Every few weeks one read of prisoners who had used its mass of outside piping and gutters as a means of getting over the giant perimeter wall; the escapers' main hazard apparently was that the inner walls were so weak that they would tend to crumble and alert the guards. For many years 'Roeland Street', as we called the jail, had been Cape Town's main remand prison, but a newly built medium security prison on the outskirts of the city had recently taken over most of its functions and personnel. In earlier days we had had to conduct interviews in Roeland Street in the warders' billiard room, but the billiard tables had been transferred along with the warders and the prisoners, and as there was now plenty of space available a special consulting room had at last been provided. All the better, some of us felt, to tape-record our consultations with.

As I waited for Alan to be brought in, I opened my brief-case and placed a large notebook and ball-point pen on the table. How many stabbings and shootings had been re-enacted in that cold little room? I wondered. Every day clients stood in it in front of their lawyers. Some stuttered, some shouted, some whispered. They waved their arms to show how they had defended themselves from attack by the deceased; or they threw their hands towards the ceiling and called on God to be their witness that they had not even been near the scene of the crime; or they remained numb and uncomprehending while their lawyers impatiently tried to gouge information from them. A ball-point pen would become an imaginary knife, and

45

the more liberal lawyers would even offer their back or chest or neck as a target and say: 'Now, imagine I'm the deceased . . .'

Alan came in and stood pale and smiling in front of me. The warder remained in the doorway for a while and then went back to his duties in the interior of the prison. Alan sat down and after overcoming a temporary embarrassment began to speak rapidly. The words poured out in an excited tumble. He wore a lecturer's jacket with leatherbacked elbows, and his carefully modulated English voice and disciplined academic's mind seemed to match his appearance, yet he laughed frequently and excitedly and was so manic that our interview seemed more like a celebration than the first step in the preparations for a major trial. The forthcoming charges of sabotage seemed unimportant and far away; all that mattered was that he could see people again.

We discussed his detention, the cells he had been in, the interrogators and police guards. He spoke uninhibitedly about the assault upon him, describing how he had held out for some time, feeling the pain getting worse and worse until eventually it had reached an unendurable level. He believed that moment had come when his ankle had fractured, although he had not realised this at the time. In his statement to the police he had mentioned what had been done to him, but still he was very disappointed with himself and felt that possibly if he had been prepared for it he might have withstood the assault better.

I told him it seemed he had added very little to the information which the police already had at their disposal, and that they would regret having touched him. The consul's visit had already received much publicity and there was bound to be continued interest in his case. Of course, if he had been a captive in Eastern Europe or Black Africa, the British Foreign

Office might well have raised an outcry on his behalf, but still, it was something that they had intervened at all.

Alan's animation increased rather than decreased as we spoke. Even when we dealt with painful topics he bubbled with a peculiar happiness, which strongly reminded me of my own euphoria when I was released from solitary confinement.

We spoke about Adrian's absence from the dock that morning, and Alan declared he had no doubt whatever that Adrian would be a witness for the State. I shook my head and said I found it impossible to believe. Well, he replied with an uncharacteristic guffaw, he had never shared the general pro-Adrian feeling, but perhaps he might have been prejudiced because the two of them had been competitors in so many fields.

Our interview came to an end, and after noting requests for toilet items and newspapers, I went to the door to call the guard. Alan's tall, straight figure was led away and I felt like calling out to the warder: take me too, that is where I belong. Yet a sense of happiness hidden inside me acted as a reminder that I had still to see Stephanie, and I negotiated my way out of the men's section of the prison with a growing sense of exhilaration.

I felt bolder than I had done at any time since my release. Friends who shared my convictions would, I thought, approve of my being involved again, even if only as a lawyer. It was good to feel that I could still be active and of use.

As I walked out of the main entrance of the prison I visualised Stephanie's face once more—the beautiful, innocently radiant portrait that I had seen in the newspaper, that would soon be alive and talking to me. Satisfied that my nails were clean, my tie straight and my hair combed, I walked round to the women's section of the jail.

Chapter 6

Peering through the eyehole in the entrance door to the women's section, I saw a small yard and a large, old leafy tree. *Prring*—I gave the bell a long bold push and looked inside again. A young pretty-faced wardress, her khaki uniform pulling tightly against a large bosom, walked towards me and asked who was there. I picked up my briefcase and answered her in Afrikaans.

'This is Advocate Sachs and I've come to see Miss Stephanie Kemp on legal business.'

'What do you want?' she asked.

'I'm a lawyer and I want to see my client, Miss Kemp. She came in here today.'

'Hang on.'

She went away, and I spent the next few minutes peering at the tree, wondering whether I should ring the bell again. Eventually the wardress returned carrying a large bunch of keys. She unlocked the door, let me in, and locked it again.

'Are you a lawyer?' she asked.

'Yes, I'm an advocate.'

'Who do you want to see?'

'Miss Stephanie Kemp.'

'Oh, Kemp. She came in today. Follow me.'

I went with her across the yard and through a door into the

office section of the jail. Women prisoners stood in a row at the end of a corridor, chatting quietly to each other, while wardresses appeared and disappeared through a door that led to a yard inside. I was shown to a small office and asked please to wait there. The furniture was dirty brown and faded, the electric light hung too low on a piece of dusty flex, and the chair creaked as I sat on it, yet though the place was shabby and depressing and though I was impatient to see Stephanie, I felt less caged-in than I had done in the cold freshly-painted men's section.

'This way, Kemp,' I heard a voice command in another part of the building.

I opened my briefcase and took out a notebook. Footsteps sounded along the passage and I stood up to face the wardress and her charge as they entered the room.

A young girl with long dirty hair and wearing worn dark-blue jeans walked quickly into the room. Her over-large blouse was crushed and hung shapelessly over her chest and shoulders. She moved aggressively, and I noticed that her face was rough and blemished. Rushing towards the table where I was sitting, she started to speak to me in a harsh accented voice.

With a sense of dismay I realised that this was Stephanie. The soft luminous picture which I had carried in my mind was shattered by the thin unattractive person who stood before me, and I cursed myself for yet again in my life having succumbed to romantic illusion.

'Christ, Albie man, but it's marvellous to see you.' Her words came out in a hard quick flow, and I was embarrassed by the use of my first name in the presence of the wardress. 'Hell, boy, what a day it's been . . .'

'Mr Bernadt instructed me,' I interrupted, desperately trying to counteract the impression made by her familiarity, 'to consult with you this afternoon.'

'Oh, Himie. Gee, it was terrific seeing him there this morning. I was so excited, I threw my arms around him. He's so sweet. He asked if I wanted him to apply for bail and I didn't know what to say . . .'

As Stephanie enthusiastically told me about her appearance in court that morning, the wardress walked away and I began to feel easier. I broke into her excited torrent to suggest that we both sit down. She sat and carried on talking without pause, thrusting her head towards me and waving her fingers to emphasise her points. Apparently she had not even known she was going to be brought to court because that bastard 'Spyker'—she gestured contemptuously—had told her the night before that she wouldn't be charged for another three months. In the morning two men had come for her and they'd taken her along a passage and told her nothing and then all of a sudden she'd seen Alan and Spike and two other detainees.

She'd joined them, she told me merrily, and they'd all gone up some stairs and she'd seen Himie, who had seemed to be very embarrassed when she'd flung her arms around him. The discussion about bail had followed and then she'd still been talking and laughing to Alan when she heard someone telling her to keep quiet and a policeman had looked across and said she must turn round and face the magistrate. She hadn't even realised she'd been in court till the whole thing was over and she had gone downstairs again. Then she'd noticed Adrian wasn't there and hadn't been able to understand why till Alan had explained he would be a State witness. What did I think of that, hey? And could I get hold of her bag? It had been put into the car that morning, a Cortina, and the police hadn't given it back to her.

She laughed brightly as she talked and I became increasingly aware of that manic spirit which seemed to light up all detainees on their release from solitary confinement. On my first night out I had babbled to friends until late in the morning, finding that the joy of being free had temporarily blotted out all the pain and depression of the previous half year.

Stephanie told me that she felt fantastic. She could have run twice as far as I had when I had dashed to the sea, she declared. Colour came into her face as she said this and she began to look softer than she had done earlier. Her eyes were alive and although her manner and language were still edged with an unnatural coarseness, she was less aggressive than she had been at first. Ideas danced around in her mind and she chased gaily from one theme to the next.

What did I think of Adrian? she asked again with a laugh. After she'd been inside for a while the police had told her that Adrian had made a statement, but she simply hadn't believed it.

Then, from the questions they'd put to her, it had become plain he must have talked and she'd begun to get worried. They'd said Adrian had wanted her to make a statement and she'd thought she could use this as a pretext for seeing him. She hadn't believed them of course, but had demanded to hear it from his own lips. They'd taken her to him and he'd stood there the way he did, with his hands in his pockets, and she'd said to him, 'Adrian, the police tell me you've become a quisling.' The police had been absolutely furious when she'd said this, their faces had turned dark with anger, but Adrian had just shrugged and said he supposed it could be called that, but he didn't see any point in her not giving evidence, especially as there was so little she knew anyhow. He'd given that sort of half-embarrassed smile of his and she'd kept thinking he was trying to get some message across to her. Then he'd offered her a cigarette and she'd said, 'Gee, Adrian, you've got cigarettes!' and he'd been extremely embarrassed because he'd been able to smoke while she hadn't. The police had chipped

51

in that she could have had cigarettes too if she'd made a statement. She'd been pretty upset by the whole episode, but had tried not to let them know how she felt and had said she still refused to make a statement.

I sat back in my chair, not attempting to take notes at this stage, but listening carefully to her description of the many pressures used by the police to break down her resistance. There was an expressiveness to her narrative which made the confrontations between her and the security policemen come alive. She made no attempt to analyse the experience, but presented a series of pictures illuminated by what seemed to me to be an extraordinary clarity of detail.

One day a short while after her encounter with Adrian, she told me, the police had taken her to a little room in Caledon Square, the police headquarters. It must have been a storeroom of some kind, because it was full of suitcases and typewriters, and when she'd got there it must have been about eleven in the morning. They'd started off by making her stand for hours on end while a lieutenant from Johannesburg named Viktor had subjected her to an aggressive political harangue. She'd been told before that the Cape Town men had been soft but the Johannesburg men would be tough, and Viktor had seemed to live up to this prediction. He'd gone on for hours, never repeating himself once, and she'd had to admire the intelligent level on which he'd spoken. He'd looked so healthy with a sort of open Aryan face that it had made her sick, but what he said had been impressive. At first he'd been extremely angry, so that she'd told him early on that not only did he speak like a Nazi, but looked like one, after which he had smiled behind his hand and then begun to relax a bit.

She described the scene without any self-awareness and I felt like smiling behind my own hand as I pictured the incident. After standing for about four hours, she continued, she'd felt her back getting very sore. Viktor had been speaking about Hyde Park at the time, and this had reminded her of the sit-downs by the nuclear disarmers in London. She'd decided that she too would sit, and told him she was going to do so because of her sore back. Then she'd sat on the floor and Viktor had tried to lift her by her arms, but she'd remained completely limp. She'd told him the situation was ridiculous for both of them, and he let her go, saying she could sit for five minutes. When the five minutes were up he said she could sit until he had finished his cigarette, but when the cigarette was finished he hadn't said anything more about the subject.

It had only been when Captain Rossouw came in just before supper time that she'd been made to stand again. She couldn't bear Captain Rossouw. He was always cold and hostile and always shouted at her. On that occasion too he'd sort of barked at her when he came into the room. Why was she sitting? he'd asked loudly. Didn't she realise she wasn't allowed to do so? Viktor had answered that he had only permitted her to sit for five minutes, and the Captain had ordered her to get up again. During the whole time she'd only been allowed out of the room once to go to the toilet and at no stage had she been given anything to eat. When she'd asked for food Rossouw had said he thought she was on hunger strike and she'd replied she'd broken it the previous night and anyhow that was all the more reason for her to eat.

During the evening the police had taken it in turns to interrogate her. She'd been made to stand all the time and Rossouw had told her his men had been treating her too well —this was a war and the sooner she realised it the better. He was very sorry, he had said, that 'they' used women to do 'their' dirty work, but if she chose to behave like a man she would be treated like a man, just as he wouldn't hesitate to treat professors and lawyers and women all in the same way. She hadn't realised then what he'd been getting at, and in any event hadn't wanted any special treatment just because of her sex. In fact all this aggressiveness towards her had been having the opposite effect to that intended. At the beginning of the day when the interrogation had started, she'd felt very weak and insecure and probably if they'd spoken to her decently she'd have made a statement, especially since they seemed to know everything anyhow. But their hostility had made her angry and she'd told them she wouldn't let them intimidate her.

At one stage Rossouw had got up and opened the door and then asked her if she knew why he'd done that. She'd said no, but she assumed it was because of the stuffiness in the room from all the smoking. He'd answered that she was wrong, he was opening the door to protect himself from any accusation she might try to make against him.

'Spyker' had come in and out at this time and kept on wheedling and whining in an attempt to persuade her to make a statement. She'd felt embarrassed for him because he'd so obviously been trying to impress the Captain, but really was too stupid to impress anybody. He seemed absolutely to worship the Captain, and she couldn't stand the way he always humiliated himself in his pathetic attempts to please his master. He'd then asked Rossouw if he could be left alone with her, and Rossouw had hesitated for a moment, looked down, and stormed out of the room in a terrible rage. Later on, it had been after she'd returned from the toilet, she remembered, 'Spyker' had told her that he was completely devoted to his job, which he was doing to the best of his ability for his country and his children. He'd begged her time and again, 'Please, please make a statement.' All he'd been able to do had been to repeat the sentence over and over again, and she felt sorry for him, because he didn't have the intellect of someone like Viktor, who could keep up a high-powered conversation for hours. Another policeman had come in and asked her why she had refused to make a statement and she told him their bullying tactics had destroyed any chance of her doing so.

She'd realised from the start of the interrogation that morning that she was in a very difficult situation because of all they knew about her activities, and had thought to herself that if she made a statement it could only have made her position worse, especially as they wanted her to be a witness. Without a statement from her she couldn't see how they could force her to give evidence, and anyway she'd wanted to see her lawyers before saying anything at all. When she told them this, they'd said she had no rights at all any more and they had become her lawyers now. She hadn't known whether to believe them or not since she didn't know much about the law, and in fact all the time she hadn't been able to tell if they'd been speaking the truth or not.

Viktor had eventually returned and had then spent most of the evening arguing with her. He had been much less reasonable at this stage, and had kept making insulting remarks about Jews. When she'd told him he was being anti-Semitic he'd answered that he didn't agree with Hitler, but one part of Hitler's policy he did agree with was the Final Solution. In the morning he'd spoken with great sophistication, admitting there were aspects of the Government's policy he might not agree with and so on, but in the evening he'd been much cruder and more threatening. He'd confidently told her that the detainees would all hang for their part in the Station Bomb case, and that this time the police would see to it that they got a judge who knew his duty, because in the Rivonia case the judge had let one of the accused get away and had let the others off with life sentences. He wouldn't like to see a rope round her pretty little neck and she would be well advised, he had warned her, to cooperate with the police to avoid this happening.

By then she'd been standing for most of the day and the whole of the evening, and had become pretty exhausted. Viktor had kept on and on at her till after midnight, when 'Spyker' had suddenly turned up and told Viktor the Captain wished to speak to him. Viktor had gone, and she had then been alone in the room with 'Spyker'. She still hadn't expected anything special, but had been pretty tired and angry because of the way they'd been treating her.

'Spyker' had started off quietly, simply pleading with her. Then he'd got up off a suitcase on which he'd been sitting and had placed himself right in front of her. He'd told her he still liked her and had in fact had a soft spot for her ever since he'd been sent to detain her. He didn't want to do this to her, he had continued, but he had to do his duty. He knew she didn't like him and after this would hate him even more. He knew she hated him, he knew she hated him. Again and again he'd repeated this statement and eventually she'd felt so fatigued and so annoyed by the way he'd kept saying this that she'd muttered desperately: 'Yes, I do hate you!' It seemed as though he'd been waiting to hear these words, for suddenly he'd shouted at her: 'Are you going to make a statement?' and then when she'd said 'No,' he'd started hitting her.

At the time she had been standing looking down at the floor and he'd struck her in the face hard with both hands. His palms had been open and his arms rigid from the elbows, and by swinging them vigourously to and fro he had been able to slap her fiercely from both sides. She hadn't felt any pain then, only fright and surprise and it had been the coldness of the attack that had upset her as much as the actual violence, since he hadn't even been angry but had dealt with her methodically and without feeling. Immediately after striking her several times in the face, he had grabbed her hair and pulled her to the ground. Then he'd started bashing her head against the floor. She'd been shocked and terrified, and had told him:

56

'Van Wyk, I'll talk.' She hadn't shouted it, just sort of groaned the words, but he hadn't taken any notice and had kept on beating her head downwards. She'd felt she was falling a long distance, and everything was turning and going black and she thought she was becoming unconscious. After that she'd become confused, and couldn't remember what happened for a short time until she'd heard someone say, 'Get up!'

She'd managed to get to her knees and place her hands on a table, and she'd wanted to vomit. Someone had said: 'That won't help you.' Somehow she'd got to her feet, possibly someone had helped her, and then she'd heard 'Spyker' saying once more, 'Will you make a statement?' She'd said she would, and noticed that he'd been panting. 'Who will you make it to?' 'Spyker' had asked. She'd looked up and seen Viktor standing behind him with his jacket off, and had said, 'To Viktor.'

Viktor had told her to sit down on the chair, which she had done, but then she'd started shaking violently. Someone, she wasn't sure who, had said, 'Stop acting', and she'd tried to control her shaking. Viktor had seated himself on the other chair and had told her to move closer to him. She'd tried to do so but hadn't been able to, and he'd got up and helped her. Then he had scolded her for calling him 'Viktor', saying it had probably been a slip, but in future she had to be careful to call him 'Lieutenant Viktor'. She must put her hand in his, he had said, because he wanted her to trust him and regard him as her friend. All the Security policemen were her friends, he had added.

Viktor had then mentioned sympathetically that he didn't like to see her looking like that, and she'd asked him if she could borrow his comb. While she combed her hair he'd left the room to get pencil and paper, and she'd noticed clumps of hair coming out in the comb. When Viktor returned he'd seen a pile of this hair lying on the floor, but all he'd done was kick it under the table without saying anything. He hadn't seemed particularly keen to take a statement there and then, and had asked her what the matter was with her eye. Leaning forward he'd touched her on the face; it was very tender and she'd winced. What had happened, he had demanded aggressively, when he had been out of the room? He had kept on badgering her with this question, using such an angry voice that she had always answered, 'Nothing, nothing happened.' She was sure he'd known what had taken place, for it must have been obvious to him, and she feared she would merely be beaten up again if she said 'Spyker' had assaulted her.

After a little while he had started trying to take down a statement but she had been so incoherent that he'd stopped and simply let her talk on. She couldn't be sure exactly what she'd said to him or for how long she'd spoken, but she could recall asking him what the time was and that he had said ten past one. He must have felt there was no point in continuing with the interrogation, since he had escorted her back to her cell and had told her he would see her again. The building had been quiet because of the late hour and as she had got undressed she'd heard the nearby City Hall clock strike two.

Her neck was stiff and she'd felt confused and sick. When she lay down she hadn't been able to put her head on the one side, and altogether she'd felt very sore and scared. She'd never been involved in violence in her life before and the experience had shocked her deeply.

Later she'd woken suddenly to see 'Spyker' standing in the doorway of her cell. It was unusual for the police to come into her cell when she was sleeping, so she was terrified, immediately expecting further ill-treatment.

'Spyker' has asked if she was ready to make her statement,

but she had begged him to let her sleep. He had looked at his watch and said it was five a.m. and that he would return at six. Too terrified to sleep, she had lain awake till six, but 'Spyker' hadn't come. Later she'd got dressed and had spent the whole of the morning anxiously waiting for him to appear.

Chapter 7

From time to time a wardress would walk past the doorway of the shabby room in which we were sitting, but otherwise there were no interruptions to Stephanie's narrative. At first I said hardly anything, and my notebook remained empty, but later I began to comment on what she said and ask some questions. I pointed out that Van Wyk must have assaulted Alan immediately after he had beaten her up, and then have returned to her cell again as soon as he and his colleagues had finished with Alan. There was no doubt about his devotion to duty, I commented grimly, not every man was prepared to work right through the night to protect his country and his children.

After we had discussed Alan's assault, I asked her to continue with her story, because apart from its importance for her case there were many people in South Africa and abroad who wanted to know exactly what had happened to her. The students were especially interested, I added. She seemed surprised and pleased to hear this, and before going on mentioned that she'd thought people would be critical of her because she'd made a statement. Possibly if she'd been prepared for the assault she might have been able to withstand it better, she said, but she'd been taken so much by surprise that her morale had been seriously affected.

She told me that the assault had taken place in the early hours of Sunday morning, and that on the Monday she'd been taken to the same little room and again left alone with Viktor. This time she'd told him what 'Spyker' had done and he'd said, 'So it took only one clout to get you to make a statement.' Being thrown on the floor and having one's head beaten was hardly one clout, she'd replied. Viktor had answered with a smile that he didn't think it had been necessary to assault her, a sign of weakness on van Wyk's part,—he'd have succeeded in getting her to talk without using violence. In any event, he'd added, he would much rather have her crying on his shoulder. Then he'd taken down her statement which had been fairly full but not too long.

She had admitted to Viktor that . . . I interrupted and explained that as far as the pending criminal case was concerned she should forget about anything she had said to the police after her assault. The prosecution would have the greatest difficulty if it tried to put her statement in as evidence against her, and it would be as well for her to think about her defence without worrying over matters that wouldn't feature at the trial.

She was puzzled by my intervention and after a momentary silence darted off into further descriptions of what had happened to her. On the Tuesday morning, she told me, 'Spyker' had called to take her to a new cell at Wynberg police station. Until the night when he'd struck her, he'd always been friendly and had given her cigarettes and said how much he liked her, but after the assault he'd been cold and hard. He had seemed to make a special point of telling her lies to frighten and confuse her, and would tease and mock her in a specially malicious way. She was scared of him, and yet whenever she thought of him she just felt overwhelming pity because he tried so hard to prove he wasn't weak and stupid, particularly in the presence of his hero Captain Rossouw, who treated him like a little dog that had to be protected all the time. It had been really awful to see 'Spyker' whining and cringing in front of Rossouw, saying the same stupid things over and over again, and trying to make a good impression. As a policeman she'd no time at all for him, but as a person she felt really sorry for him because he was so inferior to the others, and the only way he could get her to talk was through physical violence. It was pathetic—he'd had to assault her to prove to the others he wasn't stupid. Meanwhile the others must have known exactly what was going to happen, but had done nothing about it.

The spontaneity of these observations and the natural insight and charity which they revealed impressed me deeply. I had seen Sergeant van Wyk several times in court, and had found him to be diffident and tense, but otherwise not particularly remarkable. He was tall and dark, with a narrow, unfriendly face and a long, thin, hard figure, which possibly accounted for his not very complimentary nickname of 'Spyker' (the Afrikaans word for 'nail'). In the witness box he always stood very erect, answering questions in a flat, slightly choking and toneless voice and all the while staring rigidly in front of him. Many of the security policemen were jaunty and eager to display what they regarded as their capacity for wit, but van Wyk was invariably dour and withdrawn. Even his short black moustache, I thought, was humourless. I had cross-examined him on a few occasions, but never on anything substantial. Then, after my detention he had had the opportunity to do the questioning. I had refused to answer his questions, as I had done with all the other interrogators, but he had nevertheless put propositions to me which were so patently and ludicrously false that even his colleagues had been embarrassed. He had never threatened me personally with violence, but in recent years I had heard many complaints against him by others. There had also been a strong rumour to the effect that he was a police link with a lunatic-type group which called itself the K.K.K. and terrorised left-wing and

62

liberal opponents of apartheid by firing shots through windows, interfering with motor cars, making abusive phone-calls in the middle of the night and writing obscene, threatening letters, especially to women. Whether or not he had any connection with this group, and the evidence had only been circumstantial, he undoubtedly belonged to that class of policemen euphemistically characterised by the Bench as being over-zealous.

Stephanie told me of her journey with van Wyk to Wynberg police cells, and emphasised how low her morale had been at the time. She had been terrified of van Wyk, but the move to Wynberg seemed to have helped her a lot. She'd felt much safer there and in her cell had found what she described as 'that pompous stuff' I had scratched on the side of the cell door when I had been detained there.

I was amused and a little put out by her description. 'I, Albie Sachs,' I had written, 'was detained here in solitary confinement for standing as advocate and citizen for justice for all.' Below I had kept a calendar of the days, while above the door I had in a more cheerful style scratched: 'Jail Is For The Birds.' As a lawyer I had been careful not to write anything which could have been used in evidence against me.

The words had helped her immensely, she continued, and she'd felt that if I could fight back, so could she. After she'd been in the cell for a few hours, Snyman, the Station Commander had come round to look at her and had immediately asked her about her bruised eye. She was amazed and relieved that he'd asked about her injury, because in the previous two days a number of policemen had come round on inspection in the cells and they'd all asked her if she'd had any complaints and not one of them had said a word about her black eye, even though it had stared them in the face. She'd told Snyman about the assault and had said she'd been too terrified to make an official complaint in case she was beaten up again.

He'd assured her that nobody would touch her while she was a prisoner in his cells, and on the next day he had come to her with a magistrate, who had taken a full sworn statement from her. The magistrate had been quite friendly, but at the same time had asked her what she had expected—if the police had caught a murderer they would have been entitled to be rough to get the evidence, and the same would have applied to her. A Government doctor had also come to see her and had made notes about her condition. He'd been very brusque on that occasion, but then a week later when all she'd had was a cold, he'd been much nicer.

The police had by now begun to press her hard to become a State witness, but she'd been feeling much better and had persistently refused. Then that morning they'd told her to pack all her things again and now here she was in 'Roeland Street.'

I thought that she might pause for a while after this long story, but immediately she went off into a further rushed description of the events of that day. She was particularly concerned about her bag and was most annoyed that the police had driven off with it. Could I see to it that they gave it back? she asked. It had all her things in it. It had been funny suddenly being in court and not even knowing she'd been there. The magistrate had been cross with her for talking but she hadn't even realised he'd been a magistrate and had kept her back to him all the time! She'd never been in court before and it was terrific being able to talk to someone again; hell, it was marvellous to be free!

Her brightness and merriment increased as she recalled the surprise and excitement of the morning. I told her that Mr Bernadt would be handling her defence and would instruct counsel to appear for her and for Alan at the trial. She seemed unconcerned about the case against her, and I decided not to discuss it in any detail at that stage. With five weeks available for preparation whoever was briefed by Himie for the trial would have opportunity enough to go into the defence with her.

Being specially curious to find out how her conditions compared with mine, I asked if she minded telling me a bit about her treatment in the various police cells in which she had been kept. As it happened she had been in two of the three cells in which I had been held. The first had been at Maitland police station, she told me, where the police had nearly driven her mad by nagging her every exercise time to be more active and by telling her how I had always run round and round in the exercise yard. She hadn't seen what my exercise had to do with hers, or that it was any of their business anyway. In Wynberg it hadn't been so bad, because the police hadn't talked about me so much but she did remember Snyman taking her round the walls once and saying, 'Look here what Mr Sachs wrote when he was my prisoner.' He had laughed when he had showed her the scratchings and she thought he had been proud of them and rather fond of me.

From her descriptions of life at the different police stations it seemed that conditions had remained more or less the same as they had been for me. I was particularly interested to hear her opinions about Warrant Officer Snyman, who after a very harsh beginning had softened and shown humanity to me in a number of little ways. A few days after my release I had gone round to Wynberg police station to say 'hullo' to my former guards, and Snyman had seemed annoyed I hadn't gone first thing to greet him.

Stephanie was startled when I told her this. Why had I gone to see them? she asked, her brows creasing. Just because some of the police weren't as bad as the others didn't mean we should visit them, she continued. After all, basically they were all fascists carrying out a fascist policy, whatever the individual might say or feel. She spoke quickly and with feeling and reminded me that none of the detainees had asked to be placed in police cells in the first place.

I told her I'd been back not only to Wynberg but to Maitland as well. In Snyman's case I'd been genuinely grateful for some of the kindness he had shown me; little though it had been, in the circumstances it had meant a lot. But my main objective had been to force the police to see political prisoners as human beings and not just as dangerous objects and threats to the State. I had been thinking of other prisoners who might be placed in their charge, since I had known I wouldn't be the last, just as she wouldn't be the last. Somehow the whole atmosphere in a place like that changed as soon as the people in charge started to see their captives as individuals, and anything which encouraged that was to the good. I added that it had worried me, since my visits could have been regarded as unnecessary fraternisation, but I had decided to follow my feelings and had done what I felt to be best.

She did not appear convinced by my arguments, and we allowed the matter to drop. There was something else I would like to ask her before leaving, I said. She looked expectantly at me, her eyes bold and open.

Did she ever get a jersey I had sent in to her? A bright red one with a yellow stripe at the bottom?

Oh, had that been from me? She told me in a matter-of-fact way that she'd worn it a lot, in fact she'd had it on on the night of the assault, because she remembered Viktor telling her afterwards it didn't do anything for her figure and she'd looked down and seen clumps of hair on it which she'd brushed off.

She did not thank me, and I was disappointed that the gesture had not meant anything to her.

A wardress appeared in the doorway and shouted that we must please finish up because the prisoners were being locked up. I looked at my watch and saw that our consultation had

66

lasted well into the afternoon. My notebook lay open and clean on the dark table which stood between the two of us. The sudden appearance of the wardress had reminded me that whereas Stephanie was about to return to a cell, I would be permitted to go out free. It had been a sunny day and possibly I could later go for a swim . . .

We stood up and I packed my notebook into my briefcase. I told her warmly that there were many people who had followed her detention with special feeling and concern, and that they'd be extremely pleased to hear of her cheerfulness and good spirit. She'd become quite a heroine, I added with a smile, right from the time she'd been locked up.

She looked at me suspiciously and then her eyes brightened and she laughed, seemingly both pleased and embarrassed. As she stood leaning against the table, I realised again how small and thin she was and how much she had been affected by the roughness of police lock-ups.

She mustn't get alarmed, I advised her, if her moods went up and down a bit. And was there anything she needed right then?

I promised that enquiries would be made about her bag, and then, too self-conscious to shake her hand, stepped aside to allow her to leave the room before me. She strode away with quick little steps and went down the passage followed by the wardress. Suddenly she stopped and turning round to face me shouted with delight, 'Hey, there's my bag, it's come. My bag's there in the passage.' The wardress told her to shut up shouting, and she picked up the bag and happily carried it through a doorway towards the centre of the prison.

Chapter 8

The leader of the team responsible for Alan and Stephanie's defence was Wilfred Cooper, a lithe, ambitious advocate regarded as one of the leading trial lawyers at the Cape Bar. Before starting to practice he had been a public prosecutor and had developed a fierce cross-examining style which had led many of his colleagues to call him by the nickname 'Tiger'. His court manner had lost none of its attack, and his lively temperament, which he always harnessed fully to his client's cause, drew many people to watch him in action. Yet the main bases of his success were probably less spectacular: the fanatical thoroughness with which he always prepared his cases and the flair he had for adjusting rapidly and sensibly to the shifting fortunes of a trial. His appearance was strikingly youthful, but he had the penetrating caustic voice and verbal facility of a much older man. The wide interests of his earlier years— he was now approaching forty—had given way to a passion to be a respected advocate, and one day possibly, a judge.

The pending sabotage trial threatened to raise many tricky issues for the defence, but if well handled could materially enhance counsel's reputation. Many of our colleagues would have found a way out of accepting such a brief, but Himie was confident that even if he disagreed profoundly with their views, Wilfred would do wholehearted and intelligent battle for his clients.

Himie asked me to act as Wilfred's junior, and despite my reluctance to be involved in the case, I agreed. This meant that I would be obliged to stay on in South Africa for several months longer than I had planned, but with summer approaching and my anxiety abating slightly I was not too unhappy about it.

Altogether there were four legal teams appearing on behalf of the five accused, and the array of counsel alone would have secured special interest in the case. Accused number one was Edward Daniels, a 30-year-old photographer, who was both the oldest and the only Coloured person among the accused. Accused number two was David ('Spike') de Keller, the handsome 23-year-old son of a wealthy Cape Town businessman. Accused number three was Anthony Trew, the university graduate whose arrest had been reported at the same time as that of Stephanie, and the last two accused were, respectively, Alan and Stephanie. The case was set down for six weeks in the number one criminal court of the Cape Supreme Court, and the Attorney-General entrusted the prosecution to a dour but capable senior assistant.

The defence teams worked independently of each other, and Himie, Wilfred and I met frequently in Wilfred's chambers to work out the lines we would follow on behalf of our accused. Each of us usually had some information to pass on to the others—Wilfred providing news and gossip from the Supreme Court, Himie intelligence from the other attorneys, and I requests and ideas from our clients. The office in which we worked was large and bright; blue wall-to-wall carpeting and purple and green curtains provided a contemporary setting for a massive wooden desk which was surrounded by elegant chairs, while the whole of the back wall was taken up by an imposing stretch of vividly coloured text books and law reports. A swivel chair behind the desk tilted and turned to accommodate Wilfred's restless changes of posture, and on the desk lay a brass letter opener which he would from time to time pick up and tap nervously against his hand. Himie was invariably calm and businesslike. He would arrive hunched and brisk, with a pile of pink folders under his arm; placing the folders on the desk, he would take off his jacket, light a cigarette and make a joke. Then the consultations would begin.

In front of each of us there was always a pile of documents which grew higher and higher as the trial got nearer. Using powers which Parliament had recently specially granted him, the Attorney-General had ordered that no preparatory examination be held before the Supreme Court trial. This meant that we did not know who would be the witnesses for the prosecution or what they would say. It also meant that the indictment was more important than it would have been in an ordinary trial, because it was the only source of information as to what sort of case we had to prepare ourselves to meet.

To begin with, the charges ran to several pages of Roneoed legalese and by the time the prosecution had supplied the further particulars requested by us, they constituted a bulky and complex document. As each set of papers arrived from the Attorney-General's office we would read through it with anxiety and excitement, looking for clues as to the prosecutor's plan of action.

From the start we realised that the charges were grave. All the accused were alleged to have been members of an unlawful organisation known as the African Resistance Movement (A.R.M.). As such they had allegedly conspired together and with others to commit a number of acts of sabotage, their aim being to coerce or overthrow the South African Government. The acts of sabotage committed by them or the other conspirators, the indictment declared, had taken place over a period of ten months and had included explosions or attempted explosions of a broadcasting tower, four railway signal cables, and five pylons carrying electricity power lines. In addition the accused were alleged to have planned to destroy a government garage and to have considered ways of securing the release of Robert Sobukwe (a prominent African political prisoner who was being detained on Robben Island even though he had completed his sentence). The main charge was one of sabotage, and each was alleged to have assisted in bringing about at least one explosion, but there was an alternative charge as well, namely that they had performed an act calculated to further the achievement of an object of communism: 'to wit had been members of an organisation dedicated to a scheme which aimed at bringing about political, industrial, social or economic change in South Africa by means of the promotion of disorder.' There was an important difference in the possible penalties. Under the main charge of sabotage the minimum penalty was five years' imprisonment, and the maximum sentence was death. Under the alternative charge, however, the range was from one to ten years' imprisonment, and a portion of that could be suspended.

Although it was generally understood that the accused had had a liberal rather than left-wing political orientation, no one had been surprised by the fact that the alternative charge had been framed under the Suppression of Communism Act. The Government claimed that in South African conditions communism meant racial equality and that liberalism paved the way for and led directly to communism. The terms of the Act were accordingly sufficiently wide to deal with all forms of subversion of the prevailing order, whether by a communist or not, and in fact, many known anti-communists had fallen foul of its provisions.

From the piles of paper which we received we were able eventually to extract a series of specific allegations which when boiled down and converted into plain language gave us an idea of precisely what our two clients were supposed to have done.

71

Alan was alleged to have received training in the handling of explosives and to have attempted to blow up one lot of signals cables, while Stephanie was alleged to have hired a garage for use as a workshop and to have twice driven the car used by saboteurs.

Large though it was, the indictment formed only a small part of the papers which we had to read. Some weeks before the trial the prosecution handed us photostatic copies of nearly a hundred documents which the police had found in the garage where explosives had been stored. These documents recorded in remarkable detail the activities of the organisation over a period of nearly a year, but, fortunately for the members, did not mention anyone by name. It was clear to us that the prosecution would have no difficulty in proving that the organisation had existed and what its aims and activities had been, but we felt equally convinced that the only way in which the accused could be personally implicated would be if an important member of the organisation took the stand and denounced them. One man alone seemed to fit the bill—Adrian Leftwich.

Our instructions were that our clients would plead not guilty to both the main and the alternative charges, and pursuant to those instructions we collected a large amount of material for cross-examining Adrian. He dominated our preparations. Without him the prosecution case against our two clients would collapse; with him it could hardly fail, for he was resourceful and persuasive and no court would easily believe that he would falsely implicate former friends, even if there had been minor strains between them.

The more we learnt about his behaviour during detention, the more concerned we became about the extent of his breakdown. The picture was one of consistent deterioration, leading finally to what appeared to be a complete reversal of allegiances. He had been detained during the wide-spread raid because the police had discovered incriminating documents in his flat. They had also discovered a girl in his bed, but she had been allowed to go home, where she had promptly removed some dynamite to a garage in another part of town. A policeman watching her house had reported seeing her loading cases into her car and she too had been detained for questioning. Apparently she had then been severely beaten, sustaining head injuries which had subsequently had to be X-rayed, and as a result of the assault she had given the police some information about the dynamite. Adrian had apparently broken relatively early on during his interrogation. He had been threatened with assault but not actually beaten, and had persuaded his girl-friend to tell the police where she had taken the dynamite. Thereafter he had gradually started to help the police more and more, betraying the names of members of the organisation in all parts of the country and giving an extensive account of their activities. The next stage had been to agree to put pressure on other detainees to become witnesses for the State, and finally he had gone the whole way over to the police by agreeing to be a State witness himself. On the wall of one of his cells he had written that he had learnt for the first time how weak he was, but how great was the power of love; we were more inclined to think that he had discovered for the first time how weak he was and how great was the power of the police. In the remand prison two of the accused had attempted to smuggle a note to him, but instead of responding to their call to join them, he had apparently reported the matter to the police.

The police were still holding him incommunicado under lock and key and it was expected that he would be brought straight from his cell to the witness box. Only then would we know for sure whether the stories about him were true and whether his breakdown had been complete. To me it still seemed incredible that a man of Adrian's spirit and background could actually stand up in court and testify against his most intimate friends and colleagues. Yet all the indications were that that was precisely what he would do.

Public interest in the case remained high and one daily newspaper in what was clearly a reference to Adrian ran a lead story on the dilemma facing certain State witnesses. Himie, Wilfred and I were also unable to prevent ourselves from lapsing at times into speculation about the case. Apart from the problem of Adrian, there were a number of other questions to distract us.

We often wondered who would be the judge at the trial. To the public all judges might seem alike, but to us each one was different, with his own special strengths and weaknesses, flairs and prejudices. In the long run the idiosyncracies of individual judges might well even themselves out, but a client was not interested in the long run, only in his personal case, just as the practitioner was not concerned with the development of legal science, but only with how to win his next trial. Of all the judges on the Cape Bench one was feared more than any other, and that was the Judge-President, whose bullying style in court made even a one-day matter before him seem to most counsel to be like a major war.

Wilfred had no doubt about who would be the judge at the coming trial—the Judge-President. The 'J-P', as we called him, was a large, aggressive-looking man, whose powerful rurally-accented voice blotted out all other sound in his vicinity. His impatient, domineering manner frightened witnesses, repelled or delighted onlookers, and bruised even the most hardened of counsel. At the same time he was witty, unconventional and capable of a profound and impetuous concern for people, so that all in all his behaviour on the Bench was unpredictable and fascinating. His subjective attitudes and unusual insights into human motivation were said to derive from what was euphemistically referred to as his own personal understanding

74

of human frailty, though in the opinion of many counsel his good qualities were cancelled out by what they regarded as his laziness, emotionalism and lack of staying power. Also he was accused of having an excessive love of publicity, and it could well have been this consideration which made Wilfred so sure that the J-P and no one else would take the trial. A year previously the J-P and Wilfred had clashed frequently in a well-publicised murder case which had come to be known as the Dead Baron trial; they respected each other, but both of them had tough, unyielding temperaments, and a lengthy trial involving both of them would inevitably develop into a prolonged battle of attrition.

I mentioned once to Wilfred that it might not be too bad for the accused to have the J-P as their judge, since in his younger days he had been something of a rebel and accordingly might better understand their motivation.

Wilfred shook his head emphatically and said we shouldn't delude ourselves about what we were up against.

But what about the J-P having thrown out the Public Works Department men, I persisted, when they had come to put up apartheid notices in his courts? . . . Didn't the fact that the Cape Supreme Court was the only one in the country not to have segregated witness boxes and public galleries prove his capacity for independence?

Wilfred's dissent was vigorous. We would be bluffing ourselves, he warned, if we underestimated the strength of hostility of someone like the J-P for people such as the accused. The J-P wouldn't give a damn about what anyone *said* about apartheid, but when it came to the use of explosives or to anything which threatened his own security, then he would hit and hit back hard. If he were satisfied that they were guilty, the four white accused would be hammered into the ground, because they would be seen as having interfered in something that didn't even concern them. We had to face it, if the J-P got really tough with the accused he would be supported, and be supported all the way, by the overwhelming majority of Whites in South Africa.

Another issue on which Wilfred and I disagreed was on how to regard the people who had been the members of the A.R.M. We were careful not to engage in any general political discussions for we might only have embarrassed each other if we had, but it was impossible not to talk about the kind of people involved in the trial.

Didn't I think the whole organisation rather silly? Wilfred asked one day. He referred scathingly to the contents of the documents which, he thought, were typical of the kind of juvenile claptrap that so impressed students. All those words —he shook his head—they amounted to nothing but a series of high-sounding phrases, and to make matters worse, the whole collection of highly incriminating papers had been neatly catalogued and placed right next to the dynamite, as if the intention had been to help the police as much as possible. Without going into the question of whether sabotage ever helped a cause or only intensified opposition to it, didn't I feel that even on their own terms this whole crowd had been a bit stupid, arsing around with something much too big for them, hopping in and out of each others' beds and treating the whole business as one big game? This work was for dedicated professionals, if anybody, not silly amateurs. As soon as the police said boo every one of them collapsed, half of them pushing off overseas and the rest cracking up in prison.

Was he really being fair to them? I responded. (My primary feeling was that they were brave young people in serious trouble for having challenged apartheid in the only way apparently meaningful to them.) From a technical point of view they'd been pretty effective, with an operational success of seventy per cent. Their precautions had been strong enough to prevent life or limb being endangered, which showed they weren't just reckless youngsters out for kicks. In any event, I asked, couldn't their amateurism almost be regarded as something in their favour, since it emphasised the extent to which they were volunteers motivated by idealism?

But wasn't that the point? Wilfred countered. If one was going to go in for this sort of thing, shouldn't one be professional about it or else leave it to those who were?

I replied that perhaps the best analogy was with the many middle-class people in occupied Europe during the war who had felt that the only choice open to them was to collaborate with the Nazis or to go underground. Without discussing whether or not the parallel with South Africa could be said to exist, one point of similarity was that in both cases people quite ill-equipped by training and temperament for the job had found themselves engaged in activities of a serious and illegal nature. After all, most of the resistance workers in Europe were untrained amateurs and their losses especially in the beginning were extremely high. They too had largely gone in for sabotage of a symbolical nature, and many of their compatriots had criticised them bitterly at the time for acting in a futile way which only led to severe reprisals. Yet when the war was over everybody claimed to have supported them, and suddenly they were big heroes all round.

Wilfred snorted. Heroes? he asked. Whatever course South African history took, he couldn't see any of the A.R.M. crowd ever being regarded as heroes. To begin with, they represented nobody but themselves. Just about all of them were Whites, yet they hoped to liberate people who didn't even know of their existence. And Leftwich hardly seemed to qualify as a hero . . .

We had been speaking, we would have said, without prejudice to our desire to help our clients. Perhaps, too, the manner in which we characterised the organisation would affect our strategy at the trial, in particular the kind of material we might wish to place before the court in mitigation of sentence if the accused were found guilty.

In a number of other political trials in South Africa the accused had put up what had been regarded as political defences, that is, they had admitted the deeds charged against them, but had denied the right of apartheid courts to try them under apartheid laws. There was no question of Alan and Stephanie defending themselves along such lines, especially since they had at most been relatively minor members of the A.R.M. and not those who could effectively defend the honour of the organisation. Yet at the same time it seemed very important to me that they should bear themselves with dignity and spirit. As I put it to Himie and Wilfred, what we thought of the accused mattered little, what the judge thought mattered greatly, but what they thought of themselves mattered most of all. If they regarded themselves as having been dupes and play-boys the court would soon come to the same conclusion and would punish them the harder and not the more leniently for it. Some of their true character had to come through, I argued. They had to be viewed as idealistic young people and not primarily as criminals; they were responsible for their conduct, but not for the situation which had given rise to it. If eventually they were in fact sentenced to long terms of imprisonment, one could imagine how intolerable it would be for them to go off to jail feeling whipped and defeated and not believing in themselves at all. In any event, I added, they would make much better witnesses if their morale was high.

To my embarrassment Himie and Wilfred commented that with attractive junior counsel visiting her so often at least accused number five's morale should not be in question at all.

Much of our time at this stage was taken up with examining the photostatted documents. Himie was at first so 'snowed under' that he was not able to look at them properly, so Wilfred and I summarised the contents for him. A number of do-it-yourself bomb-making instruction sheets showed that all the necessary ingredients for blowing yourself sky-high could be got for a few shillings and visits to a paint shop, a hairdresser, a grocer and a chemist. Other documents set out in detail the procedures to be followed by members in the case of an emergency—none of which had in fact been followed by the members when the emergency had arisen. A batch of letters and invoices puzzled us at first, for they merely recorded the difficulties involved with the Customs in importing a crate of glasses into the country. Later we learnt that underneath the glasses had been dozens of sticks of dynamite; the recipient must have shown some nerve while he negotiated with the harbour officials for the crate to be handed over to him.

Many of the documents dealt with the problem of toppling pylons by means of explosives. There were chemical equations, drawings of pylons, diagrams of electrical circuits, and sets of operational instructions which read like cooking recipes. Frequently the words 'shape charges' appeared, and Wilfred one day asked me what they meant. He phrased his question carefully so as not to make it seem that he was assuming that I knew anything about explosives, but in fact my knowledge was limited to what I had learnt in previous trials plus what Alan had told me in his comments on the documents. I felt I could not very well tell Wilfred that there had been no need for his delicacy, though when telling me about 'shape charges' Alan in his turn had been careful to mention that he had heard from someone else . . .

A bomb out in the open, I explained to Wilfred, would not cause much damage because the extent of any blast varied directly with the extent to which the explosives were compressed. The same bomb, however, could have a terrific explosive power if packed in a hole and pressed up against the target. Thus when railway signal cables had been attacked, it had been necessary only to tape on a few sticks of dynamite, light the fuse and run away, because only a small blast had been required. Pylons and the radio tower were made of sterner stuff, however, so here the explosives had been packed in specially shaped boxes and dug in at the feet of the object to be toppled. The charges were detonated by electric fuses attached by wire to doctored alarm clocks—as soon as the hands came round to the desired hour an electric circuit was completed and instead of the alarm going off, the bomb exploded. It was the construction of the bomb in a shape adapted to that of the target that explained the use of the words 'shape charge'.

Electric charges, alarm clocks, bombs, pylons . . . this was the world of detective stories and war memoirs, not the Cape Town in which we lived in 1964. Sitting in Wilfred's comfortable chambers it seemed impossible that our clients had moved in such a world. When we went up to the prison and actually spoke to them it seemed even harder to believe.

Chapter 9

The wardress who let us in through the prison door seemed surprised that three people should want to see Miss Kemp at one time. Were we detectives? she asked. No, we were her lawyers, we replied. Impressed by the authority and politeness of our speech, she led us to the interview room and deferentially requested us please to wait for a short while.

We seated ourselves on the faded brown chairs and placed our papers on the table. The cracks in the leather upholstery made the furniture seem old and dusty, and we brushed our suits with our hands as if to keep ourselves from getting dirty. This was Wilfred's first visit to that room for a number of years and its worn appearance clearly depressed him. He was about to meet Stephanie for the first time, and being the leader of the defence team he was conscious of the need to make a good impression on her. Himie and I had already seen Stephanie and Alan several times; it was agreed that Wilfred should now do most of the talking.

Stephanie arrived looking neat and lively. Her long combed hair rubbed loosely against her shoulders and her blouse and skirt were attractively fresh and clean. We all stood up, a chair was brought in for her, she sat down gracefully, and we all subsided.

Wilfred introduced himself and explained why we had come.

He spoke in a forceful, sympathetic voice and leaned forward as he addressed her. The appropriate stage had been reached, he said, for him to meet his clients and for all of us to discuss the case together. It would be he who would conduct the defence in court, but the team as a whole would be responsible for what he said. The case would be a hard one to fight, but by no means an impossible one. All she had to do was to give evidence . . .

All she had to—she laughed as she interrupted him—she'd never been in a court of law before and didn't have a clue about what she'd have to do.

That was why we had come, Wilfred explained patiently, giving her the kind of serious engaging look he used when answering questions from the Bench. If he might go on, he continued earnestly, he would like to summarise the charges and point out what we considered were the main issues in the case.

She looked boldly back at him as he developed his ideas. Himie was to her like a kindly and understanding father, I was politically committed to the same ideas, but Wilfred—well, she did not know how to place him.

He went on to explain to her the trial procedure and told her that for most of the time all she would have to do would be to sit and look pretty. Only after all the State evidence had been heard would the defence witnesses go into the box and even then she would be the last because she was accused number five.

As in most trials, he continued briskly, the main issue would be whom the court would believe, but she had the advantage that if the court were unsure of where the truth lay and if it felt that her story might just reasonably be true, then she would have the benefit of the doubt. At the same time, she should bear in mind that the State did not have to prove that she had actually lit the fuse on any explosives—even if she had merely, say, knowingly driven the car which had been used to convey the actual saboteurs, she would in law be just as guilty of the crime as the person who had detonated the charges. Everything depended on whether it could be proved that she had knowingly taken part in the organisation's activities; it would not be enough for the State simply to establish that she had been friendly with people like Leftwich.

Wilfred spoke confidently, watching intently to see what impact his words and presence were making on Stephanie. She showed none of the submissive dependence or defiant nonchalance usually displayed by awaiting trial prisoners, but instead sat straight in her chair, listening, with her head held erect and her body in an attitude of quiet self-sufficiency.

The words rolled on as Wilfred analysed some of the issues facing the defence. One problem she could erase from her mind entirely, he stressed, was the fact that she had made a statement to the police. She had been under duress at the time and in any event her confession had not been reduced to writing before a magistrate as required by law. Accordingly both her statement and the assault would not be canvassed at all in the pending trial—he had spoken to the prosecutor about this and had been assured that the State would not refer to her statement at all.

He paused briefly to see if his ability to get undertakings from the prosecutor had made any impression on her, but she continued to stare neutrally back at him. At a later stage, he continued, she could, of course, still bring an action for damages for assault, but that would involve a civil trial and had nothing to do with the present proceedings. His voice became louder, his speech more fluent and he began to give his words the emphasis and style of an address in court. Himie and I sat quietly at his side, backing up his exposition with our presence. The three of us formed a grave, dark-suited phalanx ranged opposite Stephanie, who looked lone and frail on her side of the table. It seemed only proper that she give some acknowledgment of her respect for us as a team, and we waited for an indication that Wilfred's ringing words were making an impact on her.

Suddenly with a puzzled, troubled look, she reacted, but her question took us all by surprise.

'What do you think of Adrian?' she asked Wilfred directly.

Interrupted in the middle of a train of thought, he kept silent for a moment. Then, recovering his poise, he answered vigorously, 'He'll probably be the main State witness and my task will be to try to discredit him sufficiently in cross-examination for the court to have a doubt about any evidence he might give implicating you.'

Stephanie remained quiet, still refusing to nod her head or give any sign that she accepted and was grateful for what was being said to her. The disturbed look remained in her eyes and I decided to add to what Wilfred had said.

'It looks as though whatever Leftwich might have represented in the past, he's completely broken now,' I said.

She seemed unsatisfied and it was my turn now to feel puzzled. Himie then spoke up, and for the first time that day got a noticeable response from her.

'Adrian is a rat,' he said emphatically. 'The whole of Cape Town's saying so. Whatever they think of his politics past or present, people are saying he's a rat for betraying his friends and associates.'

'Good, that's what I've wanted to hear,' she commented eagerly.

'He'll do anything to save his skin,' Himie continued forcefully. 'He chose to be a witness and it's our duty now as defence lawyers to show no pity or mercy to him, none at all.'

'I'm so pleased you put it like that,' she said with enthusiasm. 'I'll need time to work out my attitude to him and you make it much easier for me when you put it so simply. That's what I needed. Thank you for coming and thank you for helping me.'

She smiled at Himie and looked in a friendly way at Wilfred and myself. Clearly the trial appeared a long way off to her, and its intricacies she was prepared to leave to the lawyers. In fact the case as a whole seemed to be something that concerned us more than her; what she really wanted to know was what the moral issues were and what it all meant in terms of her life and her values.

Wilfred had dealt with most of the points he had intended to discuss, and accordingly he did not prolong his exposition much. Instead, he asked her about her conditions in Roeland Street prison. It was a real dump, she replied, but the other prisoners seemed to like her and the matron wasn't bad, though some of the wardresses were pretty arrogant. We chatted in a quiet, friendly way for a while, and then resuming his role as leader of the defence team, Wilfred stood up and announced that it had been a very useful meeting and that perhaps it was time to go. Had Mr Bernadt anything to add? Himie shook his head. Did I wish to say anything? I shook my head. Well, we would see her again from time to time and she must keep up her good spirits until the case was over.

I called a wardress, and Stephanie was taken away. Later, as we walked round the prison to the male section, Wilfred said jocularly that our client Miss Kemp was an attractive little bit and he could understand why counsel might wish to spend many hours away from chambers having consultations with her. I said nothing. Was it true, he then went on to ask, that her grandfather had been General Kemp, one of the Boer leaders in the Anglo-Boer War? Himie did not know and I said I had heard she was some relation of the general. We would have to go into that, Wilfred observed, these things all help.

We then went to see Alan, who was well-spoken and jolly and who gave us the additional satisfaction of seeming to be an appreciative and helpful client.

Chapter 10

I visited Stephanie and Alan frequently during the pre-trial period in order to keep them informed of all developments.

On one occasion when I sat in the drab consulting-room in the women's section, Stephanie arrived and startled me by saying, 'Oh, it's you.' Who, I asked, had she thought it was? The wardress had told her to hurry up, she answered, because her boy-friend was there—she'd thought the wardress had meant Andy*, but sometimes I was called her 'boy-friend' because I came there so often.

I was embarrassed, and scratched with a ball-point pen on my notebook. Should I come less often? I asked. Oh, no, she answered. She enjoyed my visits, as long as they didn't interfere with my work. I assured her they did not. Thereafter I continued to go to the prison frequently, but made a point of not doing so on the days when her boy-friend was permitted to see her.

She no longer displayed the extraordinary excitement of the first day of her release from solitary confinement, but nevertheless she remained buoyant and cheerful, and was especially spirited when speaking about her fellow prisoners and the wardresses. The coming trial seemed to her to be an amusing but not very meaningful charade which would be acted out at some future date between the defence and the prosecution.

Then one day I noticed she was unusually pale and sub-

*Not his real name.

dued. She had something to report to me, she said gravely. Her eyes were frank and open, and she looked straight at me as she spoke. The previous night she had found herself behaving peculiarly, and at some time between six and eight o'clock she'd suddenly fallen on the floor. She hadn't lost consciousness, but had got up and sat on the bed.

While sitting on the bed she'd started shaking and begun to cry loudly. Someone had taken her to the bathroom, where she'd started to scream. She'd screamed and screamed and had felt herself getting paraesthesia in the ulnar nerve distribution of both arms.

I asked her how she spelt that.

PARAESTHESIA. She repeated the letters slowly as though dictating a clinical report to me. In her work as a physiotherapist she must frequently have made such reports about her patients. She explained that the term referred to a tingling sensation down the side of her arms, and then went on with her story.

After that she'd lost track and the next thing she remembered was feeling a wet cloth on her face. She'd been talking to the other prisoners and then suddenly right in the middle of a sentence had conked out and gone to sleep.

She was completely recovered, she concluded quietly, but thought she should be given a sedative and a tonic. She also felt she might benefit from some iron tablets since she was slightly anaemic.

She looked wanly at me as I wrote down her requests. Subsequently I discovered that her bout of hysteria had partially been precipitated by a press report that shots had been fired into the house of a left-wing woman friend of hers. The main cause, however, seemed to be that at last and with great suddenness she had come to appreciate her own vulnerability.

When she'd first come to Roeland Street prison, she told me, she'd never thought about the trial or even about the assault

88

by 'Spyker'. It had just been so wonderful to be able to speak to people again that she'd never really considered what had happened to her or what was likely to come in the future. But now she couldn't think of anything else. The thought of 'Spyker', even the smallest thought of him, made her shiver and get cold all over. She tried to put the assault out of her mind, but found herself perpetually remembering how he had hit her and hit her. She saw herself as all small and helpless, while he banged and banged her head on the floor, and this one picture stayed in her mind all the time. Then when she tried to think about the case she realised she knew nothing about it, absolutely nothing, and all she saw was just a great black mass of nothing ahead of her. She told herself this was a ridiculous way to behave, but just couldn't seem to help it.

Her words drew out strong feelings of protectiveness in me. The collapse of her buoyancy made her appear woefully exposed to all the hurt and pain involved in her situation. She was guileless and inexperienced and in need of help and I felt that I was probably the only person in a position really to help her.

Her reaction to strain, I assured her, was remarkable only in that it had been delayed for so long. It had come about just in time for her to get completely fit for the case.

I moved round the table and placed my notebook on the worn surface in front of her. This was what the court-room looked like, I said, drawing an oblong diagram on the page so as to give her a visual picture of the setting in which her trial would be held. I marked the places where the accused would sit, where the judge and assessors would sit, and where counsel, the press and the public would be. I bent close to her shoulder while I drew and noticed that my free hand was within touching distance of her elbow.

The judge would wear a bright red robe, I explained, while Mr Cooper and I would have long black gowns. I went into considerable detail about the clothing and appearance of the different participants in the trial, hoping that she would find the prospect of being in court less intimidating if she could imagine herself actually there. It seemed to me that a description of the rules of procedure would be of little value alone.

When the judge came in, I continued, an usher would shout 'Silence in the court' and everyone would stand up. Then when the judge had seated himself everyone would sit down, except the accused . . .

That was one of the things she was scared of, she said quickly, she'd hate to make a fool of herself by standing or sitting at the wrong time.

I smiled and assured her she would be told exactly what to do. In fact, I said with what I regarded as a sympathetic grin, all she would have to do for the first few weeks would be in the words of Mr Cooper, to sit and look pretty.

Her brows contracted and her eyes darkened. Why couldn't she be taken seriously? she asked crossly. She was sure Alan and the others wouldn't be told to look handsome; why, just because she was a girl, must she worry about looking pretty? What had that to do with the case?

By then I had become fairly used to the directness and suddenness of her comments, so I was able to answer her firmly and smoothly. Judges were men like any other men, I told her, even if they wore extraordinary clothing and made use of strange terminology. What mattered was not that she looked pretty in the conventional, meaningless sense of the term, but that she showed a natural and attractive personality. If the judge saw her as a real person and not just as a saboteur or as accused number five, it could possibly make a substantial difference in the way he treated her. In any event, I added, it shouldn't be difficult for her to look natural and attractive; on the contrary, it would be hard for her not to do so.

90

A blush spread across her face and she looked away from me and down at her hands. They were lovely, kind hands, I told myself, with clean, sensitive fingers. And she didn't bite her nails.

I told her the case would drag on for such a long time and so slowly that she would start to think that she lived in the court-room. At the end of it all she would be so bored that it would come as a relief to go into the witness box, just to have something to do.

She questioned me extensively about the witness box. Where was it situated? How did the witness get there? Where did he go afterwards? Would the accused have the chance to question witnesses at all?

I said she needn't worry about that since Mr Cooper would handle all the cross-examination.

No, she insisted, she wasn't thinking about the case so much. If she wanted to speak to one of the witnesses, could she do so?

That wouldn't be allowed, I said, shaking my head. It would be regarded as interfering with the witness.

Couldn't she just ask Adrian one question?

No, not one. But we could always put it in cross-examination. Would she like to say what it was?

All she wanted to say was, 'Adrian, why did you tell the police everything and why did you agree to be a State witness?'

She needn't worry, that's what half the cross-examination would be about.

That wasn't the same thing. The cross-questioning would be in open court with all sorts of people watching and everyone concerned about the effect of what they said. What she wanted was thirty seconds alone with Adrian to stand right next to him and ask quietly, 'Adrian, why did you become a traitor?'

Unfortunately it would be impossible for her to do so, I told her.

Then I tore off my drawing of the court-room for her, and walked back round the table to my chair. Her eyes, I noticed, were still dark and pre-occupied.

'He's just a rat,' she said unhappily to me, 'a rat and a traitor. We must have no mercy on him, he has to suffer for what he's done.'

She looked forlornly at her hands and then glanced tentatively at me. It all seemed so stupid and futile—the words came out sadly—she couldn't see what they'd ever hoped to achieve. What had been the point of it? They'd accomplished nothing; their lives had been ruined; it all seemed so meaningless and unworthwhile.

My eyelids blinked rapidly as I thought about my reply. In previous discussions we had often come close to considering this question, but she had always appeared so confident and bright that it had never seemed necessary to go into it. My own thinking had been dominated by the same sort of doubt ever since my release from detention, and I could see that in examining the implications of Adrian's breakdown I would inevitably dig up many of my own uncertainties. I asked her if she would like to hear what I thought about the matter, and when she nodded agreement, proceeded to tell her at some length.

Chapter 11

It was true that Adrian was a rat, I said, but it wasn't enough just to leave it at that, for the question still remained: why had people once followed him and believed in him?

Anyone could break, but that didn't prove that everyone was rotten, merely that no one was indestructible. We could know this quite well in theory, but the trouble was that when we saw it happening in practice to someone close to us, we felt shocked and devastated and started to doubt not only the person concerned but also our own judgment and feelings. The distress would be especially severe if the person who broke was someone who had opened us up to new ideas and feelings, who had given direction to our idealism and absorbed all our trust and belief and whom possibly we had grown to love. When such a person collapsed everything associated with him seemed to go down and the whole world turned dark.

Yet surely it was false to allow a principle to die merely because one of its proponents had fallen by the wayside? People might break, but the ideas which had inspired them could carry on, not in an abstract way, but through other people who came forward and kept them alive. These men and women might in their turn be destroyed, or be corrupted or simply become weary, but behind them were others and still others, so that the spirit and ideas could flourish even though the generations which upheld them died out.

Perhaps one of the worst features of having been kept in solitary confinement for so long was that we started to doubt everything, not excluding ourselves, in fact especially ourselves. I knew how close I had come to breaking, and even though somehow I'd managed to hold out to the end, I wouldn't be quick to judge anyone else who gave way. The discovery of our own vulnerability and limitation was very hard to bear. We'd imagined that we were complete masters of our own fate, that we could take on the world, storm the heavens and die if necessary in the fulfilment of our ideals, and then all that happened was that we were placed in a cell where there was no world and no heaven, only ourselves, and where it wasn't a question of dying at all, but only of surviving and trying to keep up some honour. How easily we felt pain and how strongly we longed to be free of it; I was supposed to be an example of a prisoner who had triumphed over loneliness, and on no less than three occasions I had thought of suicide.

Perhaps the books we had read and the legends we had heard were responsible for some of the sense of crisis we felt when actually we came to be in captivity and isolation. We nourished ourselves for years on the lives of heroes and on their noble actions, and prepared ourselves mentally to bare our breasts and shout fire to the enemy, or to march defiantly to the gallows. Books weren't written about people who simply endured stress for a long time, for there was nothing clear-cut or remarkable about their conduct, and people preferred to read about a few moments of extraordinary bravery, rather than about months of ordinary endurance. Heroes undoubtedly had their role to play; they were the people who pushed wider the limits of what man knew he could achieve. Yet their brief acts of bravery were seized on by our imaginations and converted into dramas of perpetual courage, inspiring us for situations which just didn't arise. In practice there were no guns to face, no gallows to walk to, only an empty cell and long, long loneliness. Keyed up to face the enemy with boldness, we discovered that we hardly ever even saw the enemy and when we did he usually was just an ordinary man going about his business in an ordinary way. We were prepared to be brave in battle, but we found out that our courage was needed most when the action was at its lowest, when we were depressed and filled with self-doubt, when we had to battle merely to remember earlier boldness and to keep alive the hope of future strength.

This was where Adrian seemed to have collapsed. He'd been fine when it had come to action, to planning and organising and getting things done—for one, I certainly wouldn't even have tried half of what he'd actually done, I wouldn't have had the guts—but when he was captured and the drama stopped and he was alone, he broke down completely. The police had handled him pretty cleverly (of course with all the power they had they could hardly have gone wrong) by presenting him to the world as an example of the kind of person who opposed them and yet at the same time getting the maximum use out of him. They wanted people to believe that he was basically a bastard who had always had bad ideas, a futile creature who one day worked against the police and the next day worked for them. It was bad enough that he was responsible for the arrest of dozens of people and the crushing of a whole organisation; in some ways it was worse that he was prepared to help send close friends and supporters of his to prison in order to save his own skin; but really his greatest crime was that he was destroying the faith in him and his ideas which was held by thousands of people throughout the country. He had presented himself to the public as a champion of youthful idealism and had spoken with an authority and sincerity that had made people believe in him and trust in what he said; now, by his treachery, he was destroying the enthusiasms and beliefs of a whole generation of students and young people, and of older persons as well.

Which was the true Adrian? The one who had used his energies and talents to live a creative and positive life, or the one who now sought desperately to save himself at all costs? Both were true. Every person had both good and bad in him at the same time, though perhaps not many to the same extreme degree as Adrian. The fact that all his weakness had now come out didn't mean he'd always been a rat or that everything he'd ever said or done had to be rejected. We all had a similar problem when we discovered weakness in ourselves—in principle it didn't matter whether the weakness was in ourselves or in others—and started to doubt the validity of our ideas. The world suddenly appeared to be a dark and cruel place, and people seemed to be either uncaring exploiters or else helpless victims. Nothing really mattered and all effort towards improvement seemed futile. Fatalism crippled our spirit and we began to believe there was a hard, unalterable core to human nature that made all hope of a just society nothing more than a utopian dream, at best a useless drain on human effort, at worst a dangerous pretext for more greed and cruelty. Progress through history seemed impossible, and the only hope of meaningful human advance seemed to be through the slow evolution of man's physical being.

The difficulty was that however much our personal situation improved, once we had looked at the world with bleak, depressed eyes it was never possible to revert to the simple optimistic vision that formerly had made life joyous and full of expectation. It was remarkable, really, how changed the world seemed after we'd been in solitary confinement. We would know full well that the world had remained the same, and that it was we who had changed, and yet we couldn't help seeing things the other way round. The problem then was how to face up to our confusion and moral uncertainty, how to

overcome the feelings of bafflement and self-anger. Moral exhortations to ourselves helped very little, because what we
were after was not reiteration of the details of our beliefs, but
proof of their foundations.

Some people might be able to revert to their old ideas as
though nothing at all had happened, while others might totally repudiate everything they'd ever believed in. But for
most of us it was a question of trying honestly and fully to
examine the significance of our new experiences, and to work
out what the implications were for our views of ourselves and
of the world. There was no point in not being frank about this,
because if our ideas couldn't stand up to frankness then they
weren't worth having in the first place; on the other hand, if
our ideas were substantially sound, then new facts and experiences would strengthen rather than weaken them. It required a strong sense of purpose and probably also a creative
imagination to integrate hard unpleasant facts into a philosophy and attitude of mind that for a long time had simply
been taken for granted. To deny these facts and experiences
was to push a part of reality out of our philosophy and really
to weaken it while pretending to keep it intact. To deny our
philosophy and our previous actions, on the other hand, was to
try to eradicate our past, which was after all just as much a
part of our reality as were our present doubts. If the evidence
compelled us to abandon some of our beliefs, then we must be
courageous enough to do so, but at the same time we had to
guard against the temptation of looking for material merely in
order to give ourselves a legitimate excuse for running away
from our principles. Perhaps that was the hardest part of all,
the need to admit how easily we could be terrorised and to
acknowledge that it was not so much our ideas that were
weak but we ourselves.

Times came when we had to keep going even although
we didn't know why or what it was all about, since once we

collapsed it wasn't easy to pick ourselves up off the floor again.

That was where we needed guts—to pull ourselves through the long, lonely periods, whether in solitary confinement or awaiting trial or as a sentenced prisoner. Self-pity attacked us in all sorts of guises and from all sides.

At the risk of seeming like a preacher, and an unqualified one at that, I described to her my own experience. Feeling sorry for myself had been my greatest enemy, much greater than the police. It had demoralised me and drained off what little strength I'd had left. In order to resist it and overcome its effects I'd had to make a special effort of will, not merely to tell myself to be strong, but more important, to establish positive habits and to relate myself in an active, meaningful way to my strange new environment. I'd said to myself that not only was it dishonourable to have regrets or to blame others for my predicament, it was stupid, unhelpful and enfeebling. This was the crucial thing for all of us who were faced with this sort of problem—we had to take responsibility for our own actions, both in the past and now.

She too should see her situation in the same way. She'd done what she'd done because she'd thought it was right. Whether or not her actions had from an objective point of view been wise was a different question which she would have time enough to consider, but she couldn't blame Adrian or anyone else for her conduct. She might have been persuaded or influenced by him, but he hadn't made any decisions for her. What was more, she had in the future to continue to take responsibility for herself and her actions. It wasn't only a question of her morale and self-esteem, it was also a matter of how others might be affected, since once she involved herself in the lives of others she couldn't withdraw when or where she liked. There were people who looked to her with admiration, who knew of the assault upon her, who felt deeply for her as a person and who believed in her just as she had believed in Adrian. She couldn't now say she didn't want them to be concerned about her or about what she did; it was too late for that. By becoming politically involved she'd entered their lives and entrusted herself in a way to them. This had been her own decision, voluntarily taken, and she could not renege on it. If she did, and if she sought to escape the consequences of her commitment, then apart from the injury she would be be doing to others, she would be harming herself and denying to herself the right and capacity to be responsible for her own life, both now and in the future. The pain of Adrian's treachery she would have to bear for herself. She couldn't use it as an excuse for her own betrayal.

Chapter 12

Stephanie listened intently as I spoke. I kept my voice low so that the wardresses would not hear me, and used abstract terms just in case we were being tape-recorded. Yet my tone was serious and urgent, since the problems I dealt with affected me as much as they affected her. At times I became aware of the sound of my own voice—gentle, monotonous and pleading, and I realised that I was interposing myself in a personal way between her and her bewilderment. My hands moved quietly in the air to emphasise my ideas and she sat silently watching me.

When I had finished she said to me with a sudden display of pleasure that she was extremely pleased I had spoken to her like that. Everybody else was telling her to be cheerful and to hope for the best, and she was sick and tired of people treating her like a sweet little girl who needed protecting all the time.

We stood up and faced each other across the table. Her arms hung loosely at her side and I felt an urge to take her hands and hold them for a moment in mine before I left. Be strong, I wanted to say to her, but don't place demands that are too heavy on yourself. Or on me.

Later, when I was on the way back to my office I went over in my mind what I had been saying. As a lawyer it had not been improper for me to have tried to give her morale a boost nor to have thrown out some ideas which might have helped her get some sort of perspective on her situation. Yet clearly I had shown an earnestness and subjectivity that went beyond limits of an ordinary lawyer/client relationship. In a very personal way I was getting involved in trying to save her from disillusionment. She was not the sort of person to separate ideas from their proponents, and by urging her to be honest and steadfast I was in effect undertaking that I would be the same. In my own terms, I was now entering her life, and making a sort of promise that I would live up to what I preached. This thought made me anxious, but more than that it stirred me. I had needed to hear the words I had spoken, and if they had come from someone else I might have refused to listen. Whether or not she had benefitted from my arguments, I felt sure that I had.

Some days later I went up to the prison again. After consulting with Alan, who remained consistently cheerful, I walked over to the women's section and waited for Stephanie to be called. I felt uncomfortable as I sat in the interview room, because in the side pocket of my suit was a small red rosebud which I intended to give to her. I had picked it on impulse that morning and now I felt embarrassed by the whole idea. I knew I would not be searched and that I could probably pass the bud over without being noticed. Yet the thought of being caught trying to smuggle a rosebud into prison caused me more anxiety than if there had been a steel file hidden in my briefcase. I fidgetted with my pen, and every now and then let my hand rest against my pocket. Stephanie arrived and marched briskly to her seat, then as the wardress left she pulled a face and thrust out her tongue at the departing figure. I asked what that had all been about and was told that the wardress was damned rude to the prisoners and didn't treat anybody like a person. I put my hand in my pocket and took hold of the bud. We spoke about the forthcoming trial, and slowly I brought my hand out of my pocket and released the bud on to the table. It rolled towards her and stopped near her hands. Look what's fallen out of my pocket, I said. She cupped her fingers round the little red ball and then held it tight in her hands. I waited for her to say something, but she remained silent. We continued our discussion of the case for some time, but at no stage did she make any reference to the gift. When eventually it was time for me to leave, I expected her then to thank me, but still she said nothing. Finally she walked off, and only the largeness of one fist compared to the other indicated at all that she had the bud in her possession.

I continued visiting the prison on about two or three afternoons a week. By this time the wardresses no longer bothered to supervise our consultations and one day Stephanie suddenly asked if I would like to hear some of the songs she had made up while under 90-days.

I told her that I too had made up a song to the tune of *Always*: 'I'll be living here, Always . . .'

She knew that, she said, but her songs were better. Looking covertly at the door, she began to sing in a soft clear voice.

'Ninety days . . . and the weeks drag by slowly.'

The tune was *Summertime*, and the words came out in a clear gentle soprano. Judging from the clarity of her notes, she must once have had musical training.

'Eternity . . . while they question me . . .'

She finished the song and without waiting for any comment from me started on another one.

'As long as you love me
They'll never set me free
I will not talk you see
As long as you love me.'

The tune was from *Oliver*, she explained.

'As long as I love you
I always will be true

102

To all I learnt from you
What I believe in too.'

She paused, and then continued softly with further verses. The words hovered between the banal and the poignant, but the tenderness with which she sang and the restraint in her voice made the occasion deeply affecting for me.

'But talk I did one night
I could no longer fight
They beat me till I screamed
And after that I dreamed
   I dreamed I was alone
   The terror all my own
   I did not think of you
   I told them all I knew.
And now I think of you
And how I was untrue
To all I learnt from you
What I believe in too.'

I told her that she sang beautifully but that the songs upset me—the more personal they were, the more they disturbed me, because I couldn't help thinking of her, all alone in her cell singing to herself in the same way I had had to sing to myself.

For a moment her expression was sad, and then as if she had suddenly become aware of how I might understand the song, she hurriedly explained that the words 'as long as I love you' didn't, of course, refer to me or to any particular individual. In the context of the song they meant all the people opposed to apartheid, and the whole spirit of resistance. She used especially to think of Fred Carneson and his wife Sarah, whom she'd got to know shortly before her detention. They were such a terrific couple, so mature and warm and real, and she would often imagine them giving her their support and urging her to be brave. If I ever saw them, would I give them her greetings?

Stephanie's eagerness and vitality must have inspired the Carneson's, just as their warmth and maturity had obviously encouraged her. I too had a special affection for them. Fred's extrovert good cheer and optimism had carried him through many difficult situations, and the chances were that even now the police were watching him closely with a view to cracking down when it suited them. After my release from detention he had put out a feeler to me: could I possibly help him again as I had helped him before? Filled with shame at my weakness, I had refused; I foresaw doom for him and his associates and doubted whether I could survive a further spell of isolation. Stephanie's references to him and Sarah revived some of my feelings of self-recrimination, but my main sentiment was one of pleasure at being able to share with her an affection for a couple we both admired.

I explained to her with an annoyed shrug that my ban prevented me from communicating with Fred or Sarah in any way, but I could tell people who could tell people who could tell people . . . and maybe her greetings would eventually get through to them. The trial, however, might be over by then.

As the date of the trial became closer, I noticed how much softer Stephanie was beginning to look. The presence of such a pretty young girl in prison seemed increasingly bizarre. Her cheerfulness apparently made her popular among the other prisoners, and when I paid her the last visit before trial, she told me that the women in her section seemed to be more interested in her case than in their own. (At times during previous discussions, I had got the impression that she had been more interested in their cases than in her own.) She felt that the wide press coverage had been responsible for the special excitement about her trial and told me that her fellow prisoners had promised to do up her hair specially for the occasion.

I asked if she'd made arrangements about what she'd wear, but she said her mother was taking charge of that. Himie had

104

told her mother to get her something nice and demure—she pulled a face—but her mother had good taste, so she was sure she'd look all right. She still couldn't imagine herself actually in court, but she was very pleased the case was about to start at last. Of course she was as nervous as all hell, but she supposed that was to be expected in the circumstances.

Despite her professed nervousness, however, when our discussion came to an end she seemed to me to have more of the brightness of a bride on her wedding eve than the anxiety of a prisoner about to be tried.

Chapter 13

It was a Sunday and the building was deserted and quiet when Himie, Wilfred and I met in Wilfred's chambers to do last-minute preparatory work. We took off our sports jackets because of the early summer heat, and spread out our papers with the intention of putting in a hard day's work. The period immediately before a trial was always nerve-racking—equalled for strain only by the time spent waiting for the verdict—and on this occasion we felt particularly tense. We had already gone over the ground so thoroughly that there was little more for us to do, but we seemed to feel a need to be busy, and accordingly passed papers backwards and forth to each other and perused documents which we had already read through many times. Our discussions were desultory and time and again we found ourselves deviating into speculation.

The J-P was definitely going to take the case, Wilfred informed us. This would have an important bearing on the trial, because he couldn't see the J-P allowing it to run on for six weeks.

What could the J-P do about it? Himie asked.

Put pressure on counsel, Wilfred answered. He'd make up his mind before lunch-time the first day and let us know that he thought we were wasting the time of the court. Of course he would *say* we could spend as long as we liked on cross-examination . . .

Couldn't it possibly turn out to our advantage? I ventured. There would probably be less evidence against our two accused than against any of the others and if we could crack Leftwich early on, the J-P might put pressure on the prosecution into withdrawing against our two.

Wilfred was unconvinced, and appeared to be gloomily preoccupied with the vision of having to do endless battle against an impatient judge. We continued to read the documents and each of us underlined passages and made notes of matters of special significance. The ash-tray next to Himie gradually filled up with crushed and messy cigarette stubs; a page in my notebook was soon covered with abstract ball-point doodlings; while Wilfred tapped nervously with his brass letter-opener.

At one stage when we were all momentarily unoccupied I asked if they'd heard about Alan's experience as a jail lawyer? Apparently Alan had been helping many of his fellow prisoners with their pleas in mitigation, and his greatest success had been with a man who'd been found guilty of theft but had not yet been sentenced. The plea which Alan had drafted had been so effective that the man had been given a suspended sentence, whereupon he'd left the prison—taking Alan's toothpaste with him. The incident had upset Alan a great deal, but we were highly amused by it: all lawyers complained of their clients' ingratitude and it was only fair that jail lawyers should do the same.

The morning seemed to pass slowly, and the sudden ring of the telephone came as a welcome interruption. 'Cooper,' Wilfred said in clipped lawyer's style into the mouthpiece. 'Yes . . . yes . . . I've got Himie Bernadt and Albie Sachs with me, could they come too? . . . Yes . . . yes . . . thank you. Could I ring back in a few minutes?' He replaced the receiver and told us that counsel and attorney for accused number three had arrived from Johannesburg and were wondering whether we'd care to have a drink with them at their hotel.

107

We were happy to take up the offer and drove out to the hotel where we found our Johannesburg colleagues looking surprisingly at their ease. Counsel was an urbane and friendly man with a calm, unpretentious and yet impressive manner; he had the reputation of being the most persuasive and astute of all the younger advocates in South Africa. His instructing attorney was a much larger and more nervous person, but in his own special way was equally impressive. He had a brilliant mind and eccentric ways, and his paunchy, pugnacious appearance, balding head and slightly stuttering speech were so reminiscent of Winston Churchill that anyone might have taken him for a son of the late British Prime Minister.

After we had ordered our drinks the advocate told us something of the tactics he proposed to adopt in relation to his client Anthony Trew, who, we learnt, was an unusual young man with remarkably strong moral feelings.

We reassured each other that none of our clients had anything to fear from any evidence which might be given by the others, and then spent some time discussing the rules of evidence relating to conspiracy. These rules were remarkably favourable to the prosecution, and I thought to myself how ironical the law was in its operation. Liberal judges during the war had widened the scope of evidence admissible in conspiracy trials, their aim being to assist in bringing pro-Hitler conspirators to book. The conspirators who had been imprisoned or interned at that time had now themselves become masters of the security apparatus in South Africa, and many of the counsel who had assisted them then had been appointed judges and would be applying the rules which they had once criticised. When a democratic government came to power in South Africa, would we in turn make use of laws and rules which we were now arguing against? Or would the whole judicial structure undergo such revision that the question could never arise in that form?

Our conversation was casual and not very productive, but we enjoyed the companionship and felt comforted that the burden of a long and punishing trial would be shared by us all. Eventually we thanked our hosts for their hospitality and left for lunch.

The interlude had been a pleasant one but most of the day still lay ahead of us, and our restlessness quickly returned. In the afternoon we decided to concentrate on what seemed to be the crucial feature of the trial: the cross-examination of Adrian Leftwich. We expected him to be the first witness for the prosecution, which meant that we had to have our line of questioning fully worked out before the trial began. Wilfred pointed out that we would have to handle Leftwich very carefully. Experience had shown that people who betrayed their former associates often turned against them in a very nasty fashion, and the more guilty they felt, the more savage they became. This could be very dangerous. At the same time, of course, this wouldn't be an occasion for kid gloves . . .

Himie interrupted with unusual vehemence to say that Leftwich had to be hit hard. He knew that kind of person; he thought he was big, but let himself be bullied by the first tough person who came along. The police had been pushing him around and now the defence would have to hit back and try to shake him up a little bit. Of course we didn't have the powers the police had—Himie smiled—but Wilfred wasn't the leading cross-examiner at the Bar for nothing.

The description was flattering, Wilfred answered, but unenviable. He'd prepared a detailed series of questions along the lines we'd agreed upon earlier, and would like to hear what we felt about them. What we had to bear in mind was that it wasn't Leftwich who'd be on trial, but our clients. It was no good exposing a witness's moral deficiencies if they had no bearing on his credibility. What was needed was an approach that emphasised certain features of Leftwich's make-up; first, that he had once been active in defying the laws of the land, secondly, that he was now trying to save his skin, and thirdly, that the pressure on him had been so great that he'd been prepared to do anything to protect himself, including falsely implicating our two accused. His first questions to Leftwich would be, 'You admit you were a saboteur? In fact you were a leading member of a sabotage organisation? And do you admit you betrayed the principles of that organisation?'

Then he'd take him through some of those principles, particularly those that related to not cooperating with the police. After that he'd ask if Leftwich had drawn up the exhibit which dealt with how to withstand solitary confinement—Leftwich couldn't get out of that, because his handwriting appeared on the original document—and he'd go through it passage by passage.

' "Some of the consequences are strange and unexpected and might lead to fears that you are going queer in your head." Did you write that? Was that in fact your experience? Did you not write on the wall of your cell, "I have discovered how weak I am and how strong is the power of love. Love is all"? What did you mean by that? Is that the way you would normally write?'

This was important, Wilfred emphasised, not only because it showed his general state of mind at the time, but because it had a bearing on a possible motive for falsely implicating our two accused, namely his personal rivalry with Brooks and a former strong but now embarrassing emotional entanglement with Stephanie.

' "After a time you will feel a terrible urge to talk—to anyone about anything." Was that your experience? "There may be changes in the way you see and hear. There may be fluctu-

110

ations, drifting and swirling of objects and surfaces in the visual field." Was that your experience? "You will be shouted at, insulted, told you will be hanged or kept in prison for life. You will often be threatened with torture and usually be allowed to see and speak to a man who has been tortured.' Was that your experience? Did you see your girl-friend at this stage? Did her head show signs of injury? Did you know her skull had been X-rayed? Were you worried about injury to yourself? About further injury to her? "A consequence of long isolation is suggestibility and pliability . . . Though more pleasant, attempts to sell the government line to you are more dangerous because of the doubts which may be arising in your mind." Was that your experience?'

Wilfred's voice became louder and louder and he repeated each question. His manner was cutting, precise and angry, though he still held back, conserving most of his emotion for the next day.

Wilfred explained enthusiastically that the value of the document was that it enabled us to present the effects of solitary confinement in a concrete way. Normally it was most difficult to get this across, unless one had been through the whole business oneself. Judges saw the witness in the witness box looking quite normal and without any signs of injury, and so inferred that there couldn't be anything wrong with the evidence being given. What the judges didn't understand, because it was something so alien to their experience, was the extent to which pressures could be brought to bear on a witness without there being any signs to show. That was what brain-washing amounted to, after all. If the witness went on to deny that he'd been influenced by the police in any way— which he could be expected to do in the circumstances—the defence was in a hopeless position. What was so valuable in the present case, then, was that we had Leftwich's own words and statement to put to him.

Wilfred waved the document in front of us, and then threw it on the desk. 'We'll cut Leftwich up with his own weapons,' he declared enthusiastically.

Himie and I were encouraged by this show of confidence. Once the trial began it would be Wilfred alone who would have the responsibility of presenting the defence to the court; we would be mere auxiliaries. Whatever ideas we might have would have to be converted into Wilfred's language and be put across by him according to his own personality and style.

Would we mind, Wilfred asked, if we broke up for a while and met again after supper? His mood had subsided and he spoke to us as though he were now occupied with his own thoughts. He explained that he'd like a little time on his own, first to work through his questions and then to have a short walk and get some fresh air. After supper we could get together for a last exchange of ideas and then, if we agreed, we could all have an early night.

Himie and I left the building and drove out to a sea-front restaurant some miles out of town. We strolled sedately along a wide grass-flanked boulevard and allowed our bodies to be refreshed by the pleasant early summer breeze which blew in from the sea. Brash luxury flats crammed the approaches to the beach, and palm-trees on the long green lawns gave the neighbourhood an opulent, semi-tropical character. The Judge-President lived not far away in a large house overlooking the sea; to a resident of these parts murder might seem an unfortunate incident of life, but blowing up pylons would be an inexcusable impertinence.

After we had eaten we returned reluctantly to town, where we found Wilfred sitting quietly at his desk. He told us in a casual way that while we'd been out he'd received a phone call which he thought might interest us. It had come a few minutes earlier and had been from the Johannesburg team.

112

His tone of voice was neutral as if he did not want to sound particularly concerned about what he'd heard.

They'd informed him, he continued, that their client was going to plead guilty the next morning to the alternative charge and, and this was the important thing, that the prosecution had agreed to accept this plea.

Himie and I were startled. The position of accused number three had improved drastically, for the effect of the acceptance of the plea by the prosecution was that the allegations of actual sabotage were being dropped and he would accordingly be sentenced on the basis of membership of the organisation and not as someone who had himself been responsible for any explosions.

I observed to Wilfred that this probably accounted for the calmness of the Johannesburg team that morning, and Wilfred told us that they'd apologised to him for not letting us know earlier, but that the negotiations had had to be very delicately handled at the highest levels in Pretoria, and that they'd had to take care to prevent any premature announcement which might possibly prejudice their client's chances. Even now they didn't wish us to tell anyone else.

Were there any possibilities, Himie asked tentatively, of similar pleas by our clients being accepted?

Wilfred looked seriously at us. Did we feel it something worth exploring? he queried. His voice was deliberate and restrained.

Definitely, Himie said.

Definitely, I added.

Good—Wilfred spoke now with growing excitement. He'd felt that way too when he'd heard the news, but hadn't wanted to suggest anything until we'd given our views, otherwise it might have appeared that he was merely looking for a convenient way of getting out of a heavy trial . . . We knew what some counsel were like.

For some minutes we discussed the pro's and con's of our accused pleading guilty to the lesser charge, and we came to the conclusion that it would undoubtedly be to their advantage if the prosecution were prepared to accept such pleas. Earlier on there had seemed to be no chance whatsoever of the prosecution agreeing to such a course of action, but a precedent had been established—we could not understand why and wondered whether it was connected with the fact that accused number three's grandfather had been a senior police official—and new possibilities were opened up for us. The accused might be throwing away the chances of a complete acquittal, but such chances seemed very slight, especially when set against the very positive advantage of being sentenced according to less serious charges and on the basis of a much less severe scale of penalties.

It was too late in the evening to consult with our clients or to sound out the prosecution, so we would have at most only two hours in the morning before the trial began in which to pursue the matter. Wilfred said that we had nothing to lose by approaching the prosecutor because he was an able chap who didn't throw his weight around and would at least give us a polite hearing. What he wondered though—he hesitated and his face and hands showed his embarrassment—what he thought perhaps . . . he searched for the appropriate words—wouldn't it perhaps be best . . . if he—er—went alone to see the prosecutor?

Clearly he thought that my political background might prejudice the negotiations, but equally clearly he did not wish to say so in so many words.

I told him he needn't worry: if my political background threatened to prejudice the negotiations and harm our clients I'd be quite content to keep out of the way. Himie felt that the fewer people there were, the quicker the discussions would

114

be, particularly as everything would have to be referred to the police for their decision.

We agreed, then, that Wilfred would go on his own the next morning to see the prosecutor. The chances of success seemed slight, but at least, as he had said, he would get a polite hearing.

Chapter 14

Adrian stood in the witness-box, a slight, pale figure, wearing a neat brown corduroy jacket. His hands rested comfortably on a small wooden platform in front of him, and he answered questions from the prosecution with the same brisk intelligence he had formerly displayed at student meetings. The court had been cleared at the request of the prosecution, who feared he might be intimidated by the large crowd of students present. In fact he was giving evidence with an assurance and co-operativeness which suggested that his only fear was that he might not make a good impression on the court. Whatever he did, I thought bitterly, he did well, even testifying against his friends.

From the moment he had walked into court, chatting in a friendly way to members of the Security Police, I had realised that my spontaneous feeling towards him now was one of uncomplicated hatred. If he had grown a beard or worn dark glasses or become so haggard as to be unrecognisable, my anger might have been less strong, but he was exactly as I had always known him, buoyant, serious and absorbed. The very familiarity of his stance, of his facial expressions and even of the timbre of his voice seemed to intensify my emotion. This was the same Adrian; all that had changed was his role. The extraordinary thing was that he seemed to be unaware of his transformation, for he glanced around court without showing any signs of shame or embarrassment.

Till the very last the lawyers sitting in the defence benches had hoped he might say something which would help the accused. The evidence had come out in slow question and answer form. First he had been taken by the prosecutor through his recruitment into the A.R.M. Then he had told of the organisation's activities, and finally he had referred in detail to the roles of the individual accused. Only over the identification of Anthony Trew had he seemed to hold back. He said that he had known someone under the code name of Roy, but could not say whether Roy was amongst the accused. It was this gap in his evidence which presumably had caused the prosecution to accept Trew's plea on the alternative count.

On the morning of the first day of the trial Himie and I had sat waiting anxiously in Wilfred's chambers for his return from visiting the prosecution. About an hour before the trial had been due to begin he had walked in and informed us calmly that the prosecutor had consulted with the police, who had agreed to the dropping of the sabotage charges and the acceptance of pleas on the alternative charges. Jubilant at this turn of events, we had rushed to the cells below court to get instructions from our clients. Stephanie had been brought to court so late, less than half an hour before the case had been due to begin, that it was only fifteen minutes before the Judge-President entered the court that we had finally been able to inform the prosecution that our clients were prepared to tender pleas of guilty on the alternative counts. On hearing this the J-P had ordered a separation of trials, and the case against Anthony Trew and our accused had been postponed for hearing by another judge a week later.

The trial of Daniels and de Keller, the two remaining accused, had then started. The first witness was a lieutenant who described how he had discovered dynamite and the documents now before court. There had been further police evidence about destruction of government property, and then the first of the accomplices had been called as a witness. We had all expected Adrian to appear at that stage, but instead we had seen his girlfriend come into the box. Her evidence had been damaging to the accused and she had furthermore refused several opportunities given her by defence counsel to make concessions in their favour, but relatively little attention had been paid to what she had said. What everyone in court had been waiting for was the appearance of Adrian Leftwich. Finally on the afternoon of the second day Adrian had been called as a witness for the prosecution. He had given evidence until the court had adjourned that afternoon, and now on the morning of the third day of the trial he was still telling the court what he knew about the organisation and the activities undertaken on its behalf by the two accused. Eventually he finished his evidence-in-chief and the prosecutor sat down.

Counsel for accused number one rose and the court-room waited for an onslaught on Leftwich. What occurred came as an anti-climax. The questioning was gentle and designed to get Adrian's cooperation rather than to break him down. Clearly counsel had decided to go carefully lest Adrian make things yet worse for his client. The only hostility in the court came from the Judge-President, who from time to time interrupted to pose a series of questions which indicated that what angered him was not Adrian the traitor, but Adrian the saboteur.

The court adjourned for morning tea and Adrian was left alone in the witness-box to await the recommencement of evidence. For once the police did not cluster around him, since he was now under cross-examination and they were not permitted to speak to him. Pressmen dashed out to telephone their copy to their papers, while counsel and attorneys huddled in little groups discussing the morning's evidence. I moved to a posi-

118

tion where I could see Adrian clearly and began to stare at him. I dared not be seen doing anything which could be construed as a threat to him, but there was nothing to prevent me from looking at him all the time. Anger gave me the necessary energy to hold my stare for the full period of the adjournment, and I locked my eyes undeviatingly on him. Now that nothing was happening he seemed less comfortable than he had been when giving evidence. From time to time he glanced round the court. His face was bleak, and his pale, anxious eyes bounced away when they met mine. He pursed his large lips and pushed his hand through his hair in a gesture of helplessness and self-pity, giving a slight shrug as if to ask what else he could do in the circumstances.

The Judge-President returned and cross-examination was resumed. Most of the questions were designed to show that in the A.R.M. set-up accused number one had been more of a follower than a leader. Leftwich was given a number of opportunities to agree with this proposition, but he refused them all. Even at this stage his main concern seemed to be to minimise his own role in the organisation, as if somehow it was he who was on trial and not the accused. At last came the question which thousands of people had been asking themselves for days, but which counsel had seemed reluctant to put to the one person who could answer it.

Counsel asked solemnly: with all the leading personnel of the A.R.M. either out of the country or else under promise of indemnity, did Leftwich feel happy about giving evidence against the accused?

The Judge-President intervened to ask irritably whether the witness' happiness was of any concern to the court. For a moment it seemed that the question might not be allowed, but counsel began to argue the point, and the Judge-President muttered loudly that it would probably take less time to have the question put than to have a discussion about it.

119

Adrian braced himself in the box and counsel repeated the question: 'Why are you giving evidence in this case? Do you feel unhappy about it?'

'No, I do not. I was asked by the Security Police after about 70 days whether I was prepared to give evidence. At that stage I refused. Shortly before the others were charged I was again asked to give evidence. I endeavoured to enquire who else was giving evidence. I established there were four others . . .'

What he did not mention was that he himself had persuaded the 'four others' to become State witnesses. His rationalisation was recited quickly and clearly. It seemed that he had rehearsed these words many times in his mind before coming to court, and he appeared to be as anxious to give his explanation as counsel was to hear it.

'. . . I realised that their evidence seemed, with respect to the court, to be very damning against Mr Daniels and Mr de Keller.'

Counsel: 'Possibly against you, too?'

'Yes, I am coming to that. I realised too that what we did was in itself futile and stupid, although I do not believe that the ideals underlying it were stupid or futile. I realised that my futility and stupidity had created a situation in which I was in a very serious situation—the files were kept by me . . . the writing . . . many of the documents . . . much of the evidence. I have known that in other sabotage trials the sentences have been very severe . . . I was told on a number of occasions, "We have enough to hang you," and I realised a life sentence was not out of the question . . .'

He started to speak very rapidly now and it became increasingly difficult to make out his words. Slowly he was losing control of his speech; the precise orator was giving way to the confused boy.

'. . . I realised there was enough evidence to convict myself,

120

Daniels and de Keller, and possibly the person called Roy . . .
and well, as I was . . . I'm sorry, I'm confused . . . and I
could not assess the evidence against Miss Kemp or Mr
Brooks.

'It is not an easy thing and if it is your intention to make me
break down in court I may do so.'

Counsel: 'No, I don't want you to do that.'

Leftwich resumed: 'Oh, I am sure.'

He said this in a whining, self-pitying way and then suddenly burst into tears. Sobbing strongly he put his hands to
his face and ceased addressing the court.

Counsel: 'Would the court wish to adjourn?'

Judge-President: 'You asked for this. I don't know whether
you wanted it, but it's not helping me at all.'

Leftwich pushed away his tears and gestured to counsel
that he wished to continue. His voice was broken and I found
myself overwhelmed by embarrassment and confusion.

Leftwich: 'It's not an easy thing to give evidence against the
people whom you love, who have been your friends, but,
sir . . .'

He sobbed loudly for a moment.

'. . . If I stood to get only five, seven or ten years, I would
not give it, not under any circumstances . . .'

Gripping the sides of the witness box with his hands, he
hung his head in front of him and shaking it wildly to and fro
began to shout in a high-pitched hysterical voice.

'I loathe, oh God, I loathe apartheid and all it means. This
tragedy here I place at the door of the system. I am 24 years
old. I've been stupid and I think we've all been stupid and I
think we all realise that we've indirectly, but not intentionally,
endangered human life. I don't think any of us wanted that.
Don't believe I wanted this. Not at all. I'm giving evidence
very simply because I realised the case against Eddie, the case
against Spike, was hopeless anyway. I realised I was not in a

position to give evidence against the man called Roy. As far as Stephanie Kemp and Alan Brooks are concerned, I believed they stood to get a very light sentence. If I stood a chance of getting five, six, seven, eight, ten years, I wouldn't give evidence, not against people I'm close to. But I believe if they were in my position, with all the others out of the country, and the evidence that was against me and if they stood to come out again when they were 49 or 50 years old, they would have done the same and I would have welcomed them to do so. However hard it is, and much as I loathe it and as much as I have no doubt that a seed of great bitterness has been sown in me—possibly what the psychologists call displacement activity—I have sworn to tell the truth and I have tried to do so.'

He raised his head and spoke emotionally in the direction of the dock.

'I certainly hope there will be a time when, if these people who I am giving evidence against can forgive me and understand that I do not move one jot from my ideas, when this country sees a better situation where the sort of very simple things, in a sense, selfish things, that I want for myself, but which I don't want for myself if they can't be for fifteen million other people—well, I just hope that day comes that we will all be together again. And that is why I have given evidence.'

His head sank on to his forearms and he began to sob wildly once more. By now I too was on the verge of weeping, distressed at the sight of the collapse and degradation of a person who had once seemed so noble and strong. The Judge-President, however, remained stonily unmoved, and in an angry voice declared that the court was now adjourned.

122

Chapter 15

Before cross-examination was resumed the next morning the Judge-President barked out to all those present in court that he couldn't see what the whole trial was about. No cross-examination was being directed towards establishing any defence, he declared, nor could he understand what the State evidence was about; what he wanted to know about the case he was inclined to think he knew already.

Some hours later the defence and prosecution agreed on a formula to shorten the proceedings. The prosecution amended the sabotage charge slightly so as to reduce its gravity, and the two accused thereupon pleaded guilty to the amended charge. The case was then postponed for a week so that the defence might have time to prepare its evidence in mitigation.

On the next day John Harris, the accused in the Station Bomb case, was found guilty in the Transvaal Supreme Court of murder and sabotage and was sentenced to death.

The outcome of the Harris case threw our clients into deep gloom and created an atmosphere of grimness in which defence counsel had to work. The sentence of death was pronounced three days before the case against Alan, Stephanie and Anthony Trew was due to be heard. Once more Himie, Wilfred and I met on a Sunday in Wilfred's chambers to prepare our cross-examination for the next day, but this time Wilfred was acting for Anthony Trew as well, so that we were joined in our discussions by another junior counsel and the Johannesburg solicitor. For most of the day we argued strongly among ourselves as to the best approach to adopt at the trial. Finally we agreed on a rather extraordinary line of defence: we would not, unless compelled to do so, ask a single question of any of the prosecution witnesses. We would make certain admissions so as to render it unnecessary for the prosecution to lead all its evidence, and then the accused would each make brief statements from the dock explaining why they had joined the A.R.M. Finally, the fathers of the three accused would give evidence about their children and hand in testimonials which had been received from other people as to good character.

A large crowd attended court the next day, but they must have been disappointed by the trial's swiftness and lack of drama. The judge was a quiet and, in my experience, decent man, who presided over the proceedings with grave decorum; the prosecutor seemed relieved that the tension of the previous week was over; and Wilfred conducted the defence with extraordinary caution and seriousness. Within a few hours the evidence for the State and the defence had been completed. We waited anxiously for the judge to pass sentence—again there was an anti-climax. The judge said that he wished to have a few days to consider the matter, and the case was adjourned till later in the week. The spectators filed out of court buzzing quietly about how quickly the evidence had been concluded and exchanging opinions about how well or otherwise the accused looked. Court officials then strolled over to the defence team and remarked sympathetically to us how hard it all must be for the fathers of the accused. We took this as a good sign and were further encouraged when the first edition of the evening paper presented the evidence in mitigation in a full and favourable manner. Even stronger proof that what is known as 'public sympathy' was for the first time in any of these cases beginning to swing round to the accused, was given by the way in which the largest Afrikaans popular weekly newspaper reported the trial. A five-columned headline:

BEAUTIFUL STEPHANIE TELLS OF THE MAN IN HER LIFE

stood above pictures of Stephanie and her father, and the story that followed concentrated largely on Stephanie.

'She is attractive, indeed beautiful,' it read. 'From the side she looks just like Grace Kelly, and in common with the two young men sitting next to her, she has a brilliant academic record behind her.

'A person can only wonder at how a girl like the lovely Stephanie Kemp could appear in court on such a charge. And she pleaded guilty. Like Alan Keith Brooks and Anthony Andrew Trew, that she had contravened the Suppression of Communism Act.

'In the Cape Supreme Court where she appeared this week before Judge B. F. J. Banks, 23-year-old Stephanie Kemp, daughter of an ex-principal from Malmesbury, where she herself also went to school for a time, gave an answer to the baffling question: How did she land in this situation?

'The answer is a man—Adrian Leftwich. The same Adrian Leftwich who became a State witness while his friends had to stand in the dock and take responsibility for their deeds.

'In a soft voice Kemp read her statement in the Court on Monday. "When I came to the University of Cape Town in 1960, Adrian was a leading figure in student affairs. He had a persuasive and dynamic personality and when he approached me to join the organisation I felt very flattered. He was extremely popular and I admired him tremendously at the time," she said.

'Kemp, a physiotherapist, went on to say that Adrian to her personified the spirit of idealism and integrity, and that their friendship developed into a very intimate and personal association. She wished to help him and to help humanity.

'She said that her only contact with the organisation was through Leftwich. She was always more interested in people than theoretical doctrines. Leftwich never showed her any documents and she never knew of the whereabouts of any explosives.

'In conclusion she said that her feeling for Adrian had been deep and that the whole experience had been shattering to her.

'Mr Cooper, who appeared for the three young people, told the judge that while Miss Kemp stared prison in the face, the man who was responsible would go free.

'Leftwich, who was called as first witness for the State, told of how the organisation worked and of the plans they made to blow up pylons. He also gave evidence of pylons which were in fact toppled. The organisation had a large quantity of explosives which he had hidden in various places.

'Lieut. A. J. van Dyk of the Security Police said in evidence that he found a large quantity of dynamite in a flat in Sea Point. There was enough dynamite to blow up a large part of the building, he said.

'The parents of all three of the accused were in court. At the times when the court adjourned, Kemp and Trew looked round at the public gallery where a large number of young men and women were sitting. On a few occasions Kemp smiled at persons who recognised her.

'Kemp was for the most part very calm, but when Dr Himie Gordon, senior lecturer in medicine at the University of Cape Town, and then her father, gave evidence for her she was noticeably upset. At one stage it looked as if she were crying softly.

'All three of the fathers of the accused gave evidence for

their children. Mr H. A. J. Trew, secretary-general of the Automobile Association, told of the academic achievements of his son Anthony and also of the motor accident which changed him so much.

'Mr Trew, a short man with snow-white hair, said that the accident changed his son's outlook on life. "As a father I feel that Anthony would never have had anything to do with these people if he had met them in other circumstances," he said.

'Dr R. Brooks, a tall man with a beard and moustache, said in a strong voice that his son Alan, who had been a junior lecturer at the University of Cape Town, had been a most loving son. Dr Brooks, who practises in Southern Rhodesia, said that he was deeply shocked when he heard of his son's arrest.

'From Mr Kemp the court heard that his wife had been in Cape Town for four months. She had gone there immediately she heard that her daughter had been detained.

'When Judge Banks adjourned the court to an unspecified date in order to consider sentence, the parents of all three accused, who had been sitting just in front of them, spoke to their children. Mr Kemp and his daughter flung their arms around each other. When she went down to the cells he gave her a playful tap with his hand.

'About ten minutes later a dramatic incident occurred in the foyer of the court. Kemp came out with a policeman and was taken to her sister. She cried out with joy and they embraced each other. They stood like that for some while before Kemp went with the police to a motor car. The parents and their other daughter,' the report concluded, 'moved away quickly.'

It was unlikely that the judge would read this paper, and even if he did, its sensational style would hardly appeal to him. Yet we were amused and cheered by the way the story had been angled, and our speculations about the sentences became less pessimistic. Our clients had been fortunate in having had their pleas accepted on the less serious charge, and they were also lucky in having as their judge one of the more kindly members of the Cape Bench. At the same time we were sure that the judge would consult with his colleagues on what sentence to pass, just as the Judge-President would in the case of the two accused appearing before him refer to his fellow judges before delivering his sentence. This made me hope that Daniels and de Keller would also benefit from the 'lowering of temperature' brought about by our separate trial.

Eventually, after having waited anxiously for some days, we received a message that the judge was ready to pronounce sentence.

Himie, Wilfred and I met for the last time, and we found ourselves yet once more speculating about the sentences. The maximum allowed by law was ten years, but we felt that it was unlikely that our clients would receive anything like that. I suggested that the period would be between two years and five, probably nearer five. Himie felt it would be nearer two. Wilfred refused to mention any figure, but cautiously advised us to be neither too optimistic nor too pessimistic. On one thing we all agreed, and that was that Adrian had clearly emerged as a villain, whereas our clients had come through with their honour intact.

Wilfred went so far as to suggest that even Adrian's breakdown in the witness box had been rehearsed. He recalled Adrian's use of the phrase, 'Do you want to break me?' and said this indicated that Adrian had been preparing the way for his breakdown by trying in advance to put the blame on counsel. Then Adrian had had the cheek to say that apartheid was responsible for his being in the witness box. It was the old coward's way out, Wilfred said emphatically, blaming the system for one's own faults. And as for all the sobbing and phoney emotion . . . Wilfred shook his head in indication of his disgust.

Neither agreeing nor disagreeing with Wilfred's opinion Himie said quietly that the general view was that Adrian's sentence would be the hardest of all—he would have to live with himself for the rest of his life.

I wasn't so sure of that, I commented. Adrian had become used to being successful and would find a way out of his present difficulties just as he had done out of his past ones. In fact it was amazing how many people were already making excuses for him.

The sharpness of Wilfred's reply to my statement took me by surprise. We knew how little time he had for Mr Leftwich, he said, but if he'd been in Leftwich's shoes he'd have done exactly the same thing, and so would ninety-nine out of a hundred other people. Who would want to go to jail if he could get out of it? No, Adrian was a bloody ass to have got involved in the first place in something which had been too big for him, but it was silly to criticise him for trying to save himself afterwards. We had to face it, people were basically selfish, they sought to get on in the world, and if they landed themselves in trouble they did all they could to save their own skins. All Leftwich's talk about 'sharing democracy' and 'creating a more fluid situation in the country' had been just a lot of bull right from the beginning, a collection of fine phrases to make him feel important. In fact all he'd really been interested in was playing around with power and impressing a couple of silly starry-eyed girls whose knowledge of politics hadn't extended beyond what they'd learnt between the sheets.

The vehemence with which he expressed himself distressed me considerably, but I restrained myself from hitting back. What he had really been challenging was my own philosophy, aspects of which he himself had possibly once accepted. Yet for all his insistence that man was basically selfish, and for

129

all his ambition to be a successful advocate and then a judge, he himself had an impulsive courage and a dogged sense of right which often led him to do things that cut across self-interest.

Himie picked up his files and with a chuckle that broke the tension suggested that we get across to court to see if the judge would be as severe on our clients as their senior counsel was.

A half hour later we were sitting in court number one waiting for the usher to announce the arrival of the judge. Wilfred and I were in the bench reserved for counsel, conscious that until the judge came the spectators would be looking at the accused, at the prosecutor and at us. From time to time we straightened our long black gowns and touched at our white bibs to make sure that they were in place, and often we looked at the desk in front of us where our brief covers lay ready for the sentences to be written in. Sitting with us was the junior counsel who had been briefed to appear with Wilfred on behalf of Anthony Trew, and like us he remained silent and anxious. Reporters at the press-bench opened their notebooks, and the spectators in the crowded galleries peered expectantly at the door through which the judge would come. I looked round at the accused and saw that the three of them were chatting quietly to their parents, each nervously trying to comfort the other. Policemen were telling students who had just arrived that they must not block the doorway, while other students in the upper gallery leaned forward in their seats and spoke to one another in subdued voices.

'Silence in the court!' The usher's call interrupted the buzz and everyone rose in their seats to await the entrance of the judge. I glanced quickly at the accused and saw that Alan was pale and swaying lightly from foot to foot, while Stephanie—I had an impression of long hanging hair, a polka-dotted blouse and a large white bow—stared boldly ahead of her. The

130

third looked down at his father and then faced the door through which the judge and his two assessors were about to enter.

The judge strode into the court-room, his hair silver and handsome, his crimson gown hanging splendidly round him. His face was grave, and I noticed with alarm that he did not look at the accused, which, according to lawyers' superstition, was a bad sign. He paused politely while the assessors seated themselves at either side of his throne-like chair, and then sat down. The waiting crowd sank silently back to their seats.

'Tell the accused to stand,' the judge commanded in a quiet, serious voice. Still he did not look at them, but taking out a pair of glasses from a pocket inside his robes, began to read from prepared notes.

'The accused in this case were originally charged with a contravention of the Sabotage Act . . .' He dealt briefly with the history of the case and referred to the evidence which had been led.

'It is the duty of the State,' he observed, 'to maintain law and order . . . Leftwich said that the policy of the organisation was to change the system of government and apartheid in South Africa, and that although different members had different ideas, they all hoped for a more fluid situation to be created which would give rise to the end of apartheid, and of all social, economic and political discrimination.'

We listened carefully, anxious for clues, in the judge's tone of voice or use of adjectives, to the severity of the sentences likely to be passed; but he maintained a grave monotone and his description of the evidence was neutral.

'Now it is not a crime in our country to oppose apartheid or the government,' the judge continued, 'but when unlawful means are used, more particularly violent ones, the State has a duty to protect society.' The judge paused for a moment, and

131

looking over the top of his glasses for the first time, spoke directly to the accused:

'I must say,' he said, shaking his head, 'that I have the greatest difficulty in understanding what the accused hoped to achieve by their methods.' Everyone in court seemed to follow the judge's eyes and look at the accused. They stood straight and still in the dock, lips tight, eyelids blinking occasionally, but otherwise showing no emotion at all.

'Be that as it may,' said the judge, returning to his notes, 'Lieutenant van Dyk of the Security Police gave evidence of how he found a substantial quantity of dynamite belonging to this organisation in a flat in Sea Point . . .

'The accused each read statements from the dock which this court has taken into consideration . . . Trew told of his accident and how it changed his life . . . Brooks described how he came to be a member of the organisation and referred to events such as the exclusion of non-White students from the mixed universities, the Sharpeville incident, and the banning of the African National Congress and the Pan African Congress, which, he said, gave rise in him to a feeling of frustration and the conviction that the only way to bring about change was by what he called euphemistically extra-legal means . . . Kemp told the court that she was flattered when Leftwich approached her to join the organisation . . .

'In addition to the statements by the accused themselves, evidence was given by the father of each accused. For them it is a tragic occasion, and I have sympathy for these people . . .'

There was still nothing in his judgment to indicate whether the sentence would be one year or eight, but the tone had been grimmer than I had anticipated. Sometimes, though, I consoled myself, a stern lecture preceded a lenient sentence.

'I have no doubt, however, that the accused must have known what the aims of the organisation were. Kemp for example . . .' fear burst in my stomach as he singled out Steph-

132

anie, 'must have known that the organisation was considering serious measures. I accept that the three felt frustrated, but that does not justify the offence. No one may take the law into his own hands. Such a situation cannot be tolerated.'

The judge paused again, and looked at Anthony Trew, who, he said, was only 22 years old and had a good academic record. 'I accept that he was seriously injured in an accident and that he was influenced by another person. He also did not play a major role in the organisation, and was in fact a member for only a few weeks.'

The judge looked down at his notes, and then referred to Alan, who, he commented, was slightly older, 'but has in his favour the fact that he left the organisation on his own initiative and thereafter took no further part in its activities.

'In Kemp's favour I accept that she was under Leftwich's influence, but . . .' my stomach tightened again with anxiety, 'her offence is graver because she was in the organisation for a longer time. I have taken this into account in the sentences which I propose to pass . . .' ('No, no, don't make it harder for her,' I begged softly), 'which, bearing in mind all the evidence, and everything which was said by counsel on their behalf, and all the factors which I have mentioned, are as follows . . .' I stiffened waiting for the words to be pronounced.

'Trew, I sentence you to a term of four years' imprisonment, of which two years are suspended on condition that during a period of three years you are not convicted of any offence under section one of Act 44 of 1950.

'Brooks, I sentence you to a term of four years' imprisonment, of which two years are suspended on the same condition.

'Kemp, I sentence you to a period of five years' imprisonment of which three years are suspended on the same condition . . . The court is now adjourned.'

Chapter 16

The heavy entrance door at the male section of Roeland Street prison swung open and I stepped inside to have my last interview with Alan. As I waited for him to be brought to the consulting room, I looked out of the window at the only section of the interior of the prison that could be seen by visiting lawyers—a portion of a concrete yard that led through a steel gate to another yard. From the distance came warders' harsh shouts, and I thought sadly to myself that this was the world in which Alan and Stephanie would have to live for the next two years. Footsteps approached the steel gate and I moved quickly away from the window so as not to be seen peering at what was not supposed to be my concern. The door opened and Alan, clad in prison khaki, walked in. He seemed pale and tired and when he spoke to me I felt that for the first time he was showing signs of stress. Yet though his mood seemed depressed, he spoke with resoluteness and calm, and I felt sure that his courage and independence of spirit were not in question at all. Platitudinous good wishes from me would have been out of place, and our consultation was conducted on a brisk, practical level. The only thing he wanted me to do was to try to help relieve some of the distress his parents would feel. There was an awful vicious circle of worrying, he pointed out, in which he worried about his parents worrying about him, and so on.

I said that if he liked I'd mention to his mother and father how much he'd valued their support, and then go on to hint that he'd prefer them not to go into mourning as though something disastrous or disgraceful had happened to him. He nodded agreement, and then commented sadly that he wished it were not so difficult for parents to understand the ideas and beliefs of their children. I said I wished it were not so hard for children to bear their parents' love—our poor parents had become scared of their own children, frightened of doing or saying the wrong thing; when difficulties arose all the children wanted was a quiet, natural handling of the situation, but instead the parents got over-anxious and in their determination to do right did everything wrong. He said his parents had been pretty good all along, and what he couldn't bear was the idea of their suffering on his account. I concluded the discussion by saying I'd been generalising, but that in any event he had enough to contend with without worrying about his parents at this stage—and I was sure that the people who would most agree with me when I said that were his parents.

Our consultation did not last long, and soon his khaki-clad figure was being led once more through the concrete yard, while I moved down the passage to the exit. The warder who let me out said he wished all the prisoners were as well-behaved as Brooks, and as I walked round the prison to bid farewell to Stephanie, I wondered how it was that people like this warder could see some of the country's finest citizens going to jail and yet not realise that something was wrong with society.

At the female section of the prison I had to wait for longer than usual for Stephanie to be brought to the interview room. When she came I was immediately struck by the way her new status as a convicted prisoner had changed her appearance. The khaki dress which she wore, her flat brown shoes and the absence of make-up on her face made her look like a schoolgirl.

135

Glancing at her flat chest and thin legs I said to myself: She's just a girl. Then I noticed the engagement ring on her finger and reminded myself that she was 23 years old, a university graduate, and engaged to be married.

She saw me looking at the ring and immediately asked why I had not seemed very enthusiastic when she'd told me of her engagement a week earlier.

I had come merely to say goodbye and to find out if she had any final legal or business requests to make, but she was apparently determined to have a full discussion with me, and my attempts to evade her question were unsuccessful.

Well, er . . . I admitted, . . . er . . . the morning of a serious trial hadn't seemed to me a very realistic time for an engagement.

She scoffed at my answer and said she'd have to wait only two years, which wasn't so long.

But she hadn't known at the time it would be only two years, I insisted, and well . . . er . . . it seemed a little premature.

If one kept waiting for things to happen, she retorted with a laugh, then everything was premature and one could never run one's life in one's own way.

She then proceeded to tell me some of her ideas about society and about convention, making it plain that she and her fiancé did not believe in the bourgeois idea of marriage according to which people were tied to each other by legal and proprietary chains. Either people loved each other or they didn't; when they did love each other they must do so to the limits of their being and without concern for the future. When they ceased to love each other, they must be permitted to separate. In order to be fully real, love had to be freely offered; obligation, formality and rules, because they were based either on coercion or habit, were the enemy of true feeling and accordingly would have no place in their relationship.

136

She spoke with such rapidity and enthusiasm that I found my resistance to the personal trend of the discussion being swept aside. It was pleasant to be able to speak to her without the feeling that she still had to face trial, and as for the future, well, the two-year prison sentence seemed to have no meaning for her at all. She refused to look either upon herself or upon 'time' as an abstraction, so that the coming period in prison was something to be lived out by her in the future and not a mere topic for thought for the present. The only real thing was the present, which in practical terms meant that all that mattered at that moment was the chance of having a lively discussion with her lawyer.

I asked her about children: wouldn't they suffer if parents separated and came together according to feelings of the moment.

She wouldn't have children, she assured me quickly, since she wasn't sure she'd be able to bring them up properly. Most people regarded their kids as possessions to be shown off to the world and she didn't see anything marvellous in having children just to do that. In any event she wanted to be free to develop herself as a person, and not have to spend the best years of her life changing nappies or washing plates.

I said I admired her anti-domesticity and her determination to keep her horizons wide open, but at the same time felt quite differently from her about children. During my '90-days' I'd developed an obsession about having children. My strongest fantasies had been about having children and enjoying peace; my married friends had told me afterwards that they must have been fantasies, because you couldn't have children and peace at the same time. They'd also pointed out that I'd left out a wife.

She did not smile, but shook her head and set the discussion off on another tack. What sort of a place, she asked suddenly and directly, did I live in?

I was put out by the question and tried not to answer it. What was I being so coy about? she said. She knew me only as a lawyer and wondered what I was like as a person.

I drew a diagram of my flat and showed her how it stood on stilts on the mountain slopes above the sea. It was a small flat lacking in amenities, I told her, but its cheapness and wonderful view more than made up for its disadvantages. Gradually I became enthusiastic about the description so that in the end I gave her full details even of my furnishings. I discussed the colour scheme with her: red curtains, grey carpet, thick-weave multi-striped divan covers . . .

Single or double bed?

Two singles.

Oh. What did I do in my spare time?

Was she interrogating me?

I didn't have to answer if I didn't want to.

Oh, all right. I was very fond of mountain-climbing, and, before I was banned, had done a lot of camping . . .

Oh, no, not one of those.

What did she mean?

All the men she was interested in seemed to like hiking and climbing. They expected her just to tag along, as though she didn't really count, so that they could show her how marvellous they were, sweating and making fires and carrying rucksacks.

That was me exactly. Except that more recently I'd gone in for what I called social climbing—easy ways up and down, and a good sleep on top.

She supposed I read a lot and listened to music.

Yes.

What did I read? Politics?

Not so much any more. Mainly nineteenth-century novels. Also psychology. And she?

Also novels—Dostoevsky, Tolstoy and that crowd, but mainly Sartre. What music did I like?

All kinds of classical, also modern straight-from-the-guts jazz.

Composers?

I'd changed. Formerly Beethoven, now Schubert and Shostakovich. And she?

Bach and Mozart. Especially Mozart, his tone was so pure.

There was something I ought to tell her, but please, she shouldn't repeat it.

What?

She mustn't feel disappointed if she heard I'd followed the other people who'd slipped out of the country . . .

The exchange went on for a while until I decided it was becoming too personal. We'd better get back to the purpose of my visit, I said desperately. I'd come to tie up loose ends about her personal or business affairs before she was moved. Was there anything I could do for her?

All she could think of was getting her typewriter back from the police and, possibly, trying to help her parents not to worry about her so much. They made their whole lives revolve around her and this only added to her feeling of responsibility. She couldn't take it . . .

She had to take it, I answered firmly. She called herself a progressive and this meant she had to be big enough to understand her parents and understand their love for her.

That wasn't the problem, she replied, the problem was she felt for them too much. What she did with her life should be her own affair and she couldn't bear the idea of being responsible for the way they led theirs. At all costs they shouldn't feel apologetic about her activities, or decide to give up their home just to be near her prison.

I promised to do what I could, and after taking down some particulars about her typewriter, stood up to say goodbye.

She jumped to her feet and smiling brightly thanked me for all I'd done for her. She didn't believe in speeches or painful farewells, she told me cheerfully, so she wouldn't say anything more.

Then she dashed off to call a wardress, moving so lightly and easily that it was difficult for me to think of her as a captive and to accept that soon she would be transferred to another prison, probably a thousand or more miles away. I watched her figure retreating—khaki dress, long auburn hair, dark brown shoes, at a distance she could have been any prisoner—and wondered what life would be like without the Brooks and Kemp case to occupy most of my day.

Chapter 17

A large crowd listened in court number one while the Judge-President passed sentence on Daniels and de Keller. He began sympathetically. It was bad enough for an accused to have to serve his sentence, he said, without in addition having to get a lecture from the judge. Then followed one of the most damning and sneering attacks I had ever heard in that court. If the accused thought that by their futile and stupid actions they were going to coerce anybody, he boomed angrily, then they seriously mistook the temper of the South African people. The fact that individuals like Leftwich—and he wondered if calling him a rat wasn't being unfair to the *genus rattus*—had got away without punishment, in no way diminished the crime of the accused. Only the fact that there had been no injury to life or limb, and this probably due more to good fortune than to good foresight, had caused him not to consider imposing the supreme penalty. Daniels had stated that apartheid was the cause of much juvenile delinquency, but how Daniels hoped to improve the situation by becoming a super-delinquent himself he couldn't see. Neither of the accused had shown any signs of remorse and they had been too cowardly to go into the witness box and take the court into their confidence as to their motivation. In de Keller's case he'd reluctantly accepted that there might have been a lesser degree of guilt. Nevertheless stern punishments were called for. For

Daniels the sentence was fifteen years and for de Keller ten years.

These words were spoken with such indignation that even as he left the court-room the Judge-President seemed furious. The two accused showed no signs at all of emotion, but Daniel's mother began to weep and a crowd of friends and relatives gathered round to comfort her. I left the court feeling sick. The sentences had been severe and in addition the Judge-President had from a position of strength mocked and jeered at the accused. Where was his own courage? I asked myself bitterly. Not many years earlier he had sentenced a prison warder to a heavy term of imprisonment for having brutally killed a convict, and had called for a judicial enquiry into the whole prison system. Now, in the new climate, when torture was becoming part and parcel of investigation procedures by the political police, he stayed silent on the question of abuse of power. I felt that if a case of police torture were brought to his attention his indignation would be more likely to fall on the victim than on the police.

When I got back to my chambers I telephoned the prison to find out if Miss Kemp was still there. In a friendly way the matron informed me that the prisoner had not yet been moved and that her lawyers could certainly still come and see her. This was good news, and by the time I drove up to the prison my spirits had revived somewhat.

Stephanie seemed gloomy when she came into the consulting room, but she brightened as she saw me. I told her that the formal purpose of my visit was to get her to sign a request to the police for return of her typewriter, but there was no reason why we shouldn't chat for a while. She duly signed the document and I asked her why she looked so sad.

She'd heard about the sentences on Eddie and Spike, she said, and also what the judge had said to them.

I nodded sympathetically and said it seemed unfair that

142

three of them should get two years, while the other two got ten and fifteen. Still, there was one consolation—if she and Alan and Anthony Trew had had all the luck, they'd nevertheless managed to create an atmosphere which should help the other two as well.

The newspapers had been surprisingly sympathetic, I pointed out, and Vorster had been quoted as saying he'd give remission in those cases where the parents could persuade him their children had been misled by the student leaders.

Stephanie reacted indignantly to this. She didn't want any favours, she declared, and anyhow she couldn't see why her parents should be dragged into things.

Vorster had his own motives, I replied, but that didn't alter the fact that he'd been forced to look at political prisoners as human beings entitled to decent treatment.

That was just it, she didn't want special treatment . . .

It wasn't only a question of what she wanted, I said insistently, but what could be used to help a thousand and more other political prisoners.

Nothing, she was adamant, nothing would make her say she was sorry for what she'd done, or even that she'd been misled. If she'd been misled at all, it had only been because of her readiness to be misled. Just because she was White and a girl, people had sympathy for her. Ugh, it made her mad.

It wasn't for me to persuade her one way or the other, I answered, but perhaps she could continue to refuse to express any regrets herself and yet not stand in the way of her parents if they asked for remission. Her early release could set an important precedent. She knew that although political prisoners were generally the best behaved prisoners they were always treated as the worst. In particular they never got the standard remission of sentence, nor were they ever paroled. If an exception were made in her case it would be easier to campaign for the release of other prisoners. In any event, I added with a shrug, Vorster would probably make the gesture whatever she did or said.

Then she wouldn't accept it, he couldn't force her, she responded firmly.

I smiled and told her she couldn't insist on staying in jail if her release had been ordered. But, I went on, that wasn't the point. She had to see it as a precedent for others: paradoxically, it seemed that more strength and understanding would be required to accept remission than to refuse it.

There was so much she had to get used to, she said unhappily. She needed time to think things out. No sooner had she started to adjust to being in prison that she had to begin worrying about getting out.

The conversation moved off on to different themes and she became more cheerful. I was determined to keep the discussion on a non-personal plane, and yet all the time felt an urge to explore further the tentative intimacy of our previous interview. Her character fascinated and baffled me. She told her stories with an adult's vocabulary and concern for accuracy, and yet with a child's sense of excitement. Her world was populated by alive personalities each one active with feeling, and her life consisted of what to her was a series of bright emotional encounters. What mattered were the actual happenings of her existence, and her focus was always on the occurrences themselves and not on the theories which other people might seek to justify with them.

At one stage I asked her if I could get back the red jersey which I had sent in to her—who knew who might need it next? She said nothing. Why was she so silent? I asked. She shook her head and did not answer. But she couldn't wear the jersey now, I said, puzzled by her attitude. Finally she answered: she wanted to keep the jersey so she could wear it when she got out. She seemed so anxious for me not to deprive her of it that I hastened to assure her she could keep it.

144

While I was in the middle of one of what she called my 'long dissertations,' she interrupted me in the middle of a sentence and asked me about something completely different.

Was I still determined to leave the country? I nodded. But how could I leave Fred Carneson and the others? she asked in a sharp follow-up.

I told her that that was the only thing which had held me back. But there were other factors, I continued, and even though I knew it was wrong for me to leave, I was still going to go.

I had argued the matter so often with myself that I was able to speak to her with fluency and passion. I couldn't bear living here, I told her, and being so watched and powerless that I could do nothing about the awful things I saw around me. At times I choked with impotence and felt myself fading away as a person. Soon I would be thrown out of practice, so that I wouldn't be able to help even in the minor role of a lawyer. I'd be out of work, and people would say: Shame, poor Albie, he used to be such a promising lawyer, and now look at him. I would become a symbol of pathos rather than of principle, and I wouldn't be able to bear it. In the meantime what was happening to my interests? In the past I had always been involved in a variety of activities—important or not, they had been stimulating and challenging. Now I was becoming more and more concerned with trivia and self-indulgence. I could talk for hours about steak or wine or a new tie or a haircut or even about paintings. I would climb the mountain and furnish my flat and lie on the beach—and then I would realise that these pleasant recreations were starting to become the whole of my life. I could have been any person, anywhere at any time. I hadn't even had a decent argument for ages—not just about politics, but about any subject. It seemed that once it became impermissible or dangerous to challenge the central features of our society, then all daring, all creative

145

thought in any field became suspect, and people chose simply to conform. My friends couldn't understand my basic worries, such as whether or not I should leave. They saw it purely as a personal decision, like whether one should have an operation or go on a holiday. They couldn't realise that what mattered as much as anything else was the effect that leaving might have on those who were still fighting.

We spoke for some time and towards the end of the conversation I began to realise that her fondness for me was growing beyond the normal affection a client might feel for her lawyer.

When later we said goodbye she was smiling while I was serious. I left the prison feeling confused and anxious and did not know what to do. Possibly she would be transferred that night, and I would never see her again. Possibly she would still be there the next day, so that I would be able to speak to her once more. If so, what should I say? In normal circumstances words spoken carelessly or impetuously could be corrected, but now anything I said would remain frozen and unalterable in her mind for two years.

Chapter 18

In fact I saw Stephanie twice more before she was moved.
Possibly I could have seen her a third or fourth time, but the
strain of being with her and never knowing whether it would
be for the last time was proving too much for me. After having
said goodbye and wishing her luck so many times, I decided
eventually to make my next visit the last; then we could say
all we had to say to each other and end our discussions on a
positive, buoyant note. The problem, however, was: on precisely what note were we to part? Lawyer and client? 'Just
friends'? Or . . .?

It seemed too difficult for me to solve on my own, so I
arranged to meet an old friend whose judgment I valued.
She was amused when I asked her for advice, since I had a
reputation of never discussing my personal affairs with anybody. To her the answer was quite simple, and she was sure
that if I hadn't been so subjectively involved I would have
seen it for myself. I was quite wrong, she said, to regard the
situation as an either/or one: either to encourage a relationship between Stephanie and myself, or squash it completely.
On the contrary, I could behave perfectly decently and sensibly by neither encouraging nor discouraging anything. Normally, she pointed out, one wouldn't dream of intervening in
any way in the affairs of an engaged girl, but the circumstances

here were entirely abnormal. The engagement had been more of a moral gesture than a serious agreement to get married, just as my and Stephanie's feelings were bound to be distorted by the fact that we were meeting in a prison and not a coffee bar. In the next two years things would sort themselves out and Stephanie, her fiancé and I would all have a chance to see how deep our feelings were.

I saw the sense of this advice and determined to act on it.

The consulting room at the prison was as shabby as ever, yet when I looked at the worn furniture and low-hanging electric light, I told myself that there was nothing that I couldn't become sentimental about, not even this squalid place. Stephanie walked in, looking pretty despite her plain khaki dress, and I was nervous as I spoke, aware that this was to be our last discussion, and conscious of my responsibility. For the next two years she might be mulling over my final words to her . . .

I told her about the dilemma I felt myself to be in, and then firmly prevented her from interrupting to say it was all nonsense. We could both do with a lecture on the dangers which surrounded people who found themselves in romantic situations. Both of us were capable of being reckless, I told her, but that didn't matter as long as we weren't both reckless at the same time. She had to bear in mind that she was bound to think a lot about me because I was the only man she'd been allowed to see for so long. Similarly I could find myself becoming over-excited at the idea of helping her as a maiden in distress.

And what, Stephanie asked, had all this pompous stuff to do with anything? She seemed genuinely puzzled.

I said that in reality we hadn't really got to know each other at all. What did she know about how I thought and felt?

148

Nothing. About my past and how I reacted to situations? Nothing.

She laughed and asked me what I was getting so excited about. She knew what my ideas were and what kind of a person I was, and that was enough. I didn't have to make a whole song and dance about it. Anyhow, I was only her lawyer, so why all the fuss?

For a moment I began to panic. Had I only imagined that she had been showing signs of personal interest in me?

She seemed unaware of my discomfiture, however, and gradually I became more composed. I considered what I had learnt about her during the course of preparing for her trial. Her father had once been a school principal and was now a child psychologist. His family had suffered greatly in a British concentration camp during the Boer War and he was now a supporter of the present governing party. At the same time, however, he had a strong spirit of personal independence and felt a powerful protective loyalty towards his daughter. Her mother was descended from an English settler family, and though patently a kind person, had never expressed her humanitarian concern in any political form. Stephanie herself seemed to have been bright and well liked as a girl. The vice-principal of her High School had written in a testimonial that she had a delightful personality, and that she had charm and dignity combined with qualities of leadership, moral courage, loyalty, reliability and honesty; her academic standard was high and she was gifted at music and sport. At the trial the evidence which had been given in mitigation about the voluntary work she had done as a physiotherapist had been most striking: showing great initiative and enthusiasm she had organised a physical rehabilitation unit at a student-supported clinic, and her cheerfulness and zest had so inspired her

149

patients that right up to the last they had enquired about her with affection and concern.

There was something I'd been meaning to ask her for a long time . . . I said tentatively.

Her face brightened with provocative curiosity and she told me to go ahead and ask.

What were the factors, I enquired, which had led her to take an interest in politics?

She looked at me with surprise and said that of all people surely I would understand why a person living in South Africa felt she had to do something about the situation.

But most people of her background, I observed, didn't feel they had to do something.

After considering this point for a moment she said that she hadn't really thought about the matter much. Each step she'd taken had seemed perfectly logical at the time, and she was only sorry it had taken her so long to learn what was what. As a child she'd been very serious and had had a strong sense of religious dedication. For some time her ambition had been to become a missionary and go to China, and only slowly had she come to realise there were lots of things wrong much nearer home. Actually, she'd always had strong feelings of concern about poor people, but had seen poverty as something personal and unfortunate and had never considered why some people were poor and others rich. It had been the same on the question of race. She'd never been a racialist in any conscious way, but as a patriotic girl had blindly accepted that apartheid must be right because it had been the policy of the Government. As she'd grown older she'd become more aware that something was wrong, but hadn't really been able to find out precisely what. She'd always done a lot of reading and had often cried for hours over a book that had moved her. One book which had made a tremendous impact on her had

150

been Father Huddleston's *Naught For Your Comfort,* but even after reading that she hadn't been able to tie things up properly. It had only been when she'd come to university that she'd been able to see that most of what she'd objected to was related to the system of apartheid, and that as long as apartheid existed there would always be inequality and discrimination in South Africa. She'd taken part in student protests and had learnt at first hand how the police prevented people from demonstrating. Then when she'd been asked to join the A.R.M. she'd agreed immediately to do so, because it had offered her the opportunity to do something to support the Africans in their struggle for human rights.

The simplicity of her explanation moved me. There was no looking for motives and no self-consciousness, only a straightforward statement of facts as she saw them.

We spoke at some length about what life would be like for Stephanie in the coming two years. I felt that with her personality she should manage very well, and repeated to her the advice which had once been given outside my cell by a sympathetic long-term Coloured prisoner: 'Take it easy, take it slow.' She had been on her own ever since her arrest so she looked forward to being with other women political prisoners. She hoped she could study, but otherwise the future seemed completely blank to her. I told her she might as a pastime try to put on a little weight, especially in her legs, which were rather thin. She looked down at her feet and then darkly turned her head away from me, as though I had subjected her to strong personal criticism. She was a beautiful girl, I told her placatingly, and there was no reason why she couldn't be healthy as well. Her expression softened, though she still looked suspiciously at me.

Was there anything, I asked warmly, anything at all I could do for her?

She nodded her head, and I asked her what it was.

Tell her, she replied in a soft voice, that I would still be in South Africa when she came out.

Oh, no, I groaned, hadn't we been through all that already. But why not?

I couldn't say I would, because I didn't know whether I would or not.

If it were possible, why didn't I say I would be there, but possibly I wouldn't?

Because it was the other way round—I wouldn't be there, but possibly I would.

We were arguing about words.

No, it was more than that. I didn't like giving an undertaking to do something if I wasn't sure I would do it. I would rather promise less and do more.

She was just the opposite. She thought one should promise everything and then one would try for everything. If one didn't manage, at least one knew one had tried.

We could not convince each other on the point, but we did agree that we were each very pleased to have met the other. She thanked me and said she wouldn't forget how much I had done for her, and I wished her lots of courage and patience, and told her there would be many people, including myself, who would never forget her.

When we stood up to say the final goodbye, I felt that I must touch her before we parted. I said to her with a smile that I knew she would think it very bourgeois, but would she mind if we shook hands before I left?

She laughed and stretched her hand out in front of her. I took hold of it.

She had a nice friendly hand, I told her, and I was glad I'd been bourgeois.

She laughed again, and looked towards the door. Her face was bright and had a touch of the radiance which had so affected me when I had seen it in her newspaper photograph.

Our hands separated and she began to move out of the room. I picked up my briefcase.

'Goodbye, Albie,' she said tenderly.

'Goodbye, Stephanie,' I answered.

Part Two

INTERLUDE
Cape Town 1965

Chapter 19

The flame is brilliant in the room
But the room is small in the street
With doors and curtains closed
There is a lack of air.
A song in a soundproof cell
Is as silent as a clown;
A brilliant flame in a shuttered place
Has only one leg.
Now from my own house
We leave like thieves.

I wrote these lines about a furtive personal relationship in which I had been involved, but they could have been applied to any aspect of my life in 1905. The few square miles of Cape Town to which I was confined constituted what must have been one of the most brilliantly beautiful spots in the world— a huge stone mountain in the centre of a long peninsula, with forests on the one side, wild bush and heath on the other, and a string of dazzling white beaches all around. Yet everything was tainted. The beaches were segregated and the bulk of the city's amenities were reserved for Whites only. Seven miles off-shore and visible to me each day as I drove to work was Robben Island, the small desert spot on which Nelson Mandela and a thousand other political prisoners were kept. At night a lighthouse on the island would sweep a beam across the sea. Sometimes I would be on the beachfront balcony of a luxury flat, huddling in a corner so that the police could not spot me while I illegally attended a party. I would have a cocktail or a glass of brandy in my hand and would feel myself slowly relaxing under the impact of fierce beat music, of liquor and of laughing voices. Then I would see the little light of Robben Island flashing in my direction, mocking my pleasure and commanding me not to forget.

After work and on week-ends I would spend many hours on the beach, reading, lying in the sun and swimming. With a small group of friends I played cricket at the water's edge. We had our own rules, the game was fast, the surf curled round our ankles and we laughed in the fading sunlight. When the game was over I would run to the end of the beach and back —a mile exactly—splashing like a racehorse in the shallow extremities of the waves. Then I would fling my tired, sweaty body into the chilly water, dry myself and go off to drink large tankards of beer on the spacious stoep of an internationally famous hotel on a promontory overlooking the beach. Bankers, businessmen, journalists on sponsored tours, actors and retired industrialists—rich, suntanned visitors from all over the world—mingled on its verandahs with the hearty bronzed boys and girls up from the beach.

Down below a hundred yards out to sea, surf-riders, their hair bleached in the sun, their bodies tanned to a leathery brown, with huge bony knobs grown on their knees, and their minds faded to a stupor by the ceaseless rocking of the waves, would kneel for hours on their glass fibre boards waiting for a swell to bring them careering on to the beach. Coloured waiters in sweat-stained white uniforms dashed from the stoep to the bar and back, carrying heavily laden trays of drinks the one way and empty glasses the other. They hurried like automatons, keeping the White drinkers replenished with

158

liquor, enjoying only the one privilege of being able to select which of the many clamouring patrons they should serve first. One of the waiters was a medical student who had once been friendly with my brother; it pained me to order a drink from him.

Later, when the sun had set, a loud rhythm band would strike up; pretty girls in gay party frocks, escorted by handsome young men in smart, lightweight suits, would arrive and displace the semi-nude bathers from the verandah.

On the way back to my flat I would stroll past the long line of shiny American cars which had brought the dancers. My bare feet tramped comfortably on the warm paving stones, and the sharp odour of roasting meat floated up to my nostrils from family barbecues on the beach down below. Back at my flat I would put on a record and let the music soar out loud while I changed into casual sports clothes. There was no hurry. I would select a bottle of cheap Cape estate wine, get into my car and drive off lazily to a nearby steakhouse or seafood restaurant. The road wound past giant boulders, the sea lay majestically below, and as the car cruised along, I would hum the music I had been listening to and think about the evening ahead. Then I would travel round a bend and lying in front of me, right in the centre of my vision, would be—Robben Island. It was a round blob in the distance and too far away for any detail to be discerned, but my mind would conjure up the figures of the prisoners, the cliffs of the quarry in which they cut stones, and the long rows of cells in which they slept at night.

For most of the day these men would be preoccupied with their ordinary activities in the prison camp, but every now and then, for a few moments, their thoughts would turn to the mainland and to people abroad, just as from time to time my own thinking would be interrupted by the knowledge of their existence so nearby.

There was only one activity which I was able to enjoy wholeheartedly, and that was climbing Table Mountain. Each Sunday I would complete the ascent with a few friends. The natural grandeur, the physical exertion, the sense of space, and the absence of apartheid notices temporarily relieved my oppression. Once on impulse I even climbed three mountains in one day, driving myself until I could only crawl on hands and knees up the last one. A psychiatrist mountaineering companion of mine was amused: I was manifesting a common syndrome, he told me as he took me home afterwards, found in ageing men who felt impelled to attempt extraordinary physical undertakings. To prove their continuing virility? I asked. Yes, he acknowledged with a smile.

A pastime which pleasantly anaesthetised me during many evenings was playing bridge: for hours on end the cards would absorb me and exclude all other preoccupation. Since it involved attending what was for me probably a forbidden social gathering, I had to take precautions. I always sat near a door and my fellow-players learnt to refer to me by a special name when making arrangements over the telephone. The idea of playing underground bridge amused us all.

I took a number of chances during this period. There were so many prohibitions to which I had been subjected that I found it impossible to obey them all. When the pains of obedience were almost as great as the penalties for disobedience, it did not require much temptation to induce me to break the law. The ban on being at any gathering 'at which the persons present engaged in social intercourse' was so sweeping that strict compliance would have reduced my life to that of a semi-hermit. Accordingly each day I found myself in jeopardy because of ordinary social ventures. What I feared as much as the possibility of imprisonment was the prospect of being thought reckless and foolish. Once I was rebuked by a friend for attending a large party. I replied that it was safer for me

160

to be at a gathering of seventy White dancers, which was illegal, than to speak to one political person, which might have been legal. Nevertheless I was more careful thereafter.

Though public entertainments did not appear to fall within the definition of social gatherings, I felt so alienated from Whites-only sports and theatrical functions that I voluntarily refrained from attending them. Like the girl who said everything she enjoyed was either illegal, immoral or fattening, so nearly everything I liked was either banned or I boycotted. One evening I did, however, go to a concert of contemporary South African jazz. The music was hard, sophisticated and emotional; Black and White musicians played to an enthusiastically rapt Black and White audience. We all felt that in this one field a rich, modern and distinctively South African sound was being created.

On the next day the Government announced that in future all multi-racial public entertainments would be illegal. I also received a visit in my chambers from Captain Rossouw, who informed me that he was investigating a charge that I had broken my ban by attending a social gathering, to wit, a jazz concert. He carried with him an empty-looking briefcase and I assumed that it contained a tape-recorder.

Unlike earlier occasions in court where he had jovially invited me to visit him in his office, presumably with a view to extracting information from me, he was now cold and formal. I politely declined to make a statement at that stage, and as soon as he left I sought written opinions from two leading senior counsel. Fortunately they confirmed my view that a concert did not constitute a social gathering as defined in my banning notice, and after sending these opinions off to the police I heard nothing further about the matter. I was, however, much stricter with myself from then on about what gatherings I attended.

161

As the months went by I began to re-assess my position in relation to leaving South Africa. I had stayed on with a view to having a last summer holiday before my departure. Then, when summer had passed, I had decided to wait until my book was published. It seemed appropriate that the book should come out while I was still in the country, and I reasoned that the maximum punishment would probably not exceed about six months' imprisonment, which I felt I could take. Fluttering around the edges of my thoughts, too, was the idea that I would meet Stephanie again when her civil case came to trial.

Himie, Wilfred and I had been working hard on the case which had been brought against van Wyk and secondly against J. B. Vorster in his capacity as Minister of Justice. Summonses had been issued claiming £1,000 damages arising out of the maltreatment of and assault upon Stephanie during her interrogation at Caledon Square. The defendants had filed a notice of opposition and we had waited eagerly to see what their grounds of defence would be. In Alan's case their contention had been that his ankle had been fractured while he attempted to escape: if the matter had ever come to trial it would have been his word against that of four detectives, and he would have had great difficulty in convincing the judge that he had been tortured. As far as Stephanie was concerned, however, they could hardly allege that she had received her black eye while attempting to escape. Eventually, after the maximum permissible delay, the police defence to Stephanie's allegations had been filed. We had read it with excitement, indignation and satisfaction. It admitted Stephanie's lengthy interrogation, but denied that she had been deprived of food and made to stand. With regard to the assault, and this was the cornerstone of the case, van Wyk admitted that he had struck Stephanie a blow in the face, but claimed he had done so in order to pacify her, as she had become hysterical. This

162

seemed such a feeble story that we had immediately become more confident of success.

We were anxious for the case to be brought to trial as soon as possible, but there were many procedural requirements which could not be by-passed. With both sides preparing ultra-cautiously, it eventually became clear that it would not be heard within the year. Our painstaking preparations were justified when we succeeded in prising out of the defence a copy of the dossier which the police had drawn up against van Wyk after Stephanie had complained of her assault to the magistrate.

The formalities of a proper investigation had been followed, but the results had been farcical. A strong *prima facie* case of assault had been made out, van Wyk had presented an explanation of the kind which would normally have been laughed out of court, and yet the Attorney-General had issued a *nolle prosequi*, i.e. had declined to prosecute. What van Wyk had said was that he had struck Stephanie a blow in the face after she had feigned hysteria in order to provoke him into assaulting her. Even if this highly improbable—I thought the best description was 'absurd', but Wilfred preferred 'highly improbable'—story were to be accepted, van Wyk's action almost certainly amounted in law to an assault. Presumably with Stephanie still in solitary confinement, and with the police having managed successfully to avoid prosecutions in a number of similar cases, van Wyk had not bothered to concoct an intelligent statement. The refusal of the Attorney-General to take action made it easier to understand now what Vorster had meant when he had asserted in Parliament that all allegations of assault were thoroughly investigated and invariably found to be baseless.

One could never predict with certainty the outcome of a trial, and we had to bear in mind that the climate in the country would not favour any findings which might bring the

163

police into disrepute, but nevertheless the evidence and pro-
babilities seemed so overwhelmingly to support Stephanie's
claim that we felt strongly confident of success.

It was at about this time that I had an encounter that
proved to be both heartening and amusing for me. A phone
call alerted me to be ready for a visitor whom I had long been
hoping to meet. I put on a dark suit and tie for the occasion
and repeatedly patted my hair to ensure it was sleek and tidy.
The briefs, textbooks and law reports which normally cluttered
my desk, were packed away, the curtains were drawn as
widely as possible so as to emphasise the view of the mountain and city, and my pictures were dusted and made to hang
straight; I did not wish my visitor to get a poor impression
either of myself or of South African barristers. At the appointed time there was a knock at the door and into my room
walked Mr William Collins, chairman, as he announced jovially, of Collins publishing house. He was tall and good-looking,
but to my surprise his hair was untidy, his suit casual, and
he looked neither at my pictures nor at the view. I rushed forward and before he could say much else, grabbed his elbow
and pulled him towards the door. He was so taken aback by
the suddenness of my move that I was able to hustle him out
of the room before he could protest. By the time he had recovered sufficiently to push me away, I had apologised for
greeting him so strangely, but—and I pointed back to my
room—I had to be careful of microphones. He began to smile
once more, and his good humour returned, even if for some
while it remained edged with wariness.

After we had spoken together for some time in the empty
office of a colleague of mine, he relaxed properly. He told me
of his firm's plans to publish my book, which he thought was
jolly good, but mentioned their fear that there might be repercussions for me. I answered strongly that I'd given the
matter careful thought and was fully prepared for any conse-

164

quences, and that my only concern was that the book should come out if it were good enough.

There was a further contretemps when my colleague unexpectedly returned to his room, but by this time my visitor had so fully entered into the situation that he was less embarrassed than I.

After he had gone I glowed with the knowledge that I was going to become an author and that the police were going to be exposed. I was filled with overwhelming goodwill for this Englishman who had navigated his way into my world and was about to sail out of it once more. Possibly one day I would see him again in London, perhaps I would never get there. In any event the punishment which had been inflicted on me would now rebound on those who had been responsible for it. They had not broken me completely, nor had they destroyed my capacity to fight back. The police would feel humiliated by my exposure of their conduct and even more by the fact that they had failed to prevent me from accomplishing it. It was not often that I had occasion to cheer and to pat myself on the back, but when it did arise I was not going to stint myself on my private celebration.

The book was due to be published early in 1966, which was more or less the time when it was expected that Stephanie's civil action would be heard. I hoped that nothing would happen before then to disturb my life, and received some reassurance from the announcement that the Government was thinking of suspending the operation of the 90-day law.

Then we heard that after its successful use during three years in countering subversion and sabotage, the 90-day law had in fact been suspended, but my tension rose again, when it was announced shortly afterwards that Minister Vorster would pilot through Parliament a bill to enable the police to detain potential witnesses for 180 days. The law as eventually passed provided that any potential witness for the State might on the warrant of the Attorney-General be held in solitary confinement under police control for up to 180 days. So now instead of a 90-day law we had a 180-day law, which, Mr Vorster declared, was designed primarily to protect witnesses from intimidation. His critics, of whom very few were now willing to speak out, indicated that the main source of intimidation was likely to be the very persons into whose care the witnesses would be placed.

The police claimed that all was quiet in the country and that after a few small mopping-up operations the forces of subversion would be knocked out for several years to come.

Politically 1965 had been a time of quiet, but towards the end of the year events took place which were to explode the surface serenity of southern Africa. In November the White government of the British colony of Rhodesia unilaterally declared independence. Pro-apartheid colleagues of mine were alarmed by this move, since they feared it might provoke a spirited retaliation from Britain, and that South Africa would become involved. Later on the British Government seemed to set their fears at rest by re-affirming an earlier pledge not to use force and by stressing that Britain's relations with South Africa were not to be prejudiced in any way by sanctions against the illegal régime in Rhodesia. My colleagues relaxed and smugly supported the despatch of oil through South Africa to Rhodesia.

At the same time as this news appeared in the press we read that the South African Political Police had secured what was for them a triumph by capturing Bram Fischer, the last major political figure known to be active underground in the country. An elderly and widely respected Q.C., a communist and former leader of the Johannesburg Bar, Bram Fischer had declared he could serve justice best by going underground, and for nine months the police had been searching for him in vain. Now that they had caught him, and perhaps because like

166

them he was an Afrikaner but unlike them was an opponent of apartheid, they presented him to the public in as humiliating a light as possible. Those of us who knew him as a fine lawyer and a brave and kindly man, grieved.

The Security Police soon 'swooped again', as the papers put it, this time in Cape Town. Their prey was Fred Carneson, whom they flew up to Pretoria, and Caroline and Brenda, two attractive and intelligent young women who, when most Whites were moving rightwards, had begun to support the anti-apartheid cause. A little while later they 'swooped' again, this time taking into custody a number of African men, including Zollie Malindi, who had been kept in the same police station as myself during a portion of my 90-day detention.

Two other newspaper items at about this time aroused my special interest. The one, which I read with a feeling of deep irony, was that Daniel Rossouw, now a major and described as a down-to-earth man with a fine sense of humour, had been put in charge of the Security Police in Cape Town.

The other, which produced a more profound reaction in me, was to the effect that Stephanie Kemp, a 24-year-old physiotherapist who had been convicted in the Cape Supreme Court of belonging to an unlawful organisation, had after serving one year of her sentence been released from prison.

Chapter 20

I was emotionally unprepared for Stephanie's release, and in my excitement and confusion tormented myself with imaginary confrontations with her. The news report made no mention of where she was going or what her plans were, and after agitatedly wondering how I could get in touch with her I decided eventually to send a telegram to her parents' address several hundred miles from Cape Town. It was not easy to find the right form of greeting, since the police were probably intercepting and looking at her mail, and it seemed dangerous to let them know of our interest in each other; furthermore, I did not know how she felt towards me after a year's absence, and did not wish to say anything which could prove embarrassing to either of us. Eventually I decided on the simple words, 'Welcome Out—Junior Counsel,' and cabled them to her. Then I waited anxiously for a response.

Several days passed and I heard nothing. A Sunday paper carried as its main story the information that Stephanie intended to proceed with her damages claim against the Minister of Justice, but again no news was given of her whereabouts.

Himie told me he expected her to come to Cape Town for legal consultations, but he was unable to be precise about when and for how long. As the period in which I had no news of her grew longer, I began to prepare myself for disappointment.

168

Five days had passed since her release, when Himie phoned me at my office to ask whether the terms of my banning order prevented me from communicating with persons who had been convicted under the Suppression of Communism Act. After checking the relevant statutory provisions, I told him that as long as the convicted persons had not been themselves banned or else placed on a special list, there was nothing in law to prohibit such communication. Apparently reassured by this information, he asked in a cheerful voice if I were free for lunch. I told him I was, and he then said he had with him two charming ladies who were hoping to have lunch with me. 'I believe you know them,' he said happily, 'Mrs Kemp and her daughter Stephanie.'

I was to meet them in the foyer of a building not very far from my office. As I hurried to the rendezvous I kept visualising the meeting with Stephanie. Would she be fat or thin, pretty or ugly, friendly or formal? And would we still have a fondness for each other? The first glance would be all-important, I thought anxiously. I strode eagerly down the street, peering as far ahead as I could to glimpse the mouth of the building where she would be waiting, but a thick lunch-hour crowd of well-dressed businessmen and office workers blocked my view. Everyone was hurrying to keep appointments or to complete their midday shopping. I raced through the stream of people, dashing past beautifully lit shop windows which displayed a glittering range of picnic baskets, silk dressing gowns, multi-coloured bathing suits, summer frocks, and beach umbrellas. Would she be as excited to see me as I was to see her? I straightened my tie, checked that my jacket was properly buttoned and sped into the foyer, where to my consternation I almost collided with the two of them.

They greeted me with exclamations of surprise and spontaneous delight. We shook hands and chatted enthusiastically. How nice it was to meet in these happy circumstances, we agreed. Stephanie and her Mom, with their smart dresses, high-heeled shoes and leather handbags, were like any mother and daughter spending a day in town. They spoke to each other and to me with animation. Stephanie's face was fuller than it had been, her skin was pale, and her hair had been cut short, but her eyes retained their curious and challenging character, and her voice was gentle and warm. Mrs Kemp stood at her side, attractive, trim and alert, eager to be helpful, yet anxious not to intrude. I wondered if she had any idea of a possible romance between her daughter and myself.

After we had stood talking for some minutes, I explained in an embarrassed way that the terms of my banning order made it illegal for me to have lunch with them both at the same time. Our meeting had been arranged on the phone, I added, which meant we had to be particularly careful. If they wished to eat first and meet me later, or if they preferred each to lunch separately with me . . .

We hadn't to worry, Mrs Kemp interrupted quickly, she had lots of things to do in town, so if we two went off then she would meet Steph later that afternoon at Mr Bernadt's office. She smiled at us both and before we could reply, darted away into the busy street. Not wishing to alarm her I had not said that Stephanie was probably being followed and that I too was possibly being kept under observation.

It was a warm summer's day, and we agreed to have lunch at an open-air restaurant in the Public Gardens. This was the first time we had ever walked together—there was something graceful, birdlike and free in her movements. Her step was youthful, but her deportment and the way she carried her bag were adult and womanly. We spoke politely and calmly to each other, but my thoughts jumped around—she's a little girl grown up . . . I've never seen her in high heels before . . . how friendly she is . . . will we ever speak seriously to each other?

170

When we walked up an avenue of freshly budding oak-trees, the dappled sunlight which flickered on her head and shoulders seemed to emphasise her physical unreality to me. She remarked simply on the greenness of the trees, and gazed around her with such seriousness and wonder that I was reminded of how pleasurable in a sheerly physical sense it was to be free. There were many special and intensely-felt emotions which only ex-prisoners could understand, and at that moment we realised that there was a whole range of experiences and feelings which we could share without having to articulate them.

Pigeons fluttered and rose as we sought out a table. Eventually we chose one beneath a large gum-tree and sat down facing each other, as we had so often done at the prison. The wood-and-iron garden chairs were unstable and the constant movement of birds and people around us increased our sense of excited unease.

This was a good time to speak to me, Stephanie said in a quick anxious voice. I looked around but no one seemed to be trying to listen to our conversation. Before her release she'd been taken to Police Headquarters in Pretoria, she continued rapidly, where Major-General van den Bergh, the physically striking head of the Security Police who during the war had been detained for pro-Nazi activities, had personally interrogated her. After warning her that if she returned to live in Cape Town he would have her placed under house-arrest, he had reluctantly agreed to let her come down, but only in order to collect her personal possessions and to see her lawyers. She'd felt she simply had to come and had given him those reasons for doing so because—her voice tightened with alarm—van den Bergh had told her the police were going to crack down on Cape Town and break it wide open.

She looked anxiously at me, and added quickly that she was worried about me and the others and felt she had to warn us as soon as possible. A waitress came to take our orders and our conversation was momentarily interrupted. When the waitress had gone I tried to calm her.

She shouldn't be too worried, I told her as reassuringly as I could, since van den Bergh had probably been referring to the arrests of Fred and Caroline and Brenda. If the police had wanted to detain more people they'd have done so already. As far as I personally was concerned, I wasn't expecting any police action because I hadn't been politically involved for over two years. I wasn't particularly proud of the fact, but it meant that I would probably be safe.

My words seemed to ease some of her strain, but she still seemed tense and stared so enquiringly at me that I wondered what it was that continued to pre-occupy her.

Suddenly she spoke again, asking questions and making assertions with such rapidity that I was unable to say anything. She'd thought seriously about the matter, she told me in conclusion, and was much more mature now than she'd been before, and accordingly was in no doubt at all that she and I ought to get married.

She stared confidently at me and declared that there was no one else in the country whom she could marry and that she couldn't think of anyone other than herself whom I could marry. She hadn't meant to say it all so quickly, she continued with the same impetus, in fact she'd meant to wait for at least twenty-four hours before discussing the question of marriage, but with the police all over the place we just didn't seem to have any time, there wouldn't even be any time for an affair, not that she wanted that now, so she thought we ought to get married right away.

At the end of this tumultuous rush of words she looked shyly at me as though embarrassed by what she had said, yet pleased that she had got it all off her mind. For my part I was over-

172

come by confusion and joy, and began desperately to work out a sensible answer.

It was too early for us to decide on something as serious and irrevocable as marriage, I told her. She seemed relieved that I had not dismissed the suggestion out of hand. It was possible that we might one day get married, I continued, but first we must get to know each other in as normal a way as possible.

We discussed the matter for some time and agreed to say nothing more about marriage until we had given our feelings a chance to be tested properly. She told me how she had decided fairly early on in prison to break off her engagement and how she had suddenly realised the extent to which she was emotionally drawn to me. She'd been surprised by the strength of her feelings, but had remembered what I'd once told her about the way in which prison could distort one's emotions. She now agreed with me about children and about having a peaceful and stable family life. As far as she was concerned she'd seen me again and was sure of her feelings, but if I wanted to wait she would respect my views. She would be in Cape Town for a week still.

I told her that the police had dominated our lives enough without now determining whether or not we should get married. We would have to be careful about meeting one another, and a week was nothing in relation to a decision which would affect us for a lifetime. We would have to move step by step. In a couple of months she would return to Cape Town for her civil case and we would then be able to see each other again and discuss it further.

She listened calmly and seemed satisfied with my approach. I asked her about her life in prison and she told me of many of her experiences. Her descriptions were concrete and episodic, connected by theme and mood rather than by strict chronology, while her memory was more attuned to personalities and relationships than to physical conditions. All her stories were alive with feeling and character, and she spoke with such warmth and insight that I was able vividly to visualise the situations she described. The more she spoke the more I admired her. She did not tell stories to make an effect or to support a complaint, nor did she seem concerned about what picture I might get of her from her descriptions. I was particularly struck by the sympathy she felt for all her fellow prisoners. She loved the political prisoners, but seemed to have a special feeling for the ordinary criminals—the more battered and demoralised they were, the stronger her emotion appeared to be. I hoped that one day she would be able to write down these memories, but felt it was premature to suggest it there and then.

During our conversation I kept an eye open for members of the Security Police, and during one of my periodical looks-around, which I had learnt to manage discreetly, I noticed that Wilfred Cooper had arrived at the café and was about to sit down at a nearby table. He caught my eye and walked over to us. He observed that Stephanie was looking fat and healthy enough, to which she answered that at least he was honest about her figure, most people just told her how well she looked. The three of us arranged to have a legal consultation the next day in Wilfred's chambers, and Wilfred returned to his table.

After we had finished eating I told Stephanie that I had to call back at my chambers to see if there were any messages for me, but that I would almost certainly be able to see her again in the afternoon. I said I thought it would be safer for her to stay in the Gardens rather than to come with me, and we agreed to meet later at a spot not far from the Supreme Court.

I was able to arrange my afternoon work so as to be free for a couple of hours, and after spending a few minutes in my office returned to join Stephanie. There seemed to be no im-

174

pediment to our marriage, I thought excitedly, save possibly for the police. And yet we had to become properly accustomed to each other first and make sure our love was an enduring one.

In the Gardens I looked round for Stephanie, but all I could see was a girl with half-closed eyes leaning back on a bench in the sun. How attractive that girl was, I remarked to myself impulsively. She stood up and my eyes remained fixed on her body, which I found myself admiring despite a certain feeling of shame. Then she turned and walked towards me and to my astonishment I saw that in fact it was Stephanie.

We walked up and down among the green lawns and trees and blue-grey ponds of the Gardens. Most of the time was taken up by my telling her of my feelings towards her, and stressing that it was not enough for us merely to like the 'idea' of each other—we had to get used to each other as people. In many ways we were still strangers, and no amount of dreaming and imagination could replace becoming physically accustomed to one another. My talk was not very romantic.

Eventually we agreed that she would come up to my office for a few minutes. I went ahead so that we would not be seen walking together—the less often the police saw us together, the less likelihood there was of her being banned.

Soon I heard her soft knock at the door. She looked curiously round the place from which I had always come when visiting her at Roeland Street jail and to which I always returned after seeing her. I took her hand and motioned her to the part of the room near the door where we could not be seen from outside. We kissed softly, and I felt her heart thump frantically against my chest.

'I knew you'd be warm,' she murmured softly, too softly, I thought, for the microphones to pick up.

Chapter 21

Some time later I managed to persuade Stephanie to record on paper some of her jail experiences. She took a big gulp of whisky, typed rapidly, and when she had finished, ran out of the house in which she had been working. I read the copy with interest and admiration. Although her writing was restrained in comparison with her oral descriptions, I felt that much of her liveliness and honesty had come through. Her story was told in the first person and addressed to me.

'Roeland Street was an old and dilapidated jail,' it read, 'where I was bitten by bugs in my bed, and where rats the size of kittens were sometimes seen cavorting in the drains. I learnt a lot there. I learnt to smuggle my meat ration to the Coloured prisoners in exchange for "twak" (cheap tobacco). I learnt to make "zolls" (rolled cigarettes) with the "twak" and then to split smuggled matches into four pieces with a pin in order to make them last longer. I learnt that even in prison I would be the victim of unwanted privilege because of my white skin. And I learnt with a certain amount of Victorian shock that when women are incarcerated in a confined space with a multitude of frustrations, sexual and otherwise, they will form lesbian relationships which may or may not involve love-making, but which will give rise to further tension and even violence.

'But Roeland Street jail was friendly and warm, and there was space. After the almost claustrophobic confinement and the hostility of three months' solitary confinement and interrogation, I felt really free and alive in Roeland Street. Although there was apartheid in sleeping quarters, during the day we mixed fairly freely with Coloured prisoners. And I loved the way in which they had virtually no respect for the Oppressors. Dr Verwoerd's household laundry was washed by the prisoners and hung out to dry on the lines which filled the prison courtyard. I wondered if Dr Verwoerd would not have sacrificed the cheap jail rate if he had heard the earthy comments made about his underwear in the crude language which was the only language Roeland Street knew. There was a certain homogeneity between wardresses and prisoners which I found in no other prison. The only noticeable difference was in the uniform and in the fact that wardresses carried fruit-box planks for beating the prisoners. But there was no difference in crudity, in the free use of foul language and in the general degradation which Roeland Street seemed to demand of its inmates.

'The White women were cooped up together in two crowded cells, but somehow we got on well together. M. was the most difficult. She was serving six months for permanently blinding a Coloured worker at whom she had thrown caustic soda. She thought the magistrate had been prejudiced for giving her such a severe sentence! She had a voracious appetite and there were continual squabbles about sharing out the food which was brought to the cells in large pots. Lovely J., a prostitute who had pushed time with some politicals at Pietersburg prison a few years previously, told me she liked political prisoners because with them she felt like a person and not like a criminal. We were a very mixed bunch but we seldom quarrelled because the population was such a shifting one.

'It turned out to be the worst jail in material terms, and yet the happiest jail because of its lack of discipline. We smoked smuggled cigarettes almost every day and it was very easy to get them. Only once in desperation we smoked tea—but not very successfully. The White women did no work and we spent our time smuggling and trying to bribe the wardresses. We communicated freely with the Coloured prisoners during the day while they worked at washing and ironing Dr Verwoerd's and other official laundry.

'When it became clear after my sentence that I was going to be transferred the other prisoners in my cell speculated with me about my possible destination. I felt sure that I would be taken to the centre of "enemy territory"—Pretoria, the home of extreme Afrikaner nationalism and racialism.

'On the Friday morning I changed into my own clothes and awaited the escort with a sense of foreboding.

'I was flown to Pretoria, but from there I was taken by car through desolate veld to "Vooruitsig" ("Prospect") a large modern jail near Kroonstad in the Orange Free State. I was locked up in a tiny cell in complete solitary confinement without even the customary Bible. I thought I would be held like this for the two years of my sentence. After four days I saw the prison doctor and told him I feared insanity. My legs kept on going numb and I had pins and needles down my arms. The doctor gave me vitamin tablets. But after a week I joined the other prisoners.

' "Vooruitsig" was modern and spacious. Although I was isolated in a section by myself during lock-up time, I ate and worked with the other prisoners and, I think, became fully integrated into their life.

'There were about thirty White women from all over South Africa in this prison. Their crimes ranged from robbery to murder, from fraud to abortion. I was surprised to find they were just ordinary people.

'J. was about my age, attractive and intelligent. At the age

178

of 21 she had shot dead her 6-month-old baby and wounded her 5-year-old daughter. She didn't know why. She had spent a few months in Tara, a mental hospital, without coming any closer to the reasons for her action, and was now serving a six-year sentence. I liked her. We worked together—we had to crochet a $9' \times 7'$ white table cloth without getting it dirty. On some days a crowd of dignified old ladies from a charitable organisation would come to view the prison and the prisoners. They would admire our work and rub the cloth to feel its texture, leaving us with a grubby part which had to be cut out and re-done. They would ask us interested questions about the art of crocheting, but they could not hide their curiosity, which was really about us and not our work. No doubt they wondered at our youth and our apparent respectability. J. and I would reply to their questions with scarcely veiled sarcasm.

'D. was a lesbian who had attached herself to J. She became madly jealous of my association with J. It took me a little while to understand the situation and before I did D. one night beat up J. with a badminton racket. It was during the lock-up and I could not see what was happening, but I clung to the bars of my cell window and listened to the terrible screams which seemed never to end. D. was put into a straight jacket after she tried to cut her wrists.

'They were locked up for six weeks in solitary confinement after that. When they again joined us I became quite friendly with D. though it was always a precarious relationship which might at any time if I said the wrong thing erupt into violence. She was a gentle person, much in need of genuine affection, but with a terrifying temper.

' "Vooruitsig" was in many ways a model prison—unlike the other prisons I knew. The women there slept in single cells which were always unlocked so that they had free access to bathrooms and toilets and they could visit each other and even go out into the large courtyard on to which the cells faced.

'One prisoner controlled a radio and record-player which were relayed through intercom. systems to all sections, except the punishment section—and the one in which I was held.

'All the prisoners had a ration of cigarettes and matches, except for two girls who had attempted to escape—and myself; once a week they saw a film—I was excluded. It was little wonder that despite the warnings which the authorities gave the prisoners of my dangerous and despicable character, I soon won their sympathy.

'One day I was taken to a room and shut up with two senior Security policemen. After being interrogated for six hours and feeling totally at their mercy, I collapsed hysterically and ran into Matron de Villiers' office. She held me in her arms until I gained some control and she gave me sal volatile and made me sit in her office until I had regained most of my composure.

'She was the senior matron, a very charming girl of 22, who had had a university training in psychology and sociology and was the only matron I came across who was regarded with affection by the prisoners and who achieved anything in the way of rehabilitation—or who even attempted the latter.

'Yet this seemed to have an adverse affect on the relationships between the prisoners themselves. I had expected a cameraderie, a loyalty among prisoners. Instead there was a lot of bickering, and a singular lack of cohesiveness. There was only one prisoner whom I really trusted emotionally and it was to her that I confided that a woman lieutenant, Lt. —, had offered to smuggle a letter out for me—an obvious and crude trap from a sadistic matron notorious for her dislike of political prisoners.

'Apart from the prisoners in for respectable crimes such as fraud and murder, there was a class of prisoners known as the "jollers" and the "battlers". The battlers were the professional

180

prostitutes who had children and probably a ponce to support. They were weighed under by their responsibilities just like any working woman who has a difficult time making ends meet. The jollers, on the other hand, were a lively bunch, who would have tattooed on their hands contrasting words like "love/hate", "joy/suffering"; they smoked "dagga" (marijuana), drank brandy or vodka and hitch-hiked from one city to the next. They had their own language and their own brand of morality which included a fierce loyalty to their chommies (friends). I was drawn to them, not only because of their tremendous zest, but because they seemed quite devoid of any racial or class prejudice. It was a strange world which they had created for themselves because society had rejected them. These women did not prostitute themselves unless they were driven to it, but rather robbed the men they picked up—so that there was only one actually convicted of soliciting (she had four children in various homes)—the rest were in for some form of robbery.

' "Vooruitsig" was physically more pleasant than other prisons because some care was taken with the uniforms of both wardresses and prisoners. At regular intervals we would form a queue at the clothes store in order to exchange worn-out clothing for new. And our dresses were altered to fit us. While I was there a new overall for White women prisoners was introduced. It was in a kingfisher-blue drip-dry material chosen by Mrs Vorster who had visited the prison shortly before my arrival and had extended a general invitation to prisoners to visit her at home after their release. We laughed as we imagined how she would react if, say, an abortionist, a prostitute, a murderess and myself rolled up at her élite Ministerial home and announced ourselves for tea, bringing with us the grime and dirt of the suburbs most of us lived in, and speaking the language of prison which she would not understand.

'At Christmas time we were allowed to receive food parcels,

but they were put into a common pool without anyone knowing who had received parcels and who not, so that no one felt neglected and Christmas became a truly social occasion. I very seriously sang "Silent Night" as a solo under the Christmas tree to an audience of the Colonel, his wife and other senior officials at the prison. We were allowed into the African side of the prison to listen to the African women singing carols and to watch them dancing.

'I felt bitter when I walked past some cells with windows boarded up where the African political women were then being held. I knew that they had not even the very slight privileges which I had, and that they saw no one except a few senior White wardresses. Their lives were entirely isolated. I felt very White and privileged, even in jail.

'I had been confused politically in some ways before my arrest. The longer I spent in prison the greater became my hatred of racial discrimination and White privilege and the more intense my desire to help smash the system. As a prisoner I had a glimpse of what life as a second class citizen must be like. I felt what it was like to be regarded as less than human; I knew what it was like to know that though superior intellectually to my captors I was yet to be treated as an inferior, to be continually frustrated. I saw naked power. I learnt to pretend deference to children of sixteen who had positions of authority over me. I learnt to hate in silence and to enjoy hating them when they did not know it. I came out of prison having lived on hate for months, not only feeling unrepentant for what I had done, but regretful that I had not done more while I had the opportunity.

'Suddenly one day I was fetched and driven all the way through the monotonous countryside-back to Pretoria. This time the journey was more interesting, for on the way we happened by chance to pass my sister and her husband who were on holiday in their Land-Rover.

182

'When I was nine years old I had stayed with relations in Pretoria. All these years I had carried with me an image of wide streets carpeted with purple jacaranda blossoms and an atmosphere of gaiety when a Jacaranda Queen rode through the streets.

'Now we entered Pretoria from the Voortrekker Monument side, a massive granite monument built to commemorate the beginnings of Afrikaner nationalism. We travelled through territory reserved for the air force and the army, and everywhere men in uniform stopped to salute our car in which Brigadier Aucamp was travelling as my escort. He was the Prisons' Security Officer and in control of political prisoners. I was being allowed to feel the might of the Nationalist Government—miles and miles of armoured cars; weapon-carrying men in uniform; camps and barracks. And then Pretoria Central prison.

'I was to spend the next two months in solitary confinement in the dark and gloomy death cell there, being allowed out for about two hours a day to wash and exercise. The uniform with which I was issued was demoralising. I struggled for a long time before I got laces for my shoes; my khaki dress was several sizes too large and in tatters. It was an ugly, despairing jail.

'Tertius was about eighteen months old and just beginning to talk. He was born in jail and called me "Nonna"—the African equivalent of the English word "Madam", used to address any White woman even if she were a prisoner. He was skinny with bandy legs and was the only person with whom I was legitimately permitted to associate, for even the wardresses had been warned not to talk to me except to issue instructions. Every day at two o'clock when I was brought down from the cell to the courtyard where the African women hung the sheets they had washed, Tertius would come running to me like a bright bubble calling, "Nonna, Nonna" in a dear trusting little voice. I adored him. He looked undernourished and I used to find him eating soil—something I also saw adults doing in that jail. But I never gave him bread (which was a luxury to Africans in prison) because I did not wish to buy his affection. Instead I used to smuggle bread to his mother when she was hanging up the sheets.

'I never managed to make any contact with the handful of White prisoners at the Central, but I quickly established a warm, meaningful relationship with the African women. Some of them brought my food and emptied my sanitary bucket (a humiliating experience for me) while with others I managed to conduct fairly substantial conversations behind the lines of sheets. They all knew of John Harris and informed me very sympathetically of his execution on the day he was hanged in the men's prison next door. I went on a day's hunger-strike (totally unnoticed by anyone) as a token of respect to him.

'It was in that cell that I had the worst nightmares and woke up screaming at night. It was also there that I discovered that I was in love with you and the discovery frightened me at first because I did not know if my feeling for you, a feeling born in jail, would last outside. And I did not know how you felt and thought I might be hurt later.

'When I stood on top of the locker on the cell I could see out of the window and had an unimpeded view of the prison staff making the most of the last days of summer as they lay around a glittering swimming pool. One evening I saw a fox terrier fall into the pool and swim for hours around and around, desperately. I stood on top of the locker and cried as I had no bell in my cell and was completely alone in the top floor of the jail and could not be heard if I called. When the dog was eventually rescued by a boy his back legs were frozen and he could not walk.

'At night I sometimes sang, enjoying the sound of my own voice, and to old songs from life outside I made up new words

184

appropriate to jail life. I listened with disgust to the night wardresses berating in foul language the African women; and in horror on one occasion I heard Matron Nel go into the cells and shout at the women to lift up their dresses and bend over, after which came the sound of blows. In the mornings a stream of prisoners would file past my door accompanied by the foul smell of the lidless overnight buckets which they carried on their heads. If the wardress absented herself for a moment I would hear a soft rush of feet to my door and see an eye at the spyhole, and then a pair of lips whispering hurriedly, "*Môre, Nonna. Hoe gaan dit?*" ("Morning, Nonna, how are you?") Downstairs there would be a clutter of tin dixies as the food arrived. The screams of wardresses supposedly upholding the dignity and self-respect of prisoners as the Prison Regulations required. Silence. Then beautiful voices singing to some god to lead them to the light. More shouts as they were herded outside to start the day's work.

'I could really talk to only two people there—Brigadier Aucamp who came to see me often and who though usually facetious, nonetheless understood a lot and represented my own cultural background; and the Methodist minister who considered jail the wrong environment for conversion and so discussed Jane Austen with me at our fortnightly meetings. But I often lay on the bed, having imaginary conversations with whoever took my fancy.

'I received a letter from Andy but felt so little communication. His idea of prison was entirely romantic and unrealistic, and he was unable to realise the depth of the disturbance caused by the frustration and isolation of prison life. Also my attitude to marriage had changed. The underlying anarchism in most of my thoughts had given way to something more responsible and stable. Instead of feeling, "Well, I'll get married and if it doesn't work out I can get a divorce," I approached marriage as an artistic creation that could be made to work if you started off with the right attitudes. And I wanted children. I wanted them not only to see them growing, but to experience the act of birth. I wanted a tangible product of love. The whole process of loving, getting married and having children seemed incredible in the arid, hateful surroundings of prison. I decided to write to Andy to break off the relationship. It had helped me a great deal during the confusion of my awaiting-trial period and it was difficult to push it aside now that my immediate needs were no longer pressing. But I felt a certain anger too that though he had been standing on the outside where he could have seen how vulnerable I was emotionally and physically, he still showed so little insight as not to know that I had been clutching at emotional straws by becoming engaged to him. Yet this is what had appealed to me—the absurd way of making gestures, of living in the present only, of taking every moment and devouring it with no regard to the moment after. Perhaps jail was succeeding in making me more bourgeois. Or perhaps I was just growing up.

'All these thoughts and ideas I had to share with someone, and then I found myself talking to you and responding to the memory of you. I knew that you would not make a decision except after careful and thoughtful consideration. You were not an impulsive person who would commit yourself hardly knowing the consequences of your commitment. At first I only talked to you but afterwards I found myself thinking of you. I could see your hands—white, small with delicate fingertips—hands either waving about in explanation or thoughtfully fingertips touching in front of you while you rested your elbows on the ugly table between us and pondered. I could see your eyelids drooping to cover even more your already guarded expression, and blinking as you spoke earnestly, or nodded your head up and down, up and down, as you listened to me. Earnestly reasoning. Always grave. And I knew you only in a small room in a tumble-down prison. I knew that in your

186

beautiful mouth there was a sensitivity and tenderness that you could not hide. Your mouth curved and was well-defined with a slightly full lower lip. I had not deliberately noted your appearance, yet it had stayed with me. I could see you walking away through the tiny prison courtyard—tall, thin with slightly hunched shoulders, your left shoulder higher; walking awkwardly. I could hear your soft, terribly polite voice speaking to the matron. I could no more get rid of the memory than if an artist had carved it out on the dark wall of my cell . . .

'Then suddenly (these things always happened suddenly) I was taken to Johannesburg and its notorious jail, the Fort. I knew it held six women who had just been sentenced for political offences and whom I had been waiting to join all this time. For months I had thought about them, imagined what they would be like and what it would be like to be with them. I had been alone and politically isolated for ten months and I looked forward with great anticipation to being with other political prisoners.

'At the Fort we were packed into a van. On the way to an unknown destination, we stopped at the Middleburg jail for a lunch of dry bread and black coffee. I saw some empty cells which were so small that a person could not stand up in them and a sisal mat could barely fit on to the floor. I wondered how people could ever survive in cells such as these.

'We did not know our destination but seemed to be driving towards Swaziland and I felt nervous and frightened.

'When we arrived in Barberton, a small, pretty eastern Transvaal town on the Swaziland border, it was evening and the countryside was very beautiful—even from the back of a van. The jail seemed modern from the outside and we jumped down from the van and went forward expectantly and unsuspectingly.

'We were met by a large deputation of matrons and officers.

I was used to this sort of V.I.P. treatment. We were taken into a room and a fat wardress and a redheaded junior matron ordered us to undress, one by one. Our clothes were thrown to the floor after being thoroughly searched. One of the prisoners was forced to "tauza", that is, to jump up into the air with her legs apart. The idea is that if you have hidden anything in your vagina, it will fall out. We stood naked in front of the wardresses while they took their time displaying their authority and power over us and attempting to humiliate us. Afterwards Miss Taljaardt, the fat wardress admitted that we were being treated like cattle—"On orders", she said.

'For weeks this sort of treatment continued. We were shouted at and every attempt was made to provoke us. We decided to give them three weeks to settle down as we felt that they were probably a bit excited at our arrival. When I next saw Brigadier Aucamp he very gallantly took the blame upon himself and said that we had been treated in this way on his instructions. But even so, they all thoroughly enjoyed their power.

'The section in which we lived, and in which some of my fellow prisoners were to live for the next three years, consisted of three tiny single cells and two larger cells. We were locked up in them behind double doors when the wardresses went off duty in the late afternoons. These cells were cramped and claustrophobic. The windows were barred and, in addition, had cages fitted over them. In the summer months, which were very hot, huge beetles would fly into the cages so that we heard a continual banging on the wire. Large, bright green moths fluttered about in our cells and from outside we could hear the incredible noise of frogs which sounded as big as pigs. We were told that in the past our section of the jail had been the haunt of a deadly "tree" snake. At one stage there was a cricket trapped in the skirting-board of my cell—and through all this I sat solemnly studying philosophy!

188

'The cells led into a main section consisting of a room where we ate and washed the laundry, a bathroom and a tiny boiler room where we made the coal fire to heat our water. We had many discussions on how best to start a fire—not all of us had been Girl Guides.

'There was a small courtyard leading off our section where we were allowed to walk in the sun—at first not at all, then for a quarter of an hour per week, but eventually for the regulation one hour per day. We never moved out of the section except once a week when we were permitted to venture up the passage to the matron's office to see Brigadier Pretorius, the O.C. of the prison. We were supposed to lay our complaints before him, but often I was rewarded for the audacity of doing so by receiving a long lecture on the Bible and my sins.

'Armed guards patrolled outside our cells. Once when one of us tried to shut a window, a guard shouted to her, "*Pasop, ek sal jou kop skiet*" ("Be careful, I'll shoot your head"). When we were not washing our weekly quota of laundry, we were confined to our double-locked cells. They were so cramped that we could barely fit in the tables which we had won after a struggle and at which we studied for approved University correspondence courses (mine were Philosophy, Anthropology, Psychology and Sociology). While we worked and ate we had a wardress constantly watching our small group. At first we were not allowed to talk to one another at all, and when we were caught whispering, we were accused of plotting. We had no recreations whatsoever except for our studies. When I asked when we would get the hour's daily exercise which every prisoner not working outside was entitled to, I was merely laughed at. But after fighting this issue we were allowed to walk round the courtyard for fifteen minutes every Sunday in strict silence. At first we even had a wardress sitting outside our cells at night to ensure that we did not talk.

189

'It was a dead jail. Later, when things improved a bit, one wardress brought in a very young rabbit which we fed and loved. After a week we found it dead. We vowed never to have another animal which might die. But we did, and they died.

'Gradually we learnt more about this horror jail. The beautiful panorama of sisal lands provided the setting where African women worked for long hours in the subtropical heat. Miss Taljaardt (who claimed her job was a calling from God) told us that picking sisal was just punishment for these prisoners, since not only did they suffer in the sun, but their hands became horribly infected through abrasions caused by the sisal. Every week we would count a pile of trousers coming from the African male prisoners which were covered in thickly clotted blood—evidence of brutal corporal punishment.

'We were completely isolated. We had very limited contact with other people inside the prison, just managing to smile and give the Afrika thumbs-up sign to the African men who put the cages on our windows. We received a visitor once in six months in front of a senior officer and a wardress, and wrote a carefully censored letter once in six months. Because there were six of us, we managed it so that one of us had a visit every month. So we were fairly up to date as to which of our friends had been arrested or had left the country. It was very depressing. For want of any other means of relieving our deprived social feelings, we created a world of fantasy around our university tutors whom we never met but who scribbled cryptic remarks in the margins of the essays we submitted for marking.

'We learnt to work hard which I think we enjoyed doing, because in South Africa White women are expected to leave hard physical labour to their Black servants. We washed without interruption for about eight hours a day with coarse blue soap in cement basins. At first we suffered—our hands bled and our backs ached. But soon we became fit and adept at

190

this, as well as at scrubbing and polishing the floors of our section, at making a fire in the coal stove to provide us with hot water and at mowing the lawn on Saturdays. We were proud that with so little previous experience we could cope so well and that we never complained of the amount or quality of the work given to us.

'It was tough living in that small section with the monotonous routine and unending battle against the authorities who flagrantly flouted the rules and put obstacles in our way at every opportunity. They would not pass an Anthropology essay of mine because I used the word "African"; they tried to prevent us from seeing the ministers of religion; they would not let us have knives and forks—and so it went on. Day after day, week after week. Even our food hardly changed. We had pork every day. The tea was refreshing—made from one of the local bushes.

'The only time I can remember when I really felt humiliated was when we were forced to wear long bloomers under our khaki dresses. The others had worn them at the Fort but I had not yet come across these hideously unfeminine, baggy pants which came down to my knees. But the others soon made me laugh with them by prancing ridiculously around dressed only in the bloomers and the clinging vests which went with them. And we were not allowed hair clips but had to wear purple turbans. None of this uniform was being used elsewhere in the country. Uniforms had been modernised some years previously and I am sure that this was another of the endless attempts to demoralise us.

'But from those other prisoners I learnt what the word "fortitude" meant—this word which is used vaguely and piously by people who have never seen what it involves. The women with whom I was imprisoned had endless patience and courage. They reacted to all the setbacks with remarkable resilience and remained alive and warm even in that destructive jail where everything was aimed at depersonalising us.

'Soon after we arrived at Barberton it was my 24th birthday. My place at the breakfast table was decorated with a few nasturtiums from the courtyard and there were two small gifts for me. Each was an empty camphor cream bottle, the one filled with marmalade and the other with brown government sugar, carefully collected from our meagre rations.

'This was the only jail where I never heard spontaneous singing (which is against the prison regulations but which nevertheless is usually overlooked). The African women were forced to sing a hymn before breakfast as at other prisons, and we were continually shouted at for attempting to break into song, despite our gloomy surroundings. Ironically I had to come to this prison to learn some of the South African freedom songs.

'At the end of the year I was told to pack my belongings and be ready to leave. We thought it possible that I was being taken to Cape Town for the hearing of my civil action against Vorster, and I was excited at the prospect of seeing you. As usual I was not told where I was going. I had learnt not to ask since I was seldom told the truth and my questions merely provided them with an opportunity for enjoying a cat-and-mouse game with me.

'We arrived in Pretoria and Brigadier Aucamp told me, "*Nou moet jy kophou meisie*" ("Now you must keep your head, girl"). I learnt that I was being taken to Major-General van den Bergh, the head of the Security Police in South Africa. My father had been working for my release ever since my conviction, and Vorster had agreed to release me, but van den Bergh had the final say.

'Compol Building, the Police headquarters, was an austere building, bare and unattractive inside. After waiting for half an hour I was ushered to the General's door by a very blonde young lady. I tripped slightly over the thick carpet and stumbled nervously into the room. On the walls were three large pictures of President Swart, Keevy, the Commissioner of Police and Vorster, the Minister of Justice. I felt a little nauseated. Van den Bergh invited me to sit down. He was tall and clean. I found his power strangely compelling and his uncontrolled arrogance childish. I realised that he was intelligent and clever in his use of psychological stratagems—and after seventeen months in jail I felt unsure of my own strength and judgment. He wanted me to make a statement about my friends in Cape Town and to inform on the women at Barberton, but after three hours alone with him I managed to stall for time and gain my unconditional release. He asked me to look into his eyes and claimed that by so doing I would prove to him that I was honest! I will never be sure how much of a victory I won over him. But I know that when he had finished with me I felt not much better than I had done after the physical assault on me fifteen months earlier.

'The first night out I knew that this would probably be unique for me—this experience of being released. I stayed in a hotel with my parents and we drank whisky and ate delicious food. But I do not remember details. I remember only the battering of emotions and of movement, of colour and of sound. Everything seemed confused and too loud. We talked and then went to bed; at four in the morning I got up and lit a cigarette and stood at the window and listened to the traffic.'

Chapter 22

The beach near my flat was a popular one, and we thought that if we met there just once as if by accident, we should be safe. Wearing sunglasses, a bathing costume and beach slippers, I wandered casually to the place we had chosen. It was early in the week-end and not many people had yet arrived on the beach. Stephanie was not there, so I sat down in the lee of a large rock and began to read a book I had brought with me. From time to time I looked up hoping to see her and after a while I began to feel anxious. Had she perhaps been banned or re-arrested, or forced to leave Cape Town? Then in the distance, coming towards me from a neighbouring beach, I saw the figure of a girl clad in a new deep-orange bikini; as she got nearer I realised that it was Stephanie. Her body was healthy-looking, though pale, while her legs had lost their post-90-days thinness, but her face seemed strained and I felt disappointed that the warm sun and open beach had not brought out more happiness in her. She came slowly towards me, smiling anxiously, and sat at my side.

There were two men up on the road watching her, she explained. I manoeuvred my body so that I could look at them without appearing to do so. I saw no one, and hoped that the people she had seen had merely been two tourists eyeing her attractive body. She thought they'd been policemen, she told me, and had been very worried that they'd done something to me.

We lay back on the warm, soft white sand and listened to the surf curling gently on to the beach. Our bodies warmed up slowly in the pleasant morning sun. An ice-cream seller moved lazily across the beach, saving his voice for later in the day when the temperature would be higher and the crowd bigger; dotted here and there were small groups of young men and women sprawled out on gaudy beach towels. The scene was entirely peaceful and most of the scattered sun-tanners seemed to be half-asleep, soothed into happy lethargy by the warmth being irradiated from the sand and the rock-a-bye-baby sound of the waves. Gradually our anxiety began to fade.

Drops of sweat accumulated on our necks and limbs and we decided to cool ourselves in the icy Atlantic water. We stood up and then dashed down to the sea, where panting and sticky with sand, Stephanie plunged head-first into an oncoming breaker. I waded in more cautiously after her. After the wave had passed over her, she rose up, shook the water from her hair and face, and then dived in again; meanwhile I pulled myself through the water past her and began to roll about in a deeper and calmer part of the sea. Soon our bodies were so chilled that we had to return to the beach, and as we splashed back towards the shore we looked up and saw the two men Stephanie had noticed earlier.

They were sitting half way down a set of steps which descended from the road to the beach. Both wore dark suits and they leaned against a low wall over which they could see most of the beach, including the spot where our towels lay. They were close enough for me to recognise them. The older of the two was a sergeant in the Security Police who had often assisted at interrogations, and the younger was one of their new recruits, a nattily dressed and ambitious, but not, I thought, very effectual man. I hoped that they sweated, I

195

hoped that they roasted, I hoped that they shrivelled to a dark cinder. They'd be sorry they hadn't brought costumes, I told Stephanie. The idea of seeing Security policemen in bathing trunks seemed so ludicrous that I laughed out loud, yet I felt angry that we were being spied upon while we were physically exposed and trying to enjoy ourselves. I excused myself from Stephanie and began to run energetically along the fringe of the beach, pushing my feet furiously into the wet sand and thrusting my body forward until I heaved with breathlessness. It had been in tiny prison courtyards that I had learnt to run, and after my release I had simply carried on with my 'exercise', enjoying the lonely chase into exhaustion, exhilaration and calm. I turned and loped back towards Stephanie, who, I noticed, had turned her back to me as she dried herself. I assumed that she was showing her disapproval of what she would regard as my dutiful search after health, yet although I envied the spontaneity of her athleticism, I was not prepared to forego my running, especially at that moment when its very aimlessness was likely to puzzle the two policemen.

Panting and pleasantly tired, I jumped into the water again and then walked back to Stephanie, where I sat down and stared up at the steps. To my surprise only the younger policeman was there. I looked around and with alarm noticed that the older one was walking along the beach in our direction. No, that was too much, I thought. Even on the beach they had to harass us. I hoped he got sand in his shoes. When he had advanced about twenty yards along the beach he put his hand in his pocket and took it out again. He stopped for a moment, looked at what he had taken from his pocket and moved on. We said nothing; there seemed to be no point in trying to evade him and we lay anxiously on our towels waiting for him to reach us. Then suddenly he stopped—and bought an ice-cream!

Laughing with relief, we watched him—a dark-suited figure

tramping uncomfortably on the sand, licking his ice-cream—
return to his sunny eyrie.

For some hours we lay talking to each other and enjoying
our physical relaxation, though we still resented the intrusion
on our privacy. From time to time we looked up and watched
the men take it in turns to move into the one small patch of
shade near where they sat. As the sun got higher its area contracted and by noon there was no relief at all for them; we
dipped our bodies frequently in the cold sea.

We would have liked to have kept them there all day, but
eventually our hunger and thirst became too great and we decided to go up to my flat. The path led past some large boulders and by slipping behind these rocks we managed to get
out of sight of the policemen. We then dallied for a while at
the house of my landlord, and finally went up the long line of
steps which led to my front door.

I had hoped that Stephanie would be elated at being in my
room and asked if it fitted the description I had given her in
prison. She remained quiet and tense, however, and it was only
after several minutes of strain that she admitted that she was
worried about physical contact between us at that stage. So
for the rest of the afternoon we both relaxed. We closed the
red curtains in order to keep the sun out and spent a number
of hours lying lazily on a couch listening to records. At one
stage she asked me why I was staring at her so intently and
I said I wasn't used to her at four inches. The strangeness
which we felt towards each other—except on the verbal level
—still disturbed me, but gradually our taboos were vanishing.

Suddenly there was a loud knock at the door. We jumped up,
startled and afraid. It was the peremptory nature of the knock
that alarmed me, since my friends had learnt to bang on the
door in a friendly way. Any caller had to bang hard if he
wished to be heard above the sound of the sea, but this particular knocking seemed to be unnaturally loud. Fighting

down my fear, I walked slowly to the door and unlocked it
. . . It was not the police. A friend of mine stood there. She
had come urgently to warn me that the Security Police had
been visiting a woman I knew to question her about her political associations.

From then on it was no longer possible for Stephanie or
myself to relax. We tried to forget the incident—in fact I had
already heard the news from another source—but found we
could not do so. The sun was setting and a cool evening breeze
made us shiver slightly, so we decided that I should take
Stephanie back to town. We drove along the coastal road
saying very little to each other, but in the centre of the city
were cheered to discover a large, gay crowd enjoying the
Christmas illuminations which stretched along the centre of
the main street. Huge golden stars glittered and fiery yellow
fountains rained overhead; young and old of all races thronged
the street, intoxicated by the flashing display. With children
crying and laughing, parents scolding and people milling
everywhere, we felt so safe and happy that when finally we
parted we were able to agree that apart from the interruptions
we had enjoyed the day very much.

Chapter 23

Stephanie was willing to accept in general terms that policemen would tell lies to protect themselves, but when it came to
their actually lying about *her* she was shocked and surprised.
Her indignation when reading the statements by van Wyk
and the other policemen was especially strong, because they
contained not merely exaggerations or distortions of fact, but
complete fabrications. The suggestion that she had feigned
hysteria and afterwards declared to van Wyk how glad she
was that she had been struck, caused her to exclaim out loud.
It was indeed a stupid and improbable defence, and I told
her that my only surprise was that van Wyk hadn't accused
her of assaulting his hand with her face.

Four days remained before Stephanie was due to leave and
during this period we met only in my chambers. In the office
we discussed the case, but outside in the passage or on the
landing near the lift tried to speak of personal matters.

I told her of the book I had written, and of the possibility
of my being prosecuted for it, but said that we could probably
expect to see each other again when her civil case was heard
early in the New Year. We decided that after she left Cape
Town it would not be safe for us to write to each other and
agreed that only if one of us wanted to break off the association would he or she communicate. With lawyers, clients, witnesses and messengers constantly walking or standing near us,

our conversations were cryptic and unhappy, and when finally we had to say goodbye to each other, all we could do was to shake hands as formally as we had done in prison.

My immediate sense of loss at her departure was followed by a rush of sustained elation, for I felt blessed to be associated with Stephanie and was inspired by her courage. Since my release from detention nearly two years earlier I had tended to cringe from authority, and now it was as though my spirit were straightening up and beginning to march forward again. Even the thousand political prisoners on Robben Island ceased to oppress me as much as they had done earlier, for I felt that the prisoners would not have begrudged us our happiness. How much private joy was permissible, I wondered, when there was so much public misery? Yet we did not build our happiness on the wretchedness of others, nor did we turn our backs on those deprived of the opportunity to love. If we were going to be miserable we might as well have been back in prison, where at least our suffering could have had a positive symbolical value for others.

Early in the New Year there were further arrests by the Political Police in Cape Town. A number of African workers and three White businessmen were taken into detention, one of those arrested being my landlord, and another an old school friend of my father's. Rumours circulated about the police using a special team of interrogators to break prisoners down, relying on prolonged sleep deprivation as their main technique: Fred had been interrogated for five days, after which he had had to be placed in an oxygen tent . . . Caroline had been shown transcripts of tape-recordings made over a period of a year in her house . . . her lounge had been bugged, private conversations, whispered political discussions, had been recorded . . . prisoners were being forced to make statements, everyone was being broken . . .

200

The morning and evening papers vied with each other to present Cape Town at its holiday best. One day they featured healthy long-limbed girls with small bikinis and huge grinning mouths; the next day it was dark, proud race-horses limbering up for the 'Metropolitan Handicap'; then little children building sandcastles near the sea. For several weeks there was nothing further about the detainees. Then suddenly large headlines declared that Fred Carneson, former Member of the Provincial Council, had been brought before Court on charges under the Sabotage and Suppression of Communism Acts.

The news was sad, and yet it was something of a relief to know that Fred would now at least be able to see his family and speak to lawyers. His ordeal contrasted painfully in my thoughts with my own lack of involvement. I seemed to be more isolated than ever, and the image passed through my mind of a lonely rock left far behind after a large wave had swept by. For several days I belonged neither to Cape Town's holiday-makers, nor to its prisoners. Or at least so I thought until early one morning two plainclothes policemen arrived at my flat holding in their hands an order for my detention.

Part Three

ELEGY

Chapter 24

'Hullo, Albie!' The Major beamed confidently at me, and in his guttural voice, jokingly asked what he could do me for.

This was the first raid he had organised since his promotion to head of the Security Police in Cape Town, and the efficient way in which his subordinates were bringing in their prisoners cheered him patently.

I resented his cheerfulness, his smart clothing, and the way he addressed me by my first name, but trying to keep my voice firm, I told him I wished to speak to him for a minute.

'Well, what is it? I'm a busy man, you know.' He spoke breezily but there was a harsh, mocking edge to the question. I looked at his burly body and unhandsome face which were so immediately familiar to me. He had been my main interrogator during my detention two years earlier, and ever since then I had been curiously interested in his career, as though the five and a half months of mental battling between us had bound us together in some special way. The lack of a corresponding curiosity on his part about me was disappointing. Was he hiding his feelings at being confronted with me again, I wondered, or did his new status as commanding officer blot out for him the months of jousting when he had been a mere captain?

There were just two points I wished to make, I said, forcing myself to orientate to being in his power again. I told him that at the time of my release from 90-day detention the police had indicated there would be no further proceedings against me, and that I regarded my re-arrest two years later, when nothing had changed, as a breach of that intimation. He nodded as I spoke, as if to accept the correctness of my assertion, but after I had finished he looked at me with mock sorrow and intoned in a sad preacher's voice, '*Jy moet betaal vir jou sonde, ou maat*' ('You must pay for your sins, my friend').

The second point was . . . I went on, choosing my words with care . . . it had come to my attention, or . . . should I say . . . allegations had been made that the police had been depriving prisoners of their sleep to get them to make statements. His face remained calm as I proceeded. I hadn't seen it for myself, so I couldn't say whether it was true or not, but one thing I wished to make clear was that if anything like that was tried on me, I'd see to it that afterwards people outside got to know. I didn't claim to have the right to any better treatment than other prisoners received, but I just wanted to say that I was in a stronger position to influence opinion outside than most of his prisoners were.

'Is this some kind of a threat?' he asked, assuming a mien of bored annoyance. 'The South African police are not worried by threats, especially not from your sort of people.'

It was a threat to tell the truth, I declared. The judges and lawyers knew me—I'd told the truth before, without exaggerations, and they'd believed me, and if I were subjected to any irregularities I'd tell the truth again and be believed again.

I was sleepy, anxious and uncertain, yet I felt I had to take the initiative if I were to save myself.

'What the police do is their own business,' he answered in a superior, slightly arrogant way. 'We don't need you to tell us how to carry on our investigations.' Two years earlier he had sometimes been pleasant to me, though more often he had been angry and rude, yet in his avidity to penetrate my mind

206

and subvert my resistance, he had at least always been interested in what I had been thinking. Now, however, he seemed aloof and unconcerned. 'Ours is a tough life,' he continued jeeringly. 'If we're investigating a murder case we often have to work through the night, and we certainly don't let our prisoners tell us how to conduct our questioning.' He snorted imperiously as though my suggestions were hardly worth taking seriously. I thought that his face could truly be called pig-like.

Yes, but this was quite a different situation, I answered. In the first place there was nothing urgent about the investigations, they'd been going on for months, and in the second place I'd been held not as a suspect but as a witness on the Attorney-General's warrant.

I was alarmed at his failure even to protest that he would never use illegal means against a prisoner.

'You say you haven't seen these things you talk of,' he said seemingly anxious to get me out of the room yet at the same time determined not to let me have the last word, 'so why lend your ears to the stories of others?'

I'd be happy if they turned out not to be true, I countered, remembering that he himself had once threatened me with night-and-day interrogation. I wished to mention, I continued, that his name had not been referred to as one of those responsible, but there was a group of policemen from Pretoria or Johannesburg, I wasn't sure which, whose names cropped up time and again, and it was clearly illegal to interrogate people right through the night.

'Where do you see that it's illegal?' he queried in a scornful manner. 'Show me in a book where it says it's illegal.' He snorted again.

It said so in our own case, I replied, taken aback that he should deny the unlawfulness of such interrogation. *Sachs vs. Rossouw*, I reminded him, the case brought when I had been under 90-days, about whether I was entitled to get reading matter. In their judgment the Appellate Division had ruled against me but had said quite clearly that it was unlawful to deprive a prisoner of his spiritual or physical health or to use third degree to make him talk.

'Oh, yes, but I won that case,' he said triumphantly.

But only on the point about the books, I said, suppressing my exasperation. The judges had said expressly that third degree was unlawful, and anyhow, it was a legal proposition which everyone knew.

'I'm not interested in debating these points with you,'—now he was irritated—'and I've told you not to listen to stories. You've had your chance to speak to me now, so let me get on with my work.' He pretended to study a folder in front of him, and I was escorted from the room, dazed by the indecisiveness of our encounter and unhappy about his ambiguousness in relation to the use of no-sleep torture.

Later in the morning I was taken to a cell in a police station about five miles from the police headquarters. My belongings were placed on the floor, the heavy steel door was slammed, and once more I was sitting on a mattress on the ground. I had been allowed to take books and a change of clothing with me, and the whole procedure had been so casual that I had difficulty in believing that I was back in custody.

This mood of disbelief was perpetuated when in the afternoon I was permitted to buy a newspaper and read of my own arrest. As a 90-day prisoner I had been dramatically seized by a team of seven aggressive policemen who had immediately sealed me off from the world, whereas now I had been asked to accompany two bored Security men, and was able to read about it in the press. The news report, which I looked at with a feeling of amusement combined with hysteria, mentioned prominently on the front page that as well as myself an architect, a journalist, a lecturer, and a teacher, all of whom were friends of mine, had been arrested under the 180-day law shortly after dawn that day. The publicity given to our detention pleased me, not simply because of vanity, but because I felt it was important for the public to be reminded of what the police were doing. For some years the newspapers had tended to underdramatise political arrests, as if frequency reduced rather than increased their newsworthiness.

I felt odd sitting in a cell reading about myself having been placed in a cell; it intensified my self-consciousness and sensation of unreality, and only a sense of deep irony prevented me from being overwhelmed by dismay. I seemed to be involved in an experience of continuing *déjà vu*; I was overcome by a feeling of strangeness, by a furious, baffled desire to wrench from somewhere what it was that was so intensely familiar about the situation. Yet all the time my rational self retorted that there was indeed no mystery, no displacement of consciousness—the fact was that I had been in this very situation before.

Which existence was true, and which the fantasy? I wondered. Perhaps I belonged in prison, perhaps it was only there that I could regain my sense of integrity and fight, and be at one with my ideals. Perhaps in an unjust society it was useless for a person like myself to chase after love and happiness, perhaps . . . A slam of the door, and two years of being physically free were wiped out as though they were a dream, a mere part of the imagination, while all the time my real habitat had been prison.

There was once a Chinese philosopher, I remembered wryly, who dreamt one night he was a butterfly. When he woke next morning he wondered whether he was a man who had dreamt he was a butterfly, or a butterfly dreaming he was a man.

This story ran through my mind again and again, and it stuck there and kept out other thoughts. I decided that some physical activity would help me, yet, dulled by the tiredness into which my body had retreated, I was too sluggish to move. I wondered whether I would cope: would I be stronger or weaker than I'd been the previous time? In my favour, was the fact that I was more experienced about how to survive. I knew too that the maximum period of confinement should not exceed 180 days, whereas before it could have been indefinite. Furthermore, I had a standard to maintain, a reputation as a person whom they had failed to break; vanity would give me strength, as would curiosity about the limits of my endurance. Politically, too, it meant more now for me to hold out, because in a minor way I had become something of a symbol of the ability to resist.

Yet on the negative side I had to concede that I was tired, that my resilience had been weakened by a sense of fatigue; I felt a massive revival of pain at the memory of my previous suffering, and I was despondent at the prospect of perpetual punishment. Two years of political inactivity had induced in me periodic moods of self-defeat; my militancy had run down, and I was left with less will to fight than I had had before.

As I sat analysing my gains and losses I realised that my unease and self-consciousness had been strengthened by the book I had written about my previous experience. While working on it I had been compelled to build up a complex picture of myself, and to examine precisely how I had behaved when under the stress of imprisonment and isolation; now that I was back in the sort of situation which I had been describing, I found myself repeating the phrases I had used, conscious of their inadequacy, yet almost tempted to conduct myself according to them.

There were new factors I had to reckon with, in particular, sleep-deprivation, and the fact that no one was safe from physical attack. Colleagues of mine from other centres had told me of the experiences of a large number of clients, not one of whom had been able to withstand the no-sleep torture. Those who had held out the longest had broken the hardest, whereas those who had broken down relatively early on during their interrogation had been able to limit the amount of information which they had revealed.

I wished I was less wise, that I still had the cheeky certainty which had sustained me during the early days of my first detention, that I still believed that a man could withstand anything provided he were determined enough; yet I could not undo my knowledge, just as I could not by mere effort of will transform my mood of disappointment into one of combativity.

Then there was my growing love for Stephanie. She inspired me to good thoughts and high standards of conduct, and I spoke to her in thought as if she were my conscience, but at the same time the glimpse we had had of sustained personal happiness made my imprisonment harder to bear and stimulated a greedy, overwhelming desire to be free. I wanted to be with her and was wretched at the thought of how shocked she would be on learning of my arrest. Our feeling for each other was so new and inchoate that it blurred rather than strengthened my responses, adding to the intensity of my confusion.

Again and again I had sternly to remind myself that sufficient unto the day was the evil thereof.

Chapter 25

On the afternoon following my arrest I was taken to police headquarters and placed in a cell in which I had been kept for several months two years earlier. A new coat of paint had wiped out the curses and calls for help which had formerly been scratched on the walls, but otherwise it was as I had remembered it, small, dark and oppressive.

The temperature was high in the nineties, and when I was permitted to exercise in a tiny yard at the end of the corridor outside the cell, I had difficulty in making myself run. Steep walls kept out the direct light of the sun, but the air felt heavy, and perspiration dripped down my body. When eventually a cell warder called out that I must stop running because Captain Swanepoel wished to see me, I felt relieved. I returned to the cell and, following my old practice of always dressing for interrogation, put on a clean white shirt and a pair of neat trousers. It was too hot to wear a jacket, and since it was unlikely that a serious interrogation would start at five in the afternoon, I relaxed my standards and put on slippers instead of shoes.

The cell warder escorted me to the charge office, and while following him through a gate and down some stairs, I wondered how Captain Swanepoel would behave towards me. The Captain was normally stationed at Pretoria police headquarters and had the reputation of being the toughest and

212

angriest of all the many interrogators; he was also said to be the head of the team which had recently with total success operated a series of sleep-deprivation sessions against a number of political detainees. Two men had died shortly after being interrogated by him—one was the man who had been found hanged in a cell, the other the one who had leapt from a seventh-floor window.

When I arrived at the charge office I saw a squat ugly man standing on his own and looking impatiently in my direction. He wore short pants, a sports shirt, and open sandals, so that it was difficult to think of him as a policeman. Yet his blood-shot eyes, short-cropped red hair, and thick arms, which hung like legs of meat at his side, left me in no doubt that this was Captain Swanepoel. He did not say anything when I reached him, but nodded his head in the direction of the interrogation room, and waited for me to walk ahead of him. I decided I would not go unless he spoke to me.

'Are you Captain Swanepoel?' I asked politely.

'I am Captain Swanepoel,' he replied, mimicking me in a guttural voice.

'Do you want me to go that way?' I continued quietly.

'I do want you to go that way,' he echoed harshly and sarcastically.

I walked out of the charge office and up a set of stairs which led to the landing where the interrogation room was situated. These were the stairs on which Alan was supposed to have fallen, I thought wryly, and I'm on my way to the room in which he was in fact assaulted.

Captain Swanepoel and I sat down and stared at each other. How remarkable that he should even look like a villain and a bully, I thought. His ugliness was defiant and aggressive, a weapon with which to attack the world; even the rhino-like grossness of his body seemed deliberate, as if he were inviting people around him to laugh at its absurd proportion so that he might legitimately strike them down. Redness shrouded his eyes, giving him the appearance of a diseased animal; he stared mockingly at me, apparently surprised at the softness of my demeanour and determined to provoke me out of my apparent calmness. Other strange plainclothes policemen walked in and out of the small room, stopping for short intervals to look at me as though they were appraising a piece of merchandise. Nearly all of them wore tieless shirts, open sandals, and shorts, giving the room a holiday-like character. From remarks they made to each other I learnt that they had just arrived in a team by aeroplane from Pretoria and were planning to spend some time in Cape Town. Why had they travelled a thousand miles, I wondered, when there were scores of Security men in Cape Town who could have conducted the investigations?

Their constant movement in and out of the room unsettled me, and the dazzling white panel-boards round the walls added to my discomfort. There was no formality to the questions which were put to me, and it took me some while to realise that an interrogation was actually being attempted. I was reassured by the fact that I was not being made to stand—the 'statue treatment', as prolonged enforced standing had come to be called, normally accompanied sleep deprivation—yet I felt ill at ease because of not knowing why I had been brought to the room.

'Have I been brought here for interrogation?' I asked.
'You'll see,' the Captain replied.
'What happens if I want to leave here?'
'You'll see.'
'Are you proposing to deprive me of sleep?'
'You'll see.'
A large parcel of cigarettes was brought in and placed on the table. The Captain watched me as he counted them . . . eleven . . . twelve . . . thirteen boxes, each containing fifty

214

cigarettes. That would last the members of the team several days, assuming they were heavy smokers . . .

'I'd like to make my position clear,' I said.

'Make your position clear,' the Captain jeered.

'I've been held as a witness and the law doesn't entitle you to subject me to prolonged interrogation. If I refuse to answer questions you must take me before a magistrate; that's what the law says.'

'We'll see about that.'

'There's just one other thing,' I continued. 'I don't know what your intentions are with regard to me, but I'd like to mention that if you do anything irregular I'll see to it that the whole legal profession gets to hear—the judges, the lawyers, prosecutors, the lot.'

'Don't try to intimidate us. We've been in this game a long, long time, and we're not going to be frightened by people like you.'

'That last time I was detained, one of my colleagues saw the Minister of Justice, who promised to keep a personal eye on me.'

'Ha! ha! ha! That's a good one.'

The Captain grinned at one of his assistants. Their amusement was genuine, and its smugness suggested that they were intimates of the Minister, and knew better than I what his present attitude to me was. My feeling of alarm increased.

'Now let *me* ask *you* something,' the Captain said, aggressively emphasising the 'me' and 'you'. He used his hands more now as he spoke, fat clumsy hands which closed from time to time into massive fists. 'When Fred asked you to join him again after your release from 90 days, why did you refuse?'

I was pleased that at last a specific question had been asked, because this enabled me to assert myself in a way I had been unable to do when they had merely watched me.

'I'm afraid I'm not prepared to answer any questions unless I'm brought before a magistrate in terms of the law.'

'Don't play with me,' the Captain bellowed, slamming one of his hands against the desk. 'We've got a job to do and we're not going to allow any pipsqueak Communist lawyer to stand in our way.' He let his rage subside, and grinned at me as if anticipating the pleasure of our forthcoming encounter.

Desultory questioning followed, interrupted by occasional bursts of anger from the Captain. After two hours a plate of food was brought to the room, and with elaborately mimed politeness one of the policemen placed it in front of me. I was puzzled by the exaggerated formality with which I was offered the food, but felt I should eat so that my body should continue to function normally for as long as possible.

While I was eating the questions stopped, which gave me a chance to think about the interrogators. The second-in-command of the team seemed to be a lieutenant whose name I understood to be Coetzee, a tall man whose bush jacket and neat khaki shorts gave him the appearance of a British District Officer, though his accent and style were clearly Afrikaans. His voice was cold and flat, and there was a disturbingly repressed quality to his movements which made me prefer the hot violence of the Captain to his icy ghost-like lack of animation. Whereas the Captain was perpetually agitated and alive, always making his presence felt, Lieutenant Coetzee remained withdrawn from both me and his colleagues, moving among us like a lofty automaton, hostile and disengaged, occasionally giving a crystal-cool smile, yet invariably remote and unlikeable.

There were two other lieutenants in the group; one dark, young and fierce, the other middle-aged, sallow and quiet. The younger one, Lieutenant van Rensburg, must have been about my age; he was individualistic and seemed contemptuous of people, a methodical and energetic policeman, who was

216

angry, ambitious, intelligent, and severe, and yet capable of a cynical objectivity which the others lacked. The sallow lieutenant, on the other hand, was soft and sagging, with a quiet, whining voice, and a pliable, gutless manner. He fitted in with the others, blurring the personality differences which existed between them without revealing any specific character of his own.

Finally there were a couple of young sergeants who seemed to act merely as satellites of the Captain, rushing hither and thither to do his bidding; I thought of them as apprentice bullies who delighted in the mere fact of their proximity to the Captain. Sergeant Nel was the more lively of the two, a healthy, fair-haired man with a young, stupid-looking face, personable, eager to impress, deferential to his superiors and arrogant towards me. The middle finger of one of his hands was missing and when he spoke he was unable to pronounce the 'th' sound, so that though his accent was Afrikaans, some words sounded ludicrously like Cockney. The other sergeant was very young and very ugly, but unlike the Captain who seemed to derive an aggressive pleasure from his unsightliness, this sergeant seemed trapped by his bad appearance. Occasionally he glowered at me, but he never said anything, and seemed happiest when able to fetch or carry something for the Captain. It was he who had brought in the packets of cigarettes, and he was the one who took my plate away when I had finished eating.

After supper the interrogation became more serious, yet it was still conducted on a relatively casual basis. I was now able to discern a pattern in the interrogators' movements: a pair of them would sit with me for an hour and then be replaced by another pair who would sit for another hour, and so on. The Captain was my most vigorous inquisitor, but even he seemed to be restraining himself. In previous interrogations various techniques had been tried on me; sometimes the interrogators had been angry, sometimes apparently friendly, but always they had seemed to concentrate intensely on trying to undermine my resistance in the shortest possible period. Now, however, my questioners appeared almost deliberately to be going slow, operating at a lazy tempo and with easy confidence.

'Could I please go to the lavatory?' I asked at one stage, feeling like a schoolboy wanting to leave the room.

'Why certainly, Mr Sachs.'

Again I was puzzled by the over-politeness. Some sort of instruction must have been given: allow him to eat, let him go to the toilet, don't make him stand, but . . . What sort of buts had there been? Would I be allowed to return to my cell? Would I be allowed to sleep in the interrogation room? For how long would they go on with their questioning?

Two men escorted me to the lavatory, which was some distance away along the first-floor landing. Inside the lavatory cubicle I had a moment of privacy, and decided I should try to make some record of what was happening to me. In my pocket was a diary with a little pencil, and on one of its pages I made disguised notes of the names of the interrogators and the approximate times of their shifts. I dared not spend too long, and after a reasonable interval of sitting there I emerged, washed my hands at a basin, splashed water on my face to freshen myself, and returned with my escorts to the interrogation room.

By now it was dark outside, but the strong electric light in the interrogation room shone on the white panel boards, tiring my eyes and adding to my feeling of fatigue. It was still hot and I was tense. There were little holes in criss-cross patterns on the board, and my eyes travelled compulsively along the lines of the design.

For long stretches of time nothing was said and then suddenly one of the interrogators would speak to me.

'We do all the dirty work,' one complained. 'I haven't had proper time off for three months. They send us all over the country and we're at it all the time.'

I said nothing, hoping his grumbling would continue.

'Why don't you talk now?' another pleaded. 'You're going to talk in the end, so you might as well start now and save us all, including yourself, a lot of trouble. Why don't you talk now?' he repeated. 'Why don't you talk now? Why don't you talk now?'

'Will I be allowed back to my cell?' I asked.

'You'll see. Now, Mr Sachs, why don't you talk now?'

Late in the evening the Captain returned. He had been for a walk in the Gardens, he told us, where it was very nice and cool except there were so many Coloureds, which was the one thing he couldn't stand about Cape Town. He was fresher than he had been earlier, and in his hand was a file through which he had apparently been reading and which he now handed over to Lieutenant van Rensburg.

'I see that last time you were in,' Lieutenant van Rensburg said with a sneer on his young face, 'the people here simply came to your cell and asked if you'd changed your mind about answering questions.' He shook his head contemptuously. 'And then when you said "no" they just walked away.'

'It was much harder than that,' I replied. 'They were damned tough. As I told them at the time, I thought the law was inhuman, but at least they stuck to the law. It doesn't say much for you Transvaalers that you've got to go in for irregular methods to get results.'

'I didn't know that the record down here was so clean,' Captain Swanepoel intervened. 'After all,' he smirked, 'there were allegations that Brooks and Kemp had been assaulted by one of your Cape men.'

'That doesn't excuse what you're doing.'

'What are we doing?'

219

'You're keeping me up. You're not letting me go to my cell.'

'That's a good one,' the Captain joked heartily. 'How can you say we're keeping you up, when it's you who's keeping us up. As soon as you make a statement you can go, so it's up to you. And don't tell me *we* are keeping *you* up.'

'And if I refuse to make a statement to you?'

'You'll see.'

The Captain stretched his thick legs under the table so that his toes pointed up towards me through his sandals, and then suddenly leaned forward and smashed his fist down on the table.

'You ought to be shot,' he yelled, 'all of you. You're a lot of rubbish. How dare you try to take on the South African police.' His face reddened, and he narrowed his bloodshot eyes as if to concentrate the violence of his stare. 'You know what the joke is?' he asked, laughing now with a roar and banging the table again and again. 'The joke is I learnt everything I know from you Communists. I was a Communist once myself, that's the joke. Ha, ha, ha,' he guffawed.

I was taken aback by his statement. Was he mad, believing his fantasies, trying to justify his cruelty by inventing experiences?

'The Captain was in Q-squad,' one of the lieutenants explained, noticing my incredulity.

'What squad?' I asked.

'Q-squad—the one that infiltrates subversive organisations.'

This was ludicrous—the Captain was so obviously a policeman, so gross and crude in manner, so deeply racialistic in attitudes, that he would not have been allowed near a legal liberal organisation, let alone into an underground Communist one. Perhaps he was trying to trick me into an argument. I must be careful.

'I know you people,' he continued, enjoying his rage, 'you all lead double lives. On the surface you are lawyers and lec-

220

turers and you appear to be intelligent and decent people.
But you can't take me in. I know, because I learnt from you
people. You're evil, and you've got to be wiped out. I'm not
bluffed by you people, you dirty Communist shits.' He was
letting his anger rise, enjoying the manipulation of his violence.
He leaned forward and glared at me. 'You're just a piece of
Communist shit,' he yelled.

His loss of control frightened me, yet it gave me a chance
to counter-attack.

'I'm surprised,' I said quietly, 'to find a senior police officer
using foul language like that.'

He was taken aback by my response, and closed his eyes for
a moment before continuing with his harangue.

'When it comes to swearing,' he argued in a quieter voice,
'you should have heard some of your people.'

I thought of Fred—son of a railwayman, five years in the
Army—and imagined with distress how he must have sworn
as they broke him down over five days of interrogation.

'And don't you try to provoke me,' he continued with controlled ferocity, 'I'm too experienced to fall for your tricks.
We policemen wouldn't last long if we became angry.'

His eyes looked tired, a swollen neck made his head appear
as if it sagged into his body, and his heavy limbs seemed to
drag him to the ground; yet anger gave energy to his drooping
frame, and his voice roared with activity.

I had no right to speak about manners, he declared further,
still annoyed by my retort. I was planning to kill innocent
people, including women and children, I was a typical example
of one of those people with double lives, on the surface intelligent and friendly and talking about human rights, but
underneath a devilish enemy of the State, trying to overthrow
White civilisation in Southern Africa.

What sort of civilisation was it, I asked, when the police
could lock people up more or less at will?

He shook his head in an exaggerated show of disappointment. The police were only doing their duty to protect the State from its enemies, he told me, and as a lawyer I should know that better than anyone. How is it, he wanted to know, that so many people who'd been educated at universities built by the White man, who owed everything they had—their house, their car, their learning—to the White man, should try to overthrow White civilisation? He simply couldn't make it out, people biting the hand that fed them. With regard to the Bantu it was easy to understand, for they had no moral values and knew no better. He didn't want to say they would never learn, because maybe in a thousand years they would reach the standard of the White man, though personally he doubted it. He felt sorry for them, because they were just stupid and talked about freedom when they didn't know the first thing about it and would massacre each other if it weren't for the White man's control. The people who really made him angry were those who should know better, who'd studied and even travelled all over the world and therefore should know that integration was suicide, because this was the lesson of history everywhere.

Without pausing, for his speech was in flood by now, he took up a new theme—the numbers of people whom he had arrested. Lawyers, doctors, businessmen, he rolled out their names grandly and in full as if their very eminence added to his glory. They were fools, he said, thinking they were cleverer than the South African police, which was the finest police force in the world, as everybody knew. Some people had escaped—he mentioned more names—they were cowards, too scared to fight like men. Also, they were dishonest and immoral. I would be surprised if I knew some of the things he'd learnt about them. The Black so-called leaders were the worst —did I know that one had been sent £20,000 from overseas and had handed over only £10,000, keeping the rest for himself? I was working for the Blacks and this was what they did. I was a fool and a coward, and he was surprised to see someone who called himself intelligent behaving the way I did.

The more he talked, the more enthusiastic he became, thrusting his pudgy hands in my direction to emphasise a point and grimacing like a public speaker on a platform. His contortions and the sustained volume of his address were bizarrely inappropriate to the small room in which we sat and the audience of two which listened to him, yet the mad vigour with which he poured out his views, switching without impediment of breath or logic from one point to the next, was strangely impressive. At one stage he was so carried away by his performance that he actually started to make a mock speech as though addressing an African National Congress meeting. ' "*Mayibuye!*" ' he yelled, raising, his right thumb and giving the Congress salute. ' "Last time we greeted Chief Luthuli it was to honour his becoming President of the African National Congress," ' he jeeringly quoted from a speech I had made five years earlier. ' "This time we greet him as winner of the Nobel Peace Prize, next time we will greet him as Prime Minister of South Africa." You were a big shot then,' he shouted, 'when you got cheers from a raw, half-baked audience that knew nothing about politics except what a few liberalists and Communists told them, but look at you now. You were simply a coward. We will never hand over the country to the Blacks.' He thrust his fist fiercely on the table as he said this. 'We'd all die rather than see everything we've built up over three centuries ruined by a lot of kaffirs. You've spoken a lot about votes for all, but what the Black man really wants is to sleep with all the White women and to steal all the White man's things. It's the same with the Black States in Africa; they cried aloud about apartheid, but in fact were just jealous of the good race relations in South Africa and were only after the riches of the country, the finest, happiest, most prosperous country not only in Africa but in the whole world.'

As if nothing could surpass or even equal the excellence of this statement, he fell silent for a moment, and then relaxed his tense muscles, allowing the savagery to fade from his expression.

He had attended many meetings in his time, he continued with a heavy affectionate grin to me, and he remembered well speeches which my father had made on the Johannesburg City Hall steps. There were always two groups in the audience which fought each other, he told me, so the police were ordered to break up the fights and stand in the middle. As soon as they did so, the crowd would stop hitting each other—and both sides would attack the police. He chuckled as he reminisced about his experiences as a constable, and seemed to enjoy the respite from his tirade.

Would he mind, I enquired, if I asked him something?

He said he wouldn't mind, so I asked what he thought of the book written by Ruth First on her 90-day experience, called *117 Days*. The question was mischievous, for she had written that Swanepoel's hamhanded bullying had at one stage prevented her from possibly succumbing to the wily tactics of another interrogator.

Discomfited, he hesitated over his answer, and then with a contemptuous lifting of his nostrils said the book was completely exaggerated and not worth reading. The South African police force, he continued, was not the slightest bit worried by the cries of people who ran away overseas. The police had been too soft to Ruth First and she had taken advantage of this. But nothing in the world would stop them from doing their duty.

They had only one more task to do, he confided to me, and that was to clean up the universities. After that everything would be all right in the country.

'And what about the newspapers and churches?' I asked.

'Oh, and those too, they've also got to be cleaned up.'

I thought of more bodies of which the police were likely to disapprove, but decided not to encourage this line of thought. He continued with his crude political analyses, while I listened passively.

It was nearing midnight, and as his voice boomed on I became aware of how tired I was. The personality battle had excited me, and time had passed quickly while he had been shouting, but now that his performance was drawing to an end I felt myself reacting with weariness. I yawned, and pressed my palms against the chair on which I was sitting. If the interrogation continued past twelve o'clock, I decided, then I would know for sure that it would go on forever.

On the table lay a tin box containing pins and paper clips. Without looking directly at it I casually stretched out a hand and took out one of the pins. In a film which I had seen a few months earlier the hero had resisted brainwashing by digging a nail into his palm. Perhaps, I thought, I could save myself by a similar device.

Chapter 26

By keeping my hands below the level of the table I was able to continue pricking my finger without the manoeuvre being seen. The spot at which I jabbed had become numb, yet I carried on with the prodding because it was something to do. For several hours since midnight my interrogators had maintained total silence, and the deadness which surrounded me was proving more exhausting than the yelling of Captain Swanepoel. My eyes were sore, and my body sagged, but I dared not relax, and went on pricking. Never had I known such fatigue, such a longing to close my eyes and to cease my resistance to sleep. The room was utterly quiet, and save for the periodical chiming of the City Hall clock, no sound came from outside. The walls shimmered and a blur of whiteness loomed towards me, receded into focus and then fuzzed into a blur again. I looked at the table, at the two policemen, at the walls; I glanced at my feet, at the table, at the walls, at the two policemen . . .

One of them had fallen sleep. I smiled while his companion woke him.

The pin prodded at my finger; I crossed and uncrossed my legs, moved around in my chair, and changed my position as often as possible, though I knew that the very attempt to activate my mind was tiring it. The police versus sleep . . . sleep versus the police . . .

'Mr Sachs . . .'

The voice came quietly and pleasantly to me. Damn, my eyes had closed. The soft lieutenant had noticed and had called me into wakefulness.

Again my eyes closed.

'Mr Sachs . . .'

His voice wheedled. I must stay awake, I told myself. Each time I went under the police claimed something from me. Yet how long could I last?

'Mr Sachs . . .'

It was happening frequently now, the drooped eyelids, the wakening phrase.

'Mr Sachs, why don't you talk now? You're going to in the end, so why not now?' The whining, friendly voice lulled me even as it kept me from sleep. 'Let's start now, Mr Sachs. Let's start now, Mr Sachs. Let's start now, Mr Sachs . . .' The sentence was repeated again and again. 'Get it over, Mr Sachs. Get it over. Get it over . . .' Hypnotically it continued.

I shook my head and patted my cheeks. In half an hour I would ask if I might go to the lavatory. That was a target—another half-hour of resistance should give me ten minutes out of the room, after which a further session would start.

'Mr Sachs . . . Mr Sachs . . . Mr Sachs . . .' The lieutenant's voice was kind, and what he said was not without sense. I was going to break in the end, and those who held out the longest talked the most . . .

I looked at my hands, I stared at the one lieutenant and then at the other. They too were battling to keep awake, but their shift would soon be over, whereas I would have to carry on forever, and ever. Their faces were tired, their bodies bent.

'Please, Mr Sachs . . . Please, Mr Sachs.' The words came out in a stupidly repeated monotone. 'Please, Mr Sachs . . .' I felt angry. I would not give way to this cruelty. It left no marks, they did not even touch me, but they laid siege to my mind, and broke it down, bit by bit; here they were, operating right in the heart of Cape Town, only a hundred yards from the City Hall, and who cared? Even the other four interrogators were asleep. The half hour passed slowly, and I felt better.

'Can I go to the lavatory, please?' I asked.

'Certainly, Mr Sachs.' I no longer cared why they were over-effusive.

My body felt slothful and drugged, and I walked slowly and without spirit. The route to the washroom ran past a landing which overlooked a small concrete courtyard. The drop was about thirty foot . . . I looked at the wall. I could fling myself over it, I reckoned, probably without being killed, and if my bones were broken the interrogation would have to stop. I dared not act dishonourably and yet I simply had to sleep. The conflict had grown beyond what I could bear. I wished for obliteration, a crashing, physical annihilation to end the immense tension inside me. If my body could be wiped out then the emotional anguish would cease—it would be like a suicide, but I would not die.

Yet . . . and yet possibly the police intended to interrogate me only till daylight. To jump would be melodramatic and humiliating and I would be leaping into a chaos, losing control of myself and of what happened to me.

My thoughts and impulses were confused and I realised with sadness that my capacity for making decisions had been weakened. If there were no hope at all, I reasoned, then I would jump, for though the information I had was not of much value in itself, the principle of resistance was important. The question was: when would I know for sure that all hope was gone?

The wall was only five yards away, and the feeling of being active, of doing something, should give me impetus. I hesitated. The police were near and I would have to move quickly. My arms and legs would be broken, but . . .

I walked past the wall and moved down the passage towards the toilet. *Môre is nog 'n dag,* tomorrow is another day, and I would know by then if I had any chance of surviving.

The sojourn in the lavatory provided less of an escape than it had earlier. Actions which were normally automatic, like closing the door and flushing the pan, now required the most intense concentration, and even the pleasure of being secluded from the men who had been staring at me all night was diminished, since I knew that soon I would have to return to the interrogation room. I thought of locking myself in the cubicle, but then decided that the action would be petulant and would make me feel morally inferior to my captors; the lack of dignity involved in the setting might have been amusing, but it would have amounted to an abuse of privilege which could later have been used as an excuse for preventing both myself and other prisoners from using toilet facilities.

For years I had wondered at the inertia displayed by so many Jews in the face of imminent extermination by the Nazis, and I had thought with anger that in such a situation I would certainly have rebelled. Yet here I was obeying the rules laid down by my captors, gradually accepting their domination, falling under the sway of their will. It was an example on a much smaller scale, yet the process of surrender seemed to be the same. In a muddled way I discerned many factors of similarity: the isolation, the overwhelming power of the enemy, the lack of means to fight back, the enforced habituation to passivity, the material dependence on the captors; the fatigue, the uncertainty; the tendency to rely increasingly on deliverance by some external intervention and, finally, the unwillingness really to believe that people could be cruel to other people when actually face to face with them. Theories about unconscious willingness or masochism didn't seem necessary to account for my docility in these circumstances—in fact, composure struck me as being more accusatory than wild resistance. Certainly there was no pleasure in my suffering, no feeling of sublime resignation, no martyr's ecstasy, only pain and sickness and a desire for it all to end.

The walk back to the interrogation room seemed like a retreat from one defeat to face another. It was easier to acknowledge my weakness than my capacity to endure punishment, and I began to wonder if I would hold out even until dawn. On other occasions in my life I had been up all night—once on the night before University Rag, often on New Year's Eve, once when looking for a friend lost on the mountain—but always there had been purposeful activity to keep me awake, not this attrition by silence. By subjecting me to alternating periods of violent verbal attack and total quiet, and by continually depriving me of rest, the police were beginning to dominate my physiology. I might keep going for another day, but what after that? Another day, and another and another. The drop to the courtyard . . .? I would have to act cleverly.

I took my place on my chair, and the lieutenants returned to their seats. Again they did not speak to me or say anything to each other—one picked his nails with a match-stick, while the other stared into the corner. The next shift should start soon, and they would be able to go to bed. It was strange to think that there were bedrooms in that forbidding building . . .

'Mr Sachs.' The gentle, pleading voice woke me. My eyes could have closed for no more than an instant, yet he had noticed.

According to my calculations Captain Swanepoel was due back soon. I could not imagine him sitting in silence, so that although he was the most formidable member of the team, I now looked forward to his verbal violence. Anything was pre-

ferable to the mummy stillness maintained by the two lieutenants.

'Mr Sachs,' the voice continued sympathetically, 'we know
what it's really like for you. Deep down you really want to
talk'—the words were friendly—'but there's just something
holding you back.'

Something holding me back . . . No, it was not like that,
the truth was just the opposite. 'Deep down' I wanted to say
nothing to them, nothing at all, and it was the 'just something'
which was prompting me in very rational fashion to reconsider
my position. What did they think, that I felt guilty about
what I'd done and that secretly I wanted to confess? How far
from the truth, and what an insult . . .

'Mr Sachs . . .'

I had gone under again.

'We know you really want to talk . . . we understand . . .'
Kindly, gentle.

On the hour, as I had anticipated, the Captain arrived. His
eyes were even more bloodshot than they had been earlier,
his face looked unshaven, and I realised with shock that I
had forgotten how crude he was.

'You still think you can take on the South African police?'
he asked gruffly. His irritability might have been part of a
prepared procedure—by then I was satisfied that the team
worked according to a strict programme—yet it seemed more
likely that he was suffering from ordinary human annoyance
at having had to get out of bed.

'Your actions are unlawful,' I replied with what was now a
dulled vigour.

'Oh, you're back with your lawyer's rubbish,' he said, bark-
ing out the words.

I was unable to argue as vehemently as I had done before,
yet I felt a desperate urge to assert my opposition in some
way. More and more I was beginning to think about 'after-

wards', and as far as 'afterwards' was concerned I did not want it said that I had not protested.

'It's illegal to interrogate a person for so long against his will,' I insisted.

'What's wrong with six hours?' he demanded quickly.

'Twelve hours,' I corrected him.

'Six hours!'

I was puzzled by his mistake, and looked at my watch.

'Give me that,' he yelled. 'Who said you could keep your watch?' He grabbed my arm with thick-wristed hands, and surprised me by the hardness of the grip of his flabby-looking fingers.

'Give me that,' he shouted again.

I hesitated whether to comply with his command, and felt wretched with fatigue at the thought of resistance.

'You've no right to take my watch from me,' I said firmly. 'I'm not a prisoner, I'm a witness.'

His hands started to twist the skin on my arm and his fingers pushed at the metal strap, but I pulled my arm back and covered the watch with my free hand. He glared at me with such ferocity that I thought he was going to strike me, but then suddenly he let go and said quietly that, all right, he would let me keep it for the time being.

I was elated by my success, yet felt that he had merely been testing me rather than fighting a major battle.

'You've got no right to keep me awake through the night . . .' I tried to speak loudly and with feeling, but my words sounded flat.

'That's a good one,' he interrupted angrily. 'You keep us up all night and then you've got the cheek to complain about us.'

What was happening? Everything he said was upside down.

'We're trying to do our work,' he continued, 'and you won't let us get sleep. We're the ones who should feel cross.' He

232

looked earnestly at me. 'Stop interfering with us,' he pleaded seriously.

To use his language, that was a joke, *I* interfering with *them* . . .

'What's more,' he accused, 'you're just a coward, you've got no guts at all. You attack the police when they've got no chance to answer back.'

I was tired and had difficulty in concentrating, but what he was saying was such a reversal of our actual situations that I began to feel annoyed.

'You're a coward,' he screamed, banging the table repeatedly with his ham-heavy fist '. . . a coward, a coward, a coward.'

I stared at him without being able to comprehend the purpose of his accusation. They were the cowards—six against one.

'Now, now, Albie,' he pointed a finger at me and spoke as though giving friendly advice, 'don't lose your temper.' His finger needled at me as he continued, 'It only makes things worse for you if you lose your temper, so don't get so angry.'

Was this a mad game? He had accused me of the very thing he was doing himself. Weariness made it difficult for me to reason properly, but I realised dimly that he had deliberately been distorting reality in a whole series of statements. What was his motive, I wondered; was it to anger me, or was it to confuse my thinking? I had earlier been sceptical of a rumour that pro-apartheid psychologists had been assisting the police in working out interrogation techniques, but now I had no doubt that this had been so. The Captain must have been working to a scientifically structured programme; although many policemen told lies as a routine part of trapping a suspect, I had never heard of them going in for careful distortions of time, mood and casuality in relation to facts which were insignificant in themselves. The Captain had a certain cruel intelligence of his own, but I was convinced that his natural technique was to bully rather than to deceive. He had neither the personality, style nor the education to use of his own initiative sophisticated techniques of mind control—he must have been specially trained to do so.

My back was stiff and my buttocks ached with cramp, so I took advantage of a pause in the Captain's talking to ask whether I might stand for a bit.

'You want to stand?' He was amused, and his mouth opened into a grin. 'You want to stand?' he repeated, beginning to laugh. 'Ha! ha! ha!' he bellowed. 'That's a good one. He's asking if he can stand.'

I saw that there was a funny side to my request. His prisoners were normally compelled to stand, and after hours and days of being on their feet begged to be allowed to sit, and here was I actually asking for permission to stand. I smiled back at the Captain; we shared our amusement.

'Yes, all right,' he chuckled, 'you may stand.' He could not enjoy the joke enough. 'That's a good one,' he said once more, shaking his head with pleasure.

I stood at the side of the table and stretched my arms out in an arc in front of my chest, enjoying the luxury of having been amused. My eyes were heavy and my head felt thick; being upright brought home to me how slack my muscles had become and how difficult it was for me to maintain an upright posture. I walked a few paces to the one corner of the table and then a few steps back to the other. Backwards and forwards I moved, hoping to stimulate my body into wakefulness. The Captain lit a cigarette and watched me in silence. When would I collapse? I wondered, continuing to pace to and fro. A grey light was dawning outside, and I felt proud that I had lasted out most of the night. But what of the next night, and the one after that? Ultimately I would break, for the exhaustion was becoming more than I could bear. Opposition to their interrogation seemed to have become tied to my

234

resistance against falling asleep, and eventually my physical and mental fatigue would be so extreme that I would no longer be able to exercise any will over my actions.

After some minutes I felt too tired to carry on walking, and noticing that I leaned against the table to prevent myself from falling, decided to sit down again.

'Well, how are you feeling?' the Captain asked with mock consideration.

'Not very well,' I replied.

'It will get worse,' he assured me, 'much, much worse. You'll see.'

'I suppose so.'

'You'll be begging us to take a statement. You'll see.'

'Possibly. It doesn't say much for the standard of the police that they have to rely on these sort of methods to break people down.'

'What methods?' he enquired in a calm guttural voice.

'These Nazi methods.' I was angry at the unfairness of the battle—six men against one, and they made all the rules— and was riled by his smugness.

'What methods?' he said again, looking round the room to indicate that there were no instruments of torture to be seen.

'Perhaps "Nazi methods" is an exaggeration. The Nazis were more brutal than you've been to me,' I answered, 'but in some ways your psychological torture is worse . . .'

'Aha!' he interrupted with excitement, 'I was waiting for that. They all say the same thing, I knew you'd come out with it.' He looked triumphantly at me, as though by having anticipated my accusation he rendered it devoid of substance. ' "Psychological torture",' he jeered, ' "psychological torture." "Nazi methods." You people make me sick; you haven't got any guts so you accuse us—you've got the *insolence* to accuse us—of using psychological torture and Nazi methods.' His manner was scornful and he seemed to be moving towards a new tirade. 'Anyhow,' he demanded, 'what was so bad about the Nazis? I can understand that you Communists don't like them, but why should anyone else mind what they did?'

'Because, for one thing, they killed six million Jews.'

'Ugh,' he expostulated, 'that was just a lot of stories put out by the Communist and liberal press. Why should *I* believe it?'

Indignation welled within me and I felt ashamed that I had enjoyed a joke with him earlier.

'I happened to lose whole sections of my family,' I retorted angrily. 'The Nazis just wiped them out, men, women and children.'

We glared at each other, and then he shrugged and lit another cigarette for himself. We remained quiet for several minutes, and I felt myself relapsing into total dullness. Each time I argued with him my voice became weaker and my range of ideas and expressions narrowed. The previous evening I could have debated vigorously for hours, but now after only a few minutes I was without verbal energy. My shoulders were hunched, my whole body seemed to have lost tone, and it required special effort to keep even my head from lolling.

I decided that after the Captain had finished his shift, I would ask to go to the lavatory again. One visit every four hours was not unreasonable, and they should let me go. The Captain on the other hand, might refuse me permission . . .

'Albie!' the guttural voice woke me. I had dozed again. Blinking my eyelids, I cursed myself for having gone under. The Captain was the most dangerous member of the team and I was anxious that of all of them he quite literally should not catch me napping.

Bang! The table resounded from the slam of the Captain's fist—I had dropped off to sleep again. Despite intense effort I could hardly keep my eyes open. I located the pin which I had

236

used earlier and began to use it again to stab at my forefinger, but each movement required special concentration, and the area which I prodded had lost its sensation.

'Albie!' The Captain was playing with me and grinned with satisfaction as he jerked me into consciousness again.

Clap! He beat his hands together.

I fell asleep and was woken, fell asleep and was woken.

Bang! Another smash on the table.

'Al . . . bie!' My name called out slowly and reprovingly.

Clap! 'Albie!!' *Bang, bang, bang!* 'Albie.'

The dizziness and descents into slumber seemed to be clustered in waves of total fatigue which lasted for several minutes. I survived this one and was able to regain control of my wakefulness, but each session seemed to exact a special toll of my mind and body and cause my resistance to plunge a step further. It was no longer a problem only of being overwhelmed by tiredness; my emotions were distressed and my body felt as though it were diseased.

Remaining quiet must have been as big a strain for the Captain as it was for me, for after several hours of alternating sessions of talk and quiet he stood up and asked querulously:

'What time is breakfast here?' He spoke in Afrikaans, shaking his head to keep himself awake.

'I don't know,' I replied. 'I was only brought in here yesterday.'

'Anyhow, I'm going off to shave,' he caressed his chin with his thick, meaty fingers. 'I'll see you later.'

I had the feeling that he was going to go back to bed, and it gave me a sense of minor pleasure to know that I had survived a further bout with him.

After the Captain had gone, the eager fair-haired sergeant, now suddenly on his own in charge of the interrogation, stood up and placed himself a few inches away from me. His figure loomed up at my side, and then he moved back a little so that

I would be aware of his presence without being able to see him properly.

'The Captain has been very soft to you,' he said, placing his mouth to my ear. It was disconcerting to have him half behind me, but I was too tired to turn round. 'He's a good man, and you've been lucky so far. But nuffing will save you, nuffing in the whole world.' I wanted to laugh at his mispronunciation, which was as childish as his sudden assumption of authority.

Had he been to Cape Town before? I asked politely.

Only on a rugby tour, he told me.

I turned round and noticed him rubbing his bulging stomach. He was putting on a bit of weight now, he told me, but he still played.

'What position?' I enquired.

'Centre.'

'For police?'

'No, I used to, but the ground was too far away for practice, and now I play for a team nearer home.'

He sat down and began to chat to me in a friendly way. A thing that many policemen felt very strongly about, he informed me, was that people who played in the police sports team never got any special allowance for the time they gave up or even for travelling expenses. On tour, of course, their expenses were paid, but for their weekly games they often had to travel a lot, and they felt that as they represented the police force they should at least get out-of-pocket expenses. There were quite a few senior officers who felt the same way, he assured me, and General Keevey himself had set up a special commission to investigate the matter.

While he was talking to me we heard people approaching the room, and he rapidly got up and placed himself at my side again. The door opened and Lieutenant van Rensburg and the soft lieutenant came in together. With six members in their team, my interrogators could organise their shifts so that each pair would work for only eight hours out of twenty-four, whereas I would have to work through the day and night. Daylight had come, and there was no longer any doubt that the team would not leave me until I collapsed. Indignation flickered within me, but it only added to my sense of impotence.

I asked if I could go to the lavatory. I felt that I must look at the courtyard again, as it represented my only way out.

They agreed to let me go, and I stood up and began to walk to the door. I tried to move with some dignity, but my legs dragged and my feet shuffled forward clumsily. We proceeded down the passage and I realised with surprise that I was leaning against the wall as I went along, unable to walk without support. We approached the exposed section above the courtyard, and I tried to force my thoughts into line. This was my only chance. I must walk naturally until I reached a spot opposite the courtyard, and then I must dash to the low wall and roll over it. A few more slow paces . . .

The lieutenants closed in on me, and I stumbled along the passage with their healthy bodies in a tight escort only a few inches away from me. They must have guessed my plan; perhaps I had given myself away by looking too hard at the drop, perhaps my request to go to the toilet had been badly timed. If I had been stronger I could still possibly have sprinted away and rolled over the wall, but I was so exhausted that it was painful even to contemplate such violent activity, let alone perform it.

My desperation increased as I realised that what had been sustaining me as a potential last way out now existed no more. I would get continually weaker until, inevitably, I collapsed. There was no way of voluntarily sinking into unconsciousness and my mind was being so enfeebled that it would become physiologically impossible to will further resistance. The trudge to and from the lavatory was funereal, and I wondered as I tottered alongside the lieutenants if they felt any compassion for me or shame over what they were doing.

When I sat down again in the interrogation room, my head felt empty and my body drained of sensation. I was as inert as if I slept, yet I remained upright and my eyes were open. For half an hour I sat in a stupor, aware of the configuration of my environment but entirely uninterested in it or in myself.

'I'm going to fall,' I said suddenly to the lieutenants. I rolled off the chair and sank to the floor, where I lay on my side, curled up as though in bed. The lieutenants stood up and spoke to each other, but I did not care what they were saying, for the floor was comfortable and my body rested. One of them left the room, and I heard the feet of the other pass near my head and move round the table.

A few moments later cold water splashed down on my head and body, soaking my shirt, running through my hair, and draining on to the floor around me. There was a pause and then more water rained on me, a waterfall of coolness that shocked me into alertness. I enjoyed lying helplessly on the floor, prostrate, unresisting. This was what they had done to me; the humiliation was theirs, not mine.

'Don't you try to provoke us,' a tense, angry voice said high above me. Water dripped slowly from my hair, and I continued to lie collapsed in wetness. The harassment, the bannings, the solitary confinement, the years of threat and pressure—all had culminated in this one moment when, defeated by the fatigue of my brain and body, I had finally fallen to the ground.

Chapter 27

I felt luxuriously comfortable as I lay on the dusty floor, for though I was too wet to sleep, the ground held my body like a cradle. The quiet lieutenant returned and whispered to his companion, and they both bent over me and ordered me to get up. I said nothing, but continued to lie with my head resting in my arms, determined to remain inert.

'Get up, damn you!' Lieutenant van Rensburg said fiercely into my exposed ear. I closed my eyes and enjoyed the passivity.

'Please, Mr Sachs, please get up,' the soft lieutenant urged. His voice was kind, and I thought that perhaps I should try.

Before I could move, however, hands gripped my shoulders and I was jerked upright and pulled back on to the chair. My body was too weak to remain in position, so I tumbled off the chair again and lay sprawled on the floor.

'Please, Mr Sachs,' the voice pleaded gently while kind hands manoeuvred under my back, 'please don't lie there.' I was placed on my seat again, where I stayed for a few minutes before gravity suddenly seemed to overwhelm me and pull me down to the floor. I heard a third voice speaking and realised that Lieutenant Coetzee had come in. More hands pushed and pulled my body, and as my head was jerked round I saw that Captain Swanepoel was now in the room. He looked at the empty carafe on the table and the pool of water on the floor, and scowled.

'Put him on the chair,' he commanded sleepily. As soon as I had been propped up I collapsed once more, whereupon I was yanked back on to the chair again. This time I was held upright and the Captain ordered that three chairs be put near me. The full team had assembled by then, and all six men placed themselves round me, some sitting, some standing. Five of them kept me upright with their hands and bodies, while the Captain moved about and vigorously gave them instructions. Then he placed himself in front of me; Sergeant Nel took up position once more half out of sight at my side, and the lieutenants thrust with open palms from all directions at my sagging body.

'It's no good trying to provoke us,' the Captain told me coldly. He no longer attempted to dominate me with his personality, but deployed all his energy in command, urging his team on and giving extra spirit to the encirclement of me.

My head lolled, and my eyes though half-open remained unfocused. The Captain's powerful voice boomed nearby, and I became aware of his large ugly face a few inches from mine. I closed my eyes and held them tightly shut. Strong hands leaned against my cheeks and heavy fingers and thumbs pressed against my eyelids, prising them slowly open. For some minutes we all remained in fixed attitudes, with the lieutenants and sergeants all around me and the Captain keeping my eyelids forcibly apart. Then gradually they all withdrew, the Captain took his hands off my face, and I was left sitting upright, like a statue formed by the pressure of their hands.

'Well, should we start on the statement now?' the Captain asked briskly.

I stared dully ahead of me, saying nothing. Why, I won-

242

dered, had I wasted so much energy on argument the previous evening?

The Captain ordered one of the sergeants to fetch some paper, and then told me it wouldn't take long and that it was easy once one got started. He could understand that I found it difficult to make a statement, but there came a time when there was no point in keeping it back any longer.

I remained rigid, dumb with exhaustion, neither agreeing nor disagreeing with what he said.

He admired people who thought they had principles, he continued, but everyone had to be sensible. The police were not in a hurry, and if I preferred to make my statement the next morning or the next week, it didn't matter to them, but one thing I could be sure of was that I wouldn't leave the room until I had answered their questions to their satisfaction.

The sergeant returned with a pad and ball-point pen which he placed on the table. The Captain picked up the pen and kept his hand poised, ready to write.

'O.K. Let's start . . .'

I maintained my silence. I might break, I told myself, but I would do it in my own way and my own time.

The Captain stood up and noisily marched towards the door, apparently trying to provoke me into begging him not to leave. When I failed to say anything he returned to his seat, pushed the paper and pencil aside, and said he was sorry for my sake I was being so obstinate, but nevertheless he wouldn't force me to do something I didn't want to do.

'Let me go then,' I said in a subdued voice.

Certainly, he promised, as soon as I'd made my statement I could go back to my cell, and they might even arrange for me to have a wireless.

My mouth stayed closed, my tongue lay still; I was not going to speak, not then.

The Captain whispered to the other men, three of whom left

the room. He and the two who remained looked down at their hands, and said nothing—they were going to fight silence with silence.

I glanced at my shirt and saw that it had dried out but was dirty with floor dust; my hair hung over my forehead, my trousers were creased and my chin prickled with beard. Feeling stale and devitalised, with my throat dry and my tongue lying uncomfortably in my mouth, I looked at the window, and at the walls . . .

'Albie.' My arm was being tickled; I had fallen asleep and the Captain had moved up to me and was now caressing my arm, running his fingers lightly along my bare skin. 'Albie with the long, black hair,' he said affectionately in Afrikaans, placing his face near mine, and continuing to stroke my arm.

Being tickled into wakefulness upset me more than the earlier name-calling or table-thumping had done; normally I would have withdrawn my arm or pushed away the hand that was causing me discomfort, but now I was so physically demoralised that I impotently endured the torturing sensation. I wondered if the Captain were aware of his homosexuality; it seemed somehow in his case to be related to his physical ugliness and the violence of his nature, though I was too tired to work out any specific connections.

After leaning close to me for some moments he stood up and returned to his former place behind the table. Although my body was becoming increasingly weary, the mental pressure towards sleep seemed to ease with the advance of the morning, as if some internal clock were asserting itself and declaring that the time for sleeping had passed. I would possibly be able to survive one more all-night session, I thought numbly, but that would be all. I had no alternative—I had to think in terms of 'settling' and to use my reviving strength to make the harm as slight as possible.

I would have to move slowly and cautiously in an attempt to find out what my interrogators knew and what they wanted me to tell them. Many prisoners had unnecessarily volunteered information through over-estimating the knowledge of their captors, and I had to avoid doing the same. Then I would have to prepare my statement, carefully mixing truth with lies in such a way as to make it sound plausible without in fact adding anything substantial to the knowledge which the police already had.

The Captain stared impatiently at me for some minutes and then got out of his chair. Accompanied by one of the lieutenants he walked quickly out of the room, leaving me alone with Lieutenant van Rensburg. What would happen if I also tried to leave? I stood up, my legs feeble, my body hunched, and walked with what weak resolution I could muster towards the door.

'You've got no right to keep me here,' I said as I staggered forward, 'I'm going back to my cell.'

The lieutenant dashed in front of me. 'Don't you do that,' he shouted violently, 'don't try any nonsense.' He slammed the door and pushed me back to my seat, calling me a fool.

His sudden ferocity alarmed me but when soon afterwards another member of the team came into the room, he began to relax. I had gained something from the venture, for 'afterwards' they could not say that I had voluntarily stayed on in the room or that they would have allowed me to leave if only I had asked.

The next few hours went by without any overt signs of struggle between the interrogators and myself. I was too fatigued to say much, and they were merely waiting for time to pass; when night came and I started to fall asleep again, they would become active once more. Food was brought to me, and I ate it mechanically, finding it necessary consciously to will my jaws to function. The lieutenant and his companion chatted

245

softly to each other and ignored me for much of the time, so I decided eventually to speak to them.

'What does it feel like to see a human being slowly being broken down?' I mumbled politely to the lieutenant. 'Don't you have a conscience about it?'

He took no notice of the question, and carried on speaking to his mate. A half an hour or more later he suddenly turned round to me and moved his chair near to me.

'Nothing would break me,' he said, speaking to me in a surprisingly confidential way. I had forgotten what I had said to him earlier, and at first did not know what he was referring to. 'I'm the sort of person who'd never give in if I made up my mind about something,' he continued with determination. 'I've always been like that, I've never let anyone force me into doing something I didn't want to do.' He stopped, and then presumably having realised that his words might encourage me to resist, advised me that his stubbornness had, however, got him into a lot of trouble. He repeated the phrase—a lot of trouble. It was just not worth it sometimes, he insisted, hitting one's head against a brick wall.

His lean face looked perturbed, and he continued, 'I hope all this will be over soon. What I want to do is to get on a farm and work on the land and forget all about this. I love farming, that's what I'd really like to do, not this.'

After saying these words with what seemed to me to be genuine feeling, he turned back to his colleague, and the two of them went on with their conversation.

My tiredness by then had assumed a new form. Sleepiness was no longer the main threat to my resistance, since as the day progressed something in my metabolism seemed to make it easier for me to keep my eyes open and sit upright. What alarmed me now was the lifelessness of my body and the depressed state of my feeling; my limbs and trunk felt as though they were made of wood, and my mouth and throat seemed to

246

be lined with cotton. I was able to sit motionlessly for long periods, remaining so still and unresponsive to my environment that I might have been asleep, and yet my eyes stayed open and my mind still worked slowly at a conscious level.

In the middle of the morning the tall, cold lieutenant came into the room to replace Lieutenant van Rensburg. I decided that it was with him that I should begin the process of 'settling'. They must not guess my plan, or there would be no chance of their accepting my statement at face value. I would have to pretend very carefully that I was being gradually won over by their persuasion, so that when I did speak my answers would sound spontaneous and true.

The cold lieutenant settled in the seat opposite me. Was I ready yet to make a statement? he asked in a detached, hostile way.

This seemed an appropriate moment for me to begin a cautious exploratory dialogue with him. My first target was to fathom whether their intention was to have me prosecuted or merely to use me as a witness. His answers would not be reliable in themselves, but the tone in which they were given might provide some useful indications. Though the spontaneity with which he made a statement would be no guarantee of its truth, a strained and simulated genuineness would almost certainly suggest falsehood. In a small way I would be conducting a counter-interrogation, relying upon slips of the tongue, inflexions of the voice and the patterns of his thought to give me pointers as to the true organisation of his ideas. The game would be very complicated and would spin itself out slowly. They had the advantage of superior numbers and greater freshness, but to some extent I would gain from being able to dictate the pace of the dénouement. Whatever happened I would not bluff myself that I was being clever or winning the battle between the police and myself. They were winning, and all that was left to me was to reduce the extent of their victory. My head was heavy, my body lay slumped in the chair. This, I realised, would be my last chance to fight. I must use to the maximum my fading intelligence and nerve.

What would I gain from making a statement, I asked, when they would use anything I said to try and build up a case against me?

He was clean and his khaki shirt and shorts were still neat. 'We're not interested in you,' he answered sneeringly, 'we know you've been out of things for some while, it's Fred we're after.'

In previous interrogations the police had insisted that their job was merely to investigate and that the Attorney-General decided on prosecutions. Now, apparently, they no longer even pretended that the Attorney-General had any effective say in the matter.

I felt that the lieutenant was vain and that I should take advantage of his conceit to pry further information from him. He conducted himself as though he thought he was highly intelligent, and his eagerness to get the credit for having talked me round might encourage him to reveal more than any of the others might have done.

'Of course we can't guarantee you against prosecution,' he added as a further argument, 'but if we'd wanted you as an accused we'd have taken you in long before.'

This reassurance was given without the over-emphasised earnestness that usually characterised their lies, and it fitted in with the fact that Fred had already been charged, with the result that I felt some relief. I was ashamed of the extent to which I was concerned about my personal fate rather than that of Fred and the others, yet what counted, I decided, was not whether I impulsively hoped for self-preservation, or even was spontaneously pleased at being out of the more serious danger, but whether I abandoned my values and principles under the pressure of such feelings.

248

'The other thing is,' I told the lieutenant dully, 'I can't begin to think about making a statement when I don't even know the subjects you want me to deal with. I mean, for all I know you might be wanting me to tell you things about personal friends of mine that have got nothing to do with the investigation . . .'

'Oh, no,' he interrupted, 'we're not interested in that.'

It was approaching midday on Saturday, and the police would probably be keen to have Saturday night off, as well as the Sunday. This might make them impatient to get the interrogation over and I felt I should take advantage of all these little factors. My mental processes were as sluggish as those of my body, so that my mind plodded along slowly just when it needed to be fly, but that merely meant that it was more necessary than ever for me to try hard.

'How do I know,' I persisted, 'that you won't start asking me about my non-political friends and get them into trouble?'

'But why should we do that?' he replied not unreasonably. 'We've got enough to worry about without them. Not that we're worried, of course,' he added quickly.

'That's what you tell me,' I went on stubbornly, 'but I don't even know the area you intend to cover. I don't mean the specific questions, but the range, the themes you're interested in. I'm not saying that if I did know them I would make a statement, but at least I could start considering whether or not to do so.'

We argued and bargained for several hours in an elaborate but serious game. He knew, naturally, that I must already have started thinking about making a statement, but even though I knew he knew I still had to pretend to be trying to bluff him on that score.

Eventually I learnt that there were only three things they wished me to deal with: my trip overseas when still a student twelve years earlier; my presence at a multi-racial camp nine years later; and my association with Fred. The first two items were easy to handle, for I could tell the truth without incriminating anyone, but the third was more difficult.

I thought of people whose names I could safely mention, since I would be obliged to fill out my statement with some detail. One person whose name came to mind had died some years earlier—he would have been pleased to know that he was still fulfilling a useful political purpose; others were overseas and not likely to return to South Africa until it became free. What would help me was the readiness of the police to believe that those who, as the police saw it, had run away, had been the main activists in the anti-apartheid underground. Provided I told my story reluctantly, volunteering nothing and mentioning these names only when pressed to do so, I would possibly be believed. I would of course have to say something about having worked with Fred—the safest course, I decided, would be to mention my co-operation with him during the period after the Sharpeville shootings in 1960 when he and I had been the only two people of a large group who had not been detained by the police.

My mind laboured over the statement which I would allow them to elicit from me. My thoughts were so slow that by the time I had finished formulating an idea I had forgotten how it had started, and it took me all my strength to get myself to concentrate hard enough to build up a reasonable sequence of answers. I hoped desperately that when the time of actual questioning came I would have sufficient courage and skill to counter their attempts to break me down still further.

The lieutenant and I parleyed for some while over whether I would be allowed to mention in the body of the statement that I was speaking under duress. I insisted that I be allowed to say so—it would be *my* statement and *they* could not dictate what went into it. The lieutenant said they couldn't permit me to

250

put in a lot of propaganda which had nothing to do with the case. I replied that all I wanted to include were facts which they knew as well as I did to be true, but he reiterated that it would just be an attempt at propaganda on my part. We seemed to have reached a deadlock, but eventually he said he'd better consult with the Captain on the issue.

He left the room and after a few minutes returned with the Captain, who had with him a pencil and a foolscap pad. The Captain, squat, ugly and powerful, sat down and placed the writing materials in front of him, while the lieutenant, tall, clean and cold, paced backwards and forwards behind him. The Captain had decided to be soft with me, the lieutenant said with overemphasised earnestness, so I would be able to put my allegations into the statement, even though he personally was against it because it was irrelevant.

I said I would be prepared to make a statement at five that afternoon.

'Why five?' he asked.

'Because he wants to wait till twenty-four hours are up,' the Captain guessed correctly. 'Come on, let's not waste time,' he urged, 'we'll start now.'

The extra three hours did not seem worth fighting over, and I began my statement.

'I, Albert Louis Sachs, state as follows: I am at present a 180-day detainee held at Caledon Square police station and I am making this statement under duress. The circumstances are . . .'

I spoke at some length about the time I had spent in the interrogation room, mentioning how I had collapsed and how the police had kept themselves fresh by operating in relays. I protested too about the wide scope of the enquiry, which went far beyond what was necessary for the purposes of the case against Fred, and which was a further example of illegality in their conduct.

251

The Captain had been correct earlier on—once one started it was easy. He wrote down what I said, putting the words into his language and making occasional grammatical and stylistic errors. I did not correct him, for if ever the statement came to be contested I wanted to be able to point out that much of the formulation was his not mine. At one stage he complimented me on being clear and to the point, unlike most prisoners, he grumbled, who went all over the place. I reminded him that as a lawyer I was used to dictating and receiving statements; he and I had that much in common.

He questioned me from time to time, leaning back in his chair and closing his eyes as he mentally considered what I was telling him. The procedure was brisk and he went in for none of the melodramatic stances which had characterised his earlier dealings with me. My face remained set, my voice was dull.

Someone had asked me once whether I would ever lie in order to advance my political beliefs. I had replied that I would never do so, except possibly in certain circumstances to the police, and that even then I would find it difficult. Often I had kept silent, avoiding questions, or changing the direction of a conversation, but here I was lying deliberately. It was not only permissible, I owed it to my conscience, my friends and my beliefs to do so, and yet as I mixed untruths into the statement I felt almost guilty. The Captain mentioned names and asked for more. I stuck to my list, gradually allowing him to prise most of it out of me. I had to present a picture that made sense and was consistent with what he knew—I emphasised how difficult things had been made for us by the power of the police and that we'd been able to meet only rarely. Some of the police-held myths made it easier for me to lie successfully, such as that their main opponents were White Jews, most of whom had fled the country. Finally the questioning came to an end.

252

'There is one thing I wish to add,' I told the Captain. He nodded and wrote down my final words.

'I wish to say that whatever view the court might take of his actions, from a subjective point of view Mr Carneson was always motivated by a strong feeling of idealism and by his love for all his fellow South Africans . . .' My eyeballs prickled as I thought of the battering Fred had received, of his loneliness and his consideration for all the others. He had fought on when most of us had dropped out and now he alone was to be punished for what we had all done collectively. '. . . from a poor home, he had educated himself . . . genuinely believed in justice for all . . .'

'That's more like a speech in mitigation than a statement,' one of the lieutenants commented sarcastically.

When the statement was complete the Captain tediously copied out the first pages in which I had complained of maltreatment, and then got me to initial various corrections which he had made. Would he number the pages? I asked. That wasn't necessary, he replied. I was puzzled by his refusal, but felt too weary and muddled to insist on the point.

Did I wish to swear an oath or make an affirmation? he asked, presumably priding himself on the subtlety of allowing me the option. I said I would do neither. But you must, he persevered. But I needn't, I insisted. In the end I put my signature down without doing either, thus protecting myself from a possible perjury charge. The interrogation was over.

Lieutenant van Rensburg conducted me back to my cell. I walked slowly, feeling tired and defeated. The building and the objects in it seemed strange, and I moved along the passage and down the stairs feeling like a creature deprived of animation or independent spirit. As I mechanically passed through the charge office, I suddenly felt that I was back in a world in which I had the power to act. It might get me into further trouble, but there was no alternative . . . I broke away from the lieutenant and walked to the sergeant in charge.

'I want to lay a complaint of maltreatment,' I said in a flat, weak voice. 'They've kept me up through the night without sleep, look at my face it's unshaven . . .'

The lieutenant grabbed me, his face vicious with rage. 'Come here, you fool,' he muttered angrily, 'go back to your cell.' He pushed himself between me and the bemused sergeant, and shoved me towards the exit. 'Get over there.' A cell warder was called, and I saw the lieutenant speaking energetically and anxiously to the sergeant.

My cell was airless and musky with the smell of rotting fruit. I sat on the mattress which lay on the floor, and began to make notes of my experience during the previous twenty-five hours. I was not as sleepy as I had thought I would be, but my mind seemed to have become stuck, and my feelings had died. I would try to carry on protesting, I decided, but I would only be able to do so in an automatic way. Nothing seemed to matter; the only reality was my overwhelming sense of failure and fatigue.

I scratched a few words on the wall describing what had happened, and whenever a cell warder came round on inspection, which was every few hours, I said I wished to make a complaint. Always I received the same reply: it had nothing to do with them. But still I continued to protest. Eventually a young warrant officer who had been going from cell to cell and asking if there were any complaints, stopped at my door.

'Any complaints?' he asked perfunctorily.

'Yes,' I told him. 'I was maltreated by my interrogators who kept me awake through the night and deprived me of sleep. I collapsed several times and look at my dirty shirt and the beard on my face . . .'

'I can't see any blood,' he laughed, 'so what're you complaining about?'

'I wish you to make a record of my complaint,' I insisted.

'And I don't wish to do so,' he said jocularly, 'there's no evidence of an assault, and anyhow I'm only interested in what happens in your cell.'

The door was slammed and locked, and I lay down on the mattress, angered by his laughter, yet feebly determined to carry on complaining. My body felt distressed and restless, my muscles flaccid, paralysed, inert; even to roll over seemed an immense undertaking. I lay still, uncomfortably positioned, yet unable to move. Sick with exhaustion, I felt bereft of all feeling save for an occasional hint of misery. For forty hours I had been awake, and now that the chance had come to close my eyes I was too tired to sleep.

Chapter 28

Two days after my interrogation ended I was transferred by car to the Roeland Street jail, where I was led as a captive through the massive front entrance. I penetrated beyond the visitor's section where I had gone so often as counsel, passed through one large and two small dismal concrete yards, each of which was surrounded by a series of cells, and eventually found myself locked in a big airy room, on the door of which was written the word HOSPITAL.

During the previous two days at police headquarters I had succeeded in getting first the station commander and then the visiting magistrate to make notes of my complaint. Neither of them had appeared happy about the treatment which had been meted out to me, but at the same time they had not been indignant at what had really been a crime committed under the cloak of authority by officers of the law. The magistrate had, however, promised immediately to pass on my complaint to the Secretary for Justice. I had expected that during this period I would sleep for most of the day, but instead I had lain listlessly awake on the mattress, unable to concentrate and devoid of spirit. My mind and feelings had seemed more severely crushed than my body, which had somehow managed to function in a limited robot-like way. Only on the rare and brief occasions when someone else had been present had I been able to rouse in myself any mental initiative at all.

Now I looked curiously at my new abode. Though bare enough for a hospital room, it was luxurious compared to the tiny police cells in which I had formerly been held. The windows were barred and the door was a heavy slab of metal, yet the place was spacious and clean and it had a bed on which lay crisp white sheets.

After unpacking my things I began to rush wildly around the room, enjoying the freedom of its large area. Blotches of wan sunlight lay on the floor, and the air lacked the mustiness of my previous cell; against the wall were two lavatories modestly screened by low tiled walls, and in the corner stood a tap and basin. Before, my cell's dimensions had been two paces by three, but now there was space to run and fling my arms about.

I dashed to and fro, flighting imaginary cricket balls against the massive walls of the room, and thought with bitterness of the calm way in which my complaint had been received by the magistrate and the station commander. This was how standards came to be lowered, I reasoned, and how more and more people found themselves drawn into condoning criminal conduct by State officials. By means of a division of responsibility each functionary could carry out his particular role, and no one person need accept the whole blame. The policy-makers did not themselves participate in the actual infliction of physical indignities upon prisoners. The interrogators, on the other hand, did the 'dirty' work but could claim that as disciplined men obeying instructions, they were mere instruments of the policy-makers. As for the uniformed police, they could feel that they were not responsible for what the Security Police did, while the station commander could even point to the fact that he always passed on complaints. In practice such complaints would merely be sent from one official to the next, with no action being taken at any stage, and by this means the fiction of an inspection and complaints machinery would be maintained, along with the theory that the Department of

Justice had its own procedures for correcting abuses, whereas in fact the prisoners would be providing the authorities with a record in advance of any allegations they might make when, if at all, they were brought to court.

Later in the day when I was allowed to exercise in a yard I found that though emotionally I still felt dispirited and weak, my body craved violent activity. For the full half-hour I bounded furiously round the small enclosure and both the guard and I were surprised at the extraordinary energy I showed, which contrasted markedly with my general lack of animation. Yet even this violent exercise failed to shake me out of my mood of defeat, and when I returned to the cell I could think only with despair about the prospect which lay ahead. It seemed that after some weeks or months of further isolation I would either be charged or, more probably, be called as a witness against Fred. The judge would explain to me that if what I said was satisfactory I would be granted an exemption from prosecution, but that if I refused to give evidence I could be summarily sentenced to a year's imprisonment, with the possibility of being prosecuted thereafter. Obviously I could not go against my conscience and give evidence in these circumstances, unless the defence indicated somehow that they wished me to testify. The future seemed to be one of imprisonment followed by further imprisonment; witnesses would be broken down as I had been broken so that they could be forced to give evidence against me, and then some of them would hold out and be charged, and yet others would be detained, and so the chain of persecution would be extended, with ever more people being involved and ever more being punished.

Back in my room, I strode nervously round, examining a small cupboard, testing the toilet facilities and peering inquisitively at the walls. 'I was in here suffering from too little tobacco,' someone had written ironically. 'I was in here suffering from too much politics,' I wrote sadly underneath. I thought of the complaint of Fidel Castro who when forcibly confined to a sick-room during his days as a rebel, had declared that it was not he that was sick, but Justice. A fine statement, but how would he have fared if he had been placed under no-sleep torture? Was it that the heroes had done us a disservice by the very extraordinary quality of their courage, by inviting us to strive for standards of conduct which we could not attain? Julius Fucik had resisted savage beatings by trained S.S. men in Czechoslovakia; Odette had held out against Gestapo brutality in France; Henri Alleg had withstood electric shock torture by French paras in Algeria; in a much smaller way I myself had added to the mythology by writing of how I had survived five months of solitary confinement in South Africa. Yet it was only the successes which were publicised; the thousands and millions who had succumbed to their torturers were never mentioned, since there was no audience for defeat, and people did not want to read about evil triumphing. Symbolically and morally the Fuciks, the Allegs and the Odettes provided marvellous inspiration; from a practical point of view their heroism had its dangers, for it promoted an expectation that torture could be withstood by mere effort of will. What was required was not an idealistic hope of being brave in the face of the enemy but a realistic preparation for capture; what people had to be taught was how to kill themselves, how to lie, or how to hold out for a specified minimum time.

How would Stephanie have seen the situation? She had been fiercely self-critical at having made a statement after she had been assaulted, and had thought that if she had been prepared for the beating she might have withstood it. Yet one could never be ready for everything. As the limits of resistance became greater, so did the range of police techniques. Stephanie believed in a policy of maintaining absolutely high standards: if people could not maintain these standards in extreme situ-

259

ations then it would be the people who were wrong, not the standards. In her view principles must always remain clear and unyielding, however difficult they might be to live up to. She would be compassionate towards individuals who failed but nevertheless insist rigidly upon inflexibility of goals.

My mind worried constantly over these problems, reiterating the same arguments again and again, and making little progress. 'Politics is the art of the possible'—I hated that dictum, regarding it as a rationalisation for complacency, conservatism and dishonesty. At the same time I could not believe in virtues which though noble were abstract and unrealisable.

My thoughts became steadily gloomier, and although I knew I was suffering from depression and fatigue as a result of having been 'processed' by the police, I could not force myself to postpone this analysis or end my search for an understanding of why I had made a statement. I was just like so many clients of mine had been when faced with prosecution or bankruptcy; preoccupied with a single theme, unable to break out of the circle of my thought, compelled to exaggerate ordinary difficulties into overwhelming obstacles, and driven to visualise myself as a dwarfish and defeated man.

I wondered whether I would ever fight again, fight hard, with a buoyant, undivided self. During my previous detention I had often been confused and desperate, reaching a level of despair that I had never previously conceived of as being possible, but always I had been intellectually sure that resistance did matter and that the only point at issue was whether or not I had the courage to do what I knew to be the right thing. Now I was tending to question what this right thing was, and the sense of uncertainty and conflict in itself was totally undermining my capacity to act. During interrogation I had been to some extent demoralised by the knowledge that 'those who held out the longest broke the hardest'. Now as I wandered agitatedly round the hospital-room I found myself bewildered and depressed by another conflict; I wanted to do what was correct irrespective of consequences, yet at the same time I did not wish unnecessarily to prejudice my chances of coming out free at the end of it all. Never in my life had I felt so wretched.

Not even the thought of Stephanie helped me. She was the concrete symbol of my idealism, but she was also the principal object of my selfishness. Her passion and virtue inspired me to think in militant terms, and I felt that my exhortations to her when she had been awaiting trial, bound me to hold fast now that I was in distress. Yet the possibility of being able to enjoy love, to know peace and to have children, drove me frantically to seek a way out of imprisonment. I formulated one technical legal argument after another in an anxious search for a way out. I was ashamed of my moral wriggling, yet was not sufficiently resolute to put an end to it, and remained in a state of perpetual anxiety and self-anger.

Stephanie would be suffering desperately because of my detention, and, as I thought of her freshly out of jail, alone and vulnerable, I raged at our being again unable to communicate with each other. I wanted her to know of the strength of my love for her, and that I wished her to wait for me for at least a year; I wanted, too, to tell her that if I were sentenced to more than two years' imprisonment, she should make her life without me, otherwise we could go on endlessly each waiting for the other. We had seen each other briefly and then been separated by prison. We had seen each other briefly again and then been separated by prison again; possibly by the time I was released she would be back in jail once more, and it would then be my turn to wait for her. Perhaps, I thought unhappily, it would have been better if she and I had never met.

Every sound coming in from outside seemed to refer to and sharpen my misery. Fire-engines entering and leaving a nearby fire-brigade station filled the air with a clamour that made me anxious. Each day at lunch-time I could hear the excited shrieks of schoolchildren coming out from their classrooms on to a playground about thirty yards from my cell. I knew that they were Coloured children, and the contrast between their happy, shrill laughter and my silent, solitary wretchedness caused me to write a poem which I called 'Song of Self-Pity'

> *The laughter of brown kids at play*
> *bounces from the school across the way*
> *flying high it clears the prison wall*
> *and leaps insouciantly into my cell*
> *which is where I sit for my belief*
> *that brown kids may freely play and laugh.*

I hoped that as time passed my spirits would revive, but this did not prove to be so. The days proceeded slowly and my unhappiness continued. Food and clothing could be sent in to me by my mother, but otherwise I had no contact at all with the world outside my cell and exercise yard. I was kept in total isolation from the other prisoners whom I never saw except through a spyhole, and even then only for a moment and at a distance.

My only visitor was a magistrate who by regulation had to see me each week. The first man who came had presided over many trials in which I had appeared, and he looked at me with sympathy while I stood uncomfortably before him in short pants and sandshoes. I pressed him to find out if I could receive newspapers and a wireless, and later assumed he had passed on my request, because on the following day I was brought a pile of newspapers, which, the warders said, had been accumulating for me during the week. As soon as I was alone I looked at the headlines and felt once more the mixture of excitement and apprehension which I had known so often during the previous two years. There were articles about oil supplies to Rhodesia, and reports on crime and cricket, and in the middle of these, a story which, as soon as I read it, aroused in me violent feelings of horror and joy.

The report stated that an urgent application had been brought to a judge at his home asking him to issue an interdict restraining the Security Police, Cape Town, from unlawfully interrogating an architect, Bernard Gosschalk, while he was being held as a 180-day detainee at Caledon Square police station. In a supporting affidavit the detainee's wife, Ruth, alleged that she had been allowed to see her husband that morning and that she had been shocked by his dirty appearance and smelly body. He had told her that he had been interrogated against his will for long periods, that he had been denied opportunity to sleep and that in his cell he did not have access to toilet facilities. The judge had granted a temporary interdict in the terms requested and had called upon the police to file opposing affidavits, if they so wished, within a specified period.

I put the paper down and marched to and fro in the room, appalled at the treatment to which Bernard had been subjected, yet exhilarated by Ruth's initiative in bringing the application. I felt proud, too, of the lawyers who had prosecuted the matter on her behalf, for they had resisted the tendency, which most South African professional men had, to avoid situations which could bring them into conflict with the police. The combination of chance, courage and intelligence had made it possible for the police to be exposed; the problem now was to ensure that Ruth's application succeeded in all its stages, so that Bernard and the other detainees could be protected, and the irregular procedures made fully known.

How naïve I had been, I thought with anger, to have expected that my complaint to the magistrate would have in itself put an end to what the police were doing. On the very afternoon that the Secretary for Justice had received my report the police had started to subject Bernard to the very

sort of treatment about which I had complained. They knew I
had protested and that my complaint would be passed on to
the head of the department who would in the ordinary course
of events convey it to the Minister of Justice himself, J. B.
Vorster. Only one inference could be drawn—that the police
were confident of receiving the protection of Vorster. During
the Second World War he and Major-General van den Bergh
had been detained in the same internment camp for their pro-
Nazi activities, and it was there, according to a newspaper
interview given in 1965 by the Major-General, that they had
built up a special friendship and understanding which had
helped them so much now that they were in office. Against
this background it seemed highly improbable that the Government was merely not bothering to investigate complaints and
turning a blind eye to the activities of people like Captain
Swanepoel. Far more likely was the fact that Vorster himself
had been a party to the decision to use sleep-deprivation as a
general means of breaking down political detainees. His reasoning would probably have been that tough measures were
needed to beat a ruthless enemy, and that anyhow it was better
to keep torture under control than to allow it to get out of
hand.

I moved restlessly backwards and forwards past the newspapers, and began anxiously to consider ways and means of
smuggling out of the prison a note which could be used to
support the allegations which had been made in Ruth's application. A mere message would not be enough, what was required was a document which could be identified and used in
court proceedings. I would have to be particularly careful
since the police obviously felt free to act as they wished in
opposing the application; if Vorster were compromised by
their activities, he would have to give them full backing.

I started to compose a mental note. In a few crisp sentences
I would have to tell the essential features of the story, identi-

fying clearly the interrogation team and their style of operation. My testimony would have to be written in such a form that it could be used either to support the application already brought or else to ground separate proceedings on my own behalf. I thought with irony that this would be the most important legal document I had ever drafted. My handwriting would have to be small but legible, my accusations clear, and my language concrete and convincing.

Everything that passed between me and my mother was minutely and expertly examined by the warders, so that concealment in my daily food basket or weekly laundry bundle was out of the question. The warders were unbribeable if the bribe came from a political prisoner (with ordinary prisoners, I had been told, it was different, the price of 'dagga', for example, being only ten per cent higher in the prison than on the free market) and as for the prisoners, even if I could establish contact with them I would not be able to trust them. There seemed to be no reasonably safe way of getting the note out, and my anguish grew as I impatiently worked my way through plan after plan without discovering one that was satisfactory.

That day and the next I had to make a special effort at self control to hide from the warders my state of excitement.

I was still pondering on how to get a note out when a newspaper arrived in which the police reply to the application was set out at length. I read with fury of the warm, homely treatment which the police claimed Bernard had been receiving. The headline referred cosily to sandwiches and coffee, and there was an extract from an affidavit by Captain Swanepoel in which he spoke of a brief and friendly discussion which he had had with a cooperative Bernard. A doctor's report showed no evidence of injuries or other forms of maltreatment, though it did refer to Bernard's being apathetic and complaining of being unable to concentrate. The collective weight of the affi-

265

davits was to the effect that Bernard was being extremely well looked after; the police went further and denied even that he had said anything about his conditions or his interrogation to his wife who, they declared pointedly, was a banned person and by implication merely out to make propaganda.

The police could have avoided the issue simply by agreeing not to interrogate Bernard further, in which event the need for an enquiry by the court would have fallen away. Instead they had chosen to fight the case, which made it all the more urgent that a supporting statement from me be made available to Ruth's lawyers.

For hour after hour I made sample notes, flushing dozens of mutilated discards down the toilet. Eventually I formulated a model which seemed to be appropriately pithy in content, small in size and convenient in shape. I destroyed the model, but kept materials handy for quick use should the opportunity arise. One of my problems was that no one outside the prison would be on the look-out for a note from me, and the danger existed that any method of concealment which would defeat the eyes of the guard would also get past the eyes of the intended recipient.

A possible solution came to me by chance. I had asked for a Thermos flask in which I could keep coffee warm, and in her anxiety to be as helpful as possible my mother had sent in a flask which was much too large for my needs. I decided I would ask for a smaller one in exchange and return the flask —with one extra little piece of paper in the wrapping. I reasoned that whereas the warders would be content merely to examine the flask, my mother would clean it and re-pack it, and by simulating the different processes I was able to devise a means of locating the note in such a way that it should pass undetected by them and yet be revealed to her. I practised on the flask itself, and when I had satisfied myself that the method was reasonably safe I prepared and inserted the note.

The next day the warder who carried out the food basket agreed with me that the coffee-bottle, as he called it, was much too big for me. He took it out to give to my mother in exchange for a smaller one, and as soon as he was clear of my cell I ran round and round to celebrate the successful start of the venture. The feeling of elation did not last long, however, because soon I began to speculate on the possibilities of failure. I had seen the warders examining incoming parcels, but could only guess at how they inspected outgoing material. The basket would lie in the reception office for some time, and the flask might be mislaid or lost, or the warder might forget to ask for a smaller one, or my mother might miss the note, or be caught with it before she could get it to the lawyers—there were many ways of failure. My greatest fear was that the note would be intercepted, since then it could be interfered with and used to embarrass rather than help the application; in addition there could be unpleasant repercussions for my mother and reprisals against me.

That afternoon when the warder came round to deliver the bread and coffee which constituted the evening meal there was nothing in his demeanour to suggest that he had discovered the note. Again I had to fight down a dizzy rising of my spirits, and tell myself that many hazards still lay ahead.

During the days that followed my excitement gradually subsided. Nothing in the prison routine or the behaviour of the warders seemed to have changed, and the whole episode of the note appeared to have lost its momentousness. I became fatalistic about the outcome of my effort and found myself reverting to my earlier inertia although whenever I heard doors and gates being unlocked at the times when newspapers were brought to me my stomach tensed with anxiety. Each evening an elderly English-speaking warder would shove a paper through the bars of a window in my cell and pass some comment about the main news items of the day. Once he even told me knowingly that Harold Wilson was a Communist who had been to Russia twenty-six times and had married a Russian woman. Why couldn't Wilson recognise the independency of Rhodesia, he asked me, when the whole world had already done so?

Every day there appeared reports of oil-laden trucks crossing the South African border into Rhodesia, and there were stories, which I now found particularly upsetting, of a series of death sentences pronounced in the Cape Supreme Court. Yet there was nothing to indicate one way or the other whether or not my note had got through. Against this background of death sentences and international disputes my endeavours seemed increasingly trivial and unimportant.

The warders who brought the morning paper seemed less interested in what it said than how it looked. Once one page had a tear in it of two inches, and the warder responsible for the damage apologised with such fulsomeness that I was embarrassed on his behalf.

For a number of days neither the morning nor the evening paper carried any further news about the application, and I began to wonder why Ruth's lawyers were being so slow with their final set of replies. For a short while, however, I was distracted from preoccupation about my note by an event which happened inside the prison.

A prisoner escaped, and he did so by climbing up the wall outside my cell. I was lying on my bed when I heard a bang and saw a pair of dark-blue jeans flashing across one of my barred windows. A body was moving rapidly upwards and then I heard the movements of someone jumping across a corner. This was followed by high scraping sounds against the opposite wall, and then silence. What astonishing agility—the prisoner had leapt his way up a wall of at least thirty foot and reached the prison roof. I looked at my watch—one minute passed ... a second ... a third. Then a siren began to wail and a

268

fierce whirring klaxon sound filled my cell and the whole prison. He must have got away, I thought with excitement, since it should not have taken him more than two minutes to cross the roof to the top of the perimeter wall.

The next afternoon I heard a sound which told of the sad sequel: the pathetic clank-clank of a man walking in leg-irons. The escapist had been recaptured. The evening newspaper reported with satisfaction that he had been caught on the morning after his escape while attempting a foolish burglary.

Another sequel to the escape was that disciplinary proceedings were brought against two warders for alleged negligence in the performance of their duties. One of these men happened to be the kindest of all the prison guards, a man who was consistently decent to all prisoners, Black and White. My sympathy now swung from the escapee to him, and on learning the charges I immediately offered to help him in the preparation of his defence. Each day when he came to supervise my exercise periods I would subject him to the kind of cross-examination he was likely to get when his case was heard. Eventually he received an indictment and when he showed it to me the allegation against him seemed so improbable that I forecast that the case would eventually be dropped. This is what in fact did happen and he seemed to feel that somehow I had been responsible for his good fortune!

One lunch-hour I was surprised to see the chief warder himself arriving at my cell. He was accompanied by a bare-footed and cowed Coloured prisoner, who on receiving an abusive instruction, obsequiously deposited my food basket in front of me. The chief warder looked sternly at me, and angrily waved his officer's stick in my direction.

'You'll know what this is all for,' he said sharply. Then he began roughly to inspect the food and containers. My pulse started to hammer, but I managed to keep a neutral expression on my face.

'Major Rossouw's ordered you to get no more Thermos flasks,' he continued aggressively. He picked up a flask from the basket and examined it with exaggerated thoughtfulness.

I said nothing, but felt my legs and body become weak. The chief warder was angry, which meant that he must have known about my note, but he did not sneer which suggested that the note had not been intercepted. I wanted to cheer and jump around, yet I hid my inner delirium and stared stupidly back at him. Also I was scared. Silence was my best weapon, for it enabled me to hide both my fear and my joy. Eventually the chief warder seemed to tire of his attack, and after warning me not to try to be clever again, he strode rapidly out of the room, with the prisoner padding frantically after him. The heavy steel door was slammed, locked and bolted, and I was alone again, with mauled parcels of food lying next to me. It worked, it worked, I said jubilantly to myself, the note got through and it's being used to expose the police. With arms outspread I skated round the room, ecstatically enjoying a sensation of triumph.

I realised that there might be reprisals, but whatever they did to me could not detract from the fact that at least two of their prisoners had broken through their steel curtain. Bernard and I might be singled out for special punishment, yet we would know that we had managed to hit back and hurt them.

By evening I was still in a manic mood, and when the warder came with the newspaper I had to hold back from cheering. After he had tramped away I looked excitedly at the paper, and, as I had anticipated, I found an article in which the replies to the police denials were set out. Among the documents referred to was an affidavit by my mother to the effect that she had found in the wrappings of a Thermos flask a note written by me. The report added that the note was annexed to her affidavit and placed before court, together with a similar note from Fred Carneson alleging the same kind of maltreatment

270

by the same team of interrogators. I danced a crude ballet of happiness until, exhausted by my sudden surge of feeling, I sat down on my bed and greedily ate my food.

Perhaps I had prejudiced my chances of being released, and possibly Stephanie and I would never meet again, but what I had done was right, and she would have done the same! Only some people could be heroes, and then probably only for some of the time, but everyone could be reasonably intelligent and reasonably brave for most of the time. It was true that the area of what could be achieved through the courts was constantly being diminished, and that the role of the judges in political cases was more and more being restricted in effect to the sentencing of prisoners whose guilt had already been determined by the police. Yet for as long as the Government chose to boast of a free judiciary, opponents of apartheid would be able to fight back even after capture. Three prisoners, isolated and defeated on their own, had by means of a cooperative effort succeeded in putting the mighty Security Police on the retreat. There would be occasion enough for further humiliation; now was the time to feel proud.

Chapter 29

Friends of mine who came to the prison to welcome me out took bets as to whether I would run to the sea again. In fact I walked quietly to their car and sat glumly in it, feeling that this was no occasion for gestures of triumph.

I had spent three months in total isolation in the prison hospital, anxiously pacing around and waiting for the day when the police would come to escort me to court. My legal defence and address to the judge had been ready: I would not have given evidence, I would have protested at having been brought to court after three months in solitary confinement, I would have said something about the unlawful methods which had been used to extract a statement from me, and I would have spoken out about the unfairness of being expected to give evidence when the persons who had maltreated me sat in court to intimidate me further. Yet my defiance would have been half-hearted. I would have done what I could to have avoided being committed to prison, and I would have chosen my phrases carefully so as not to have antagonised the judge.

The inclusion in my laundry one week of my red jersey had revived my courage a bit, but I had never really recovered from the session with Captain Swanepoel and his team. My main hope, and I had been ashamed of it, had been that by making admissions Fred would save all the detainees from being called as witnesses. This is what he had in fact done. Our evidence would have related at most only to the minor charges against him, in respect of which the State case had been overwhelming in any event, and by excluding us from the case he had been able to concentrate his defence on the more serious allegations. The police presumably had felt we had been taught our lesson, and when the prosecution case had been closed nearly all the detainees had been released.

As I was driven away from the prison I thought about my next moves. Three things stood out in my mind—seeing to it that as many people as possible got to know of the treatment which was being meted out to detainees, getting in touch with Stephanie, and leaving the country.

The first proved to be the most difficult. I told my story to as many colleagues and friends as seemed interested to hear. Some were so non-committal, even sceptical, that I almost began to doubt the reality of my own experiences, others remarked blandly that I was lucky I had not received electric shock torture. Even the sympathetic ones did not fully understand how exhausting and demoralising all-night interrogation was especially when it was destined to go on forever, and how different it was from, say, being up all night dancing or working.

I reported my treatment to the Bar Council and asked them to arrange an interview, a confidential one if necessary, with Vorster. After several weeks' delay Vorster replied in sharp terms that I was a liar and a propagandist and that as a lawyer I should know that my remedy lay in taking him to court. Part of his letter was of special interest to me—it denied that in my statement to Captain Swanepoel I had complained of any ill-treatment, and said that my allegations to the magistrate had been fully investigated and found to be completely without substance. Now I was able to understand why the Captain had refused to number the pages in my statement:

he must have planned all along simply to tear up the first few of them.

I thought bitterly about Vorster's suggestion that I take him to court. Stephanie had medical evidence to support her claim, but after so many months of being held incommunicado, what proof would I be able to offer of my sleep-deprivation? If the application by Ruth had been proceeded with I might have had a chance to tell the court what had happened to me, but once Bernard had been released the whole basis of her application had fallen away. A long and bitter battle on the question of costs, in the course of which her witnesses might have been subjected to further harassment, had been avoided by an agreement that each side would pay its own costs, and the matter had been withdrawn from the roll.

There was one other person of importance in the Justice Department to whom I did speak and that was the Attorney-General for the Cape. It had been the 'A-G', as we called him who had signed the warrant authorising my detention, and in the ordinary course I would have been too embarrassed to have spoken to him again. He was a mild, softly-spoken middle-aged man, very much like Himie in manner, though lacking Himie's shrewdness and sense of humour and he and I had often had friendly clashes in court. I suspected that it had been he who had been responsible for my having been detained in the relative luxury of a hospital cell. What put me in touch with him now was the fact that I was in law entitled to receive witness fees for the period of my detention, and that he had to issue the relevant certificate.

The 'A-G' was an experienced and hard-working prosecutor, who through years of not making enemies and doing his job competently had risen to his present high position. As soon as I entered his office he apologised profusely to me—I looked at him with surprise—for having spilt a drop of ink on my claim form. My surprise vanished. I told him what Captain

274

Swanepoel had done to me and he replied courteously and sympathetically that he regretted it very much but officially could not go behind the denials of the police. He did not apologise for my arrest—I respected him for that—but he did give me the impression that he was nostalgic for the days when he had had to deal only with crime and not with politics. From a financial point of view my visit turned out to be highly rewarding, since I was paid witness fees according to the special tariff for White professional men. My additional claim for special day and night (hotel) expenses was disallowed, but nevertheless I collected a cheque for one hundred and forty pounds, which I sent on to Fred's family.

At first it seemed impossible for me to get in touch with Stephanie. I did not know where to write to her and even if I had known I would have been worried about doing so. The problem was suddenly solved by her arrival in Cape Town. She had fortuitously left her home for Cape Town on the very day of my release, and only when she turned up the next day at Himie's house had she learnt that I was no longer in prison. We were soon brought together, and felt such instant tenderness towards each other that there seemed little doubt that we would get married. If we could. In the weeks that followed we met semi-clandestinely, climbing the mountain, walking on the beach and longing for the time when we could be together without fear of the police.

Her civil case was eventually set down for trial on a day early in August, exactly two years after the date of her assault. Because of my emotional involvement with her I decided I could no longer properly act as one of her counsel, and so I withdrew from the case. I nevertheless continued to discuss the matter with her, and together with Himie advised her to avoid situations which could lead to harassment by the police in the pre-trial period. Reluctantly but obediently she followed the advice of 'her lawyers'. Then one evening she rushed up to me at our meeting-place and in an anxious voice told me I'd be very cross with her because that afternoon she'd taken part in a students' protest march. The students had been demonstrating against the banning orders which had been placed on the president of the N.U.S.A.S. after he had invited U.S. Senator Robert Kennedy to address meetings of South African students. Stephanie pleaded with me to forgive her: when she'd read about the proposed march in Cape Town she'd been unable to resist joining in. At first everything had been all right; she'd worn dark glasses and had walked behind two large women, but then right at the end when the march was almost over she'd been spotted by one of the Security policemen and had had her photograph taken. Her knees were still knocking, she told me, and please, I mustn't be cross with her. She was so abashed at her naughtiness that I laughed.

The next day a pro-Government newspaper headlined its report of the march with the news that Stephanie Kemp, the former political prisoner, had been one of the marchers. We feared that she would now be banned, in which event it would have been a criminal offence for the two of us to have communicated with each other in any way. A similar situation had arisen in connection with my landlord and myself, since after his release he had been banned and placed under 12-hour house-arrest. At the time I had jokingly remarked that I was now prohibited by law from paying him rent, but in fact it had become impossible for the two of us to occupy premises on the same property, and I had been forced to find somewhere else to live. Even this had been difficult, because I was obliged to report any change of address to the police, but fortunately one of my friends had not minded getting his name into their files, and I had moved into his flat.

From then on, Stephanie was more cautious than she had been earlier, and when Senator Kennedy arrived and spoke to large audiences of White youths, inspiring them with a freshness and seriousness that many of us had not expected of an American politician, neither she nor I had been among his hearers—I because I was banned by the Government, and she because she was banned by 'her lawyers'.

The liveliness displayed by the students cheered us, especially as it came at a time when all Whites seemed to be rallying to the Government, and soon afterwards there was further good news. After some brilliant advocacy by defence counsel followed by what seemed to me to be a most fair and careful assessment by the court of the evidence, Fred had been found not guilty of the major charges against him. The sentence imposed on him had been one of imprisonment for five years and nine months, which in the circumstances was regarded as an outstanding achievement by the defence.

By this time both Stephanie and I had become impatient at having had to wait so long for the permits we needed from the Department of the Interior to enable us to leave the country legally. We had no hope of getting passports, and had separately applied for documents known as exit permits which would authorise us to leave the country on condition we never returned. By law we were entitled to receive such permits provided that the police had no charges outstanding against us. Vorster favoured allowing a limited number of opponents to go into exile: if a fly was troubling you, he had once said, you either swatted it or let it fly out the window. It had galled us to apply for permission to leave, and on one occasion Stephanie had wept and said she wasn't going to go. There had seemed to be no other realistic prospect open to us, however, and our arrangement was that I would leave as soon as my permit arrived, and that Stephanie would go as soon as she had received her permit and completed her case. Whoever got to London first would find accommodation and prepare the way for the other.

Each day I went to my office hoping to find a letter con-

277

taining my exit permit. For weeks and then months I heard nothing at all, not even acknowledgment of my application. By then my practice had fallen away completely, partly because I did not wish to undertake cases that I might not be able to see through to their conclusion. My telephone rang rarely, few letters arrived, and not many people called to see me. When one day I heard a firm knock at my door I assumed that the caller must be a colleague who had come to discuss one of his cases with me. The door opened, and I was surprised to see the African ex-detainee who had called on me eighteen months earlier standing there.

Smiling lightly he stretched his palm forward in greeting. I took hold of it and we looked fondly at each other.

'My wife and I,' he said formally, 'and the people in the location saw in the newspapers that you were detained by the police, and we also read that you had been released after three months.'

I nodded my head in agreement, and told him that I had been badly treated at first, but that afterwards my conditions had been much better. His face was fuller than it had been when last he had called on me, but greyness seemed to have settled all over his hair.

'It's terrible,' he continued with concern, 'what the Government has done to you.'

'It's been much worse for many others,' I replied, thinking immediately of Looksmart who was dead and Denis who was serving a life sentence.

'And poor Fred, the judge was very hard on him.'

'Actually, it could have been much worse. The police were hoping he'd get fifteen years at least, and his lawyer Sam Aaron put up a marvellous fight, so Fred was very pleased with the result.'

'Life is very hard for our people now in the locations,' he said. 'The police chase everyone all the time, and their stooges brag out in the open, when before they used to try to pretend they weren't working for the Government. Also the police are paying hundreds of people to be informers, even women and little children. But still we know we will beat the Government in the end, for everyone hates all this apartheid business, even the people who work for it, and they can't lock up the whole African nation, so we will get freedom in our lifetime.'

I said nothing, but felt embarrassed and ashamed that I was soon going to leave South Africa, whereas he and all the other African men and women with whom I had shared so much for so many years, would not be able to go even if they wished to do so. Guerilla fighters had reportedly returned across the border into South West Africa, prepared to die for the liberty of their people—I was on my way out.

'We understand that you are going overseas to England,' he said gravely to me. 'Is that correct?'

'Yes.' I was burning with discomfort.

'Well, let me wish you good luck.' He shook my hand enthusiastically and smiled happily at me.

I was taken aback by the friendly and sympathetic way in which he was reacting to my proposed departure, and felt such relief that I nearly had to sit down. I realised too why he had been speaking to me with such formality—he had come to bid me goodbye, and in terms of African custom such an occasion demanded a stately and decorous expression of feeling.

'All the people in the location wish you to know that they will never forget you and what you have done for the African people. There are many of us who would like to see you off when you go, but it is very difficult and the police might make trouble, so they asked me to come up here instead and to give you our greetings. We hope you will tell the people in England about our struggle, and one day when we are free we hope we will see Albie again in Cape Town.'

279

'I will never forget you.' It seemed so inadequate. 'I feel terrible about leaving, and will always remember the African people of Cape Town. Please say goodbye to everyone for me, I think about them all the time and feel very bitter that I'm not allowed to see them any more.'

We shook hands once more, and then stood facing each other in deep emotional silence.

'My wife and I were just wondering, Albie, what you were going to do with your furniture . . .'

A few days later I stood in an empty office, ruefully looking at it for the last time. My exit permit had come through at last, and excited and sad at the prospect of going, I had rushed from floor to floor in the building bidding my colleagues farewell. Now stripped of all furnishing my room seemed desolate, like a cell. A disconnected telephone stood on the bare floor and a pile of still unsold law reports lay stacked in a corner. Chairs, bookcases, curtains, pictures, carpet and couch had all been removed and the room was dead; even the police microphones, I guessed, would have been taken away.

Epilogue

London 1966

Stephanie and I were married at the St Pancras Registry Office in London. It was a cool drizzly September day, and reporters from the British press crowded around us.

'Hold hands, please, That's lovely. Smile please. That's lovely. Look this way, please, walk that way, please. Lovely, lovely.' The photographers were kind, the reporters sympathetic. Everything was lovely. What formerly had been regarded as our crimes now became our virtues; what had been suppressed despite proof was now accepted on our mere say-so. Two years of courtship with its excitement, confusion, agony and despair, were converted into twenty minutes of easy phrases. Stephanie became The Girl Who Sued Vorster (and was paid £500 damages plus costs a week before trial) and I was The Anti-Apartheid Lawyer (who had come to England for the publication of a book on his experiences in prison).

The newsmen shook our hands, wished us luck, and hurried off to their next assignments. We kissed each other and hoped that at least we would live happily ever after.